PEDESTRIANISM

WHEN

WATCHING PEOPLE WALK

WAS AMERICA'S FAVORITE SPECTATOR SPORT

MATTHEW ALGEO

CHICAGO
REVIEW
PRESS

Library of Congress Cataloging-in-Publication Data
Algeo, Matthew.
  Pedestrianism / Matthew Algeo.
    pages cm
  Summary: "Strange as it sounds, during the 1870s and 1880s, America's most popular spectator sport wasn't baseball, football, or horse racing—it was competitive walking. Inside sold-out arenas, competitors walked around dirt tracks almost nonstop for six straight days (never on Sunday), risking their health and sanity to see who could walk the farthest—500 miles, then 520 miles, then 565 miles! These walking matches were as talked about as the weather, the details reported in newspapers and telegraphed to fans from coast to coast. This long-forgotten sport, known as pedestrianism, spawned America's first celebrity athletes, the forerunners—forewalkers, actually—of LeBron James and Tiger Woods. The top pedestrians earned a fortune in prize money and endorsement deals. The sport also opened doors for immigrants, African Americans, and women. But along with the excitement came the inevitable scandals, charges of doping—coca leaves!—and insider gambling. PEDESTRIANISM chronicles competitive walking's peculiar appeal and popularity, its rapid demise, and its enduring influence"— Provided by publisher.
  Includes bibliographical references and index.
  ISBN 978-1-61374-397-3 (hardback)
  1. Walking—United States—History—19th century. 2. Spectators—United States—History—19th century. I. Title.

GV199.4.A43 2014
796.510973—dc23
                    2013045115

Interior design: Jonathan Hahn

To Zaya Theresa Algeo
Born January 31, 2013

———

We should go forth on the shortest walk, perchance, in the spirit of undying adventure, never to return—prepared to send back our embalmed hearts only as relics to our desolate kingdoms.
—Henry David Thoreau, *Walking*

CONTENTS

PREFACE

DAN O'LEARY STAGGERED AROUND the dusty track on the floor of Madison Square Garden like a drunken man. Sweat streamed down his face, saturating the bandanna he wore tied around his neck. The thousands in attendance watched in stunned silence as O'Leary struggled to stay on his feet, his emaciated body bent like a wheat stalk in a thunderstorm. His countenance was appalling: mouth agape, cheeks hollow, eyes barely open. One spectator said he looked like a corpse. But nobody looked away. The audience was transfixed.

It was noon on Wednesday, March 12, 1879, the third day of the Astley Belt race, a six-day walking match to determine the world's champion pedestrian. This was the biggest sporting event of the year, a Gilded Age version of Wimbledon or the Masters golf tournament, and Dan O'Leary, an Irish immigrant from Chicago, was America's best hope for winning the race. He'd been circling the ⅛-mile oval inside the Garden for two and a half days, practically nonstop. He'd completed 1,624 laps—203 miles—but was still more than thirty miles behind the race leader, an Englishman named Charles Rowell. O'Leary had walked nearly three thousand miles in various competitions over the previous twelve months, and now his body was broken.

Later that afternoon, O'Leary retreated to his tent and collapsed on his bed. A doctor summoned to examine O'Leary declared him simply "used up."

At 5:36 PM, O'Leary limped to the judges' stand.

"Gentlemen," he announced, "I have finished."

The crowd gasped. Western Union carried the news instantly by telegraph across the country. Within an hour, extra editions of newspapers began appearing on street corners from New York to San Francisco, announcing the shocking news in bold front-page headlines: O'LEARY QUITS.

Dan O'Leary's withdrawal from the Astley Belt race was national news because, at the time, competitive walking was the most popular spectator sport in the United States. In the 1870s and 1880s, fans regularly packed massive arenas like the first Madison Square Garden and Chicago's Interstate Exposition Building, paying twenty-five or fifty cents apiece to watch people walk in circles for days at a time. As one newspaper pointed out, a great walking match was as talked about as the weather. (Running was sometimes allowed; however, as we shall see, it was not an especially effective strategy.)

This sport, known as pedestrianism, spawned America's first celebrity athletes, the forerunners—forewalkers, actually—of LeBron James and Tiger Woods. Dan O'Leary was as famous as President Chester Arthur (himself a huge fan of the sport). The top pedestrians earned a fortune in prize money and endorsement deals (O'Leary was the spokesman for a brand of salt), and their images appeared on some of the first cigarette trading cards, which children collected as avidly as later generations would collect baseball cards. The sport opened doors for immigrants, African Americans, and women, affording those underprivileged groups unprecedented opportunities for status and wealth. Less laudably, pedestrianism also gave professional sports its first doping scandal.

It's no coincidence that pedestrianism's rise coincided with the Industrial Revolution. Throughout the nineteenth century, rapid increases in mechanization and urbanization resulted in something previously unimaginable to all but the very rich: leisure time. For the first time, millions of ordinary people had free time on their hands, and many chose to spend it watching other people walk. What does that say about them and their times? And what does it say about us and ours that we regard them as quaint, even simple, for having done so?

In the following pages, we will examine competitive walking's peculiar appeal, its rise and fall, and its enduring influence. In many ways, pedestrianism marked the beginning of modern spectator sports in the United States. Never before had so many people attended (and, not coincidentally, wagered on) athletic events. Never before had the media devoted so much attention to them. NASCAR, the National Football League, even sports radio—all are legacies of pedestrianism.

Pedestrianism also animated the major issues of its era: American-British relations, class warfare, racial injustice, women's rights, religious zealotry. Some of these will seem all too familiar to modern readers. An international superpower gets bogged down in a war in Afghanistan, America is riven by a bitter debate over immigration, and a world-famous athlete finds himself accused of using performance-enhancing drugs. The story of pedestrianism is really the story of its time, a period of rapid technological and social change—much like our own.

Above all, however, this is the story of the pedestrians themselves, men and women who performed unimaginable feats of human endurance, walking for days and weeks on end, always under punishing conditions. What they achieved is as remarkable as the achievements of today's best endurance athletes. Their names deserve to be remembered, and they ought to assume their rightful place in the pantheon of history's great athletes.

1

WHISKEY IN HIS BOOTS

or

HE'S THE MAN

IT ALL BEGAN WITH A WAGER. One day in the autumn of 1860, two friends were enjoying a meal together when the conversation turned to the upcoming presidential election. One of the friends, a door-to-door bookseller named Edward Payson Weston, believed Abraham Lincoln would lose the election. The other, George Eddy, was convinced Lincoln would win. So they made a bet.

The stakes were unusual: whoever lost the bet would have to walk from the State House in Boston to the Capitol in Washington, a distance of some 478 miles, in ten consecutive days, arriving in time to witness the inaugural ceremony on the following March 4.[*]

It was a lark, really—just banter between friends. "I do not suppose that either of us at that time had the remotest idea of ever attempting such a task," Weston later recalled. Eddy, for his part, later confessed that, if Lincoln had lost, he would "most decidedly have preferred to get excused."

---

[*] The Twentieth Amendment moved Inauguration Day from March 4 to January 20 beginning with FDR's second inaugural in 1937.

But after Lincoln's victory, Weston decided to see if he was up to the task. As a test, he walked from Hartford to New Haven, Connecticut, on New Year's Day 1861, stopping at houses to distribute book catalogs along the way. He covered the distance of 36 miles in 10 hours and 40 minutes, including an hour-long break for dinner. "I did not feel the effects of the walk at all," Weston wrote. The next day he walked back to Hartford, handing out more catalogs as he went. He made it in 11 hours and 30 minutes. "After this," Weston wrote, "I thought I could walk from Boston to Washington without injury to myself."

Weston wasn't an especially swift walker. He was less than five feet eight inches tall, and his stride, once measured at thirty-three inches, was not exceptionally long (the average is about thirty-one). He typically covered between three and four miles per hour, and at his fastest a little more than six. (The average human walking speed is about three miles per hour. The current world record for the men's 20-kilometer walk is 1 hour, 17 minutes, and 16 seconds, a pace of 9.65 miles per hour, though, as we shall see, racewalkers don't always keep one foot on the ground when they compete.)

But Edward Payson Weston was blessed with almost superhuman stamina.

Born in Providence, Rhode Island, on March 15, 1839, Weston was just ten years old when his father abandoned the family to join the California gold rush in the spring of 1849. Later that year, young Weston himself left home to work as a vendor for a traveling musical group called the Hutchinson Family Singers.

Formed in the early 1840s by four of the thirteen children of Jesse and Mary Hutchinson, a farming couple from Milford, New Hampshire, the troupe would eventually grow to comprise all the siblings: eleven brothers and two sisters. At first the Hutchinsons sang traditional tunes, hoary standards extolling the virtues of patriotism and rural life. "My Country, 'Tis of Thee" was a favorite.

But around 1843, the Hutchinson Family Singers began doing something revolutionary: they started writing and performing their own original compositions. And these were not bland, sentimental songs. Many of them addressed the most pressing social issues of the day. The Hutchinsons sang songs advocating abolition and women's suffrage. These were America's first protest songs. It was as if the Partridge Family had morphed into Peter, Paul and Mary.

Singing about slavery in four-part harmony was controversial, of course, but even in antebellum America, controversy did not preclude commercial success. The Hutchinsons toured the United States and Britain extensively and to great acclaim throughout the 1840s and 1850s. They were paid up to $1,000 per performance, which, even divided thirteen ways, was good money at the time. They spawned many imitators, but none could match their success, much less their social impact. They are forgotten today, but the Hutchinson Family Singers were as influential to their generation as Elvis Presley and Bob Dylan would be to theirs a century later.

When ten-year-old Eddie Weston hit the road with the troupe in 1849, the Hutchinson Family Singers were at the peak of their popularity. The lad traveled with the family for a year, selling candies and souvenirs at their performances. After that, he moved in with Jesse Hutchinson Jr., who was the group's main songwriter and its manager. Weston lived with Hutchinson for about two years, attending school in Boston and working in a local theater. Thereafter he went to school only intermittently.

The young Edward Payson Weston learned quite a bit about show business during his spell with the Hutchinsons, and he would evince a flair for the theatrical for the rest of his life.

In 1852, Weston, now thirteen, returned home to Providence, where he worked variously as a newsboy on a railroad and a steamship, a clerk for a local merchant, and a jeweler's apprentice. In the spring of 1856, he once again left home for a job in show business: he joined a traveling circus. Weston was a fairly accomplished musician—he played the drums and cornet—so he probably performed in the circus band. In any event, his tenure under the big top was soon curtailed by an injury—Weston later claimed he was struck by lightning—and by the end of that year, Weston, just seventeen, embarked on a career in "the book business," as he called it.

Over the next few years he bounced around, from New York City to Hartford to Boston to Worcester, Massachusetts, selling books door-to-door and dabbling—always unsuccessfully—in get-rich-quick schemes. During this period he also worked briefly as an errand boy for James Gordon Bennett Sr., the legendary publisher of the *New York Herald*.

One day in February 1859, Weston accidentally sent a package from the newspaper to the wrong address. An hour later he realized his mistake and immediately went after the wagon with the wayward parcel. Zigzagging through the teeming streets of Manhattan, Weston ran from the *Herald* offices near the corner of Fulton and Nassau and didn't stop until he finally caught up with the wagon at Seventieth and Broadway, a distance of more than five miles. "I was so much exhausted," Weston recalled, "that I could not stand for some moments."

It was his first inkling that Weston possessed what he called "great locomotive powers." It was also a rare instance of Weston running, an exercise he professed to detest. "Walking is according to nature in his view," a newspaper would later say of Weston, "but he leaves running to animals differently constituted." When he returned to the *Herald* with the package, Bennett was so impressed that he gave Weston a raise on the spot.

By the autumn of 1860, when he made the bet with his friend George Eddy, Weston was twenty-one, handsome, and rail thin, with long black hair and piercing dark eyes. He was a dandy, a dapper dresser who draped himself in capes and was rarely seen without a gaudy walking stick. And he was a natural showman, unselfconscious and unencumbered by self-doubt. He would have made a good actor. In fact, he resembled John Wilkes Booth, the dashing thespian whose final act would end the Lincoln presidency.

Having discovered his "abilities as a pedestrian," Weston began making arrangements for his walk to Washington. He carefully plotted his course, which would take him from Boston into western Massachusetts, then south through Connecticut, New York, New Jersey, Pennsylvania, and Maryland before finally arriving at the Capitol. He would depart on February 22—Washington's Birthday—and, by his reckoning, would arrive in Washington late on the morning of March 4—just in time to see Lincoln take the oath on the East Portico at noon.

But his itinerary left little margin for error. Weston would have to walk nearly fifty miles a day for ten straight days in the middle of winter on roads that were often barely passable in the best of circumstances. Even the slightest setback would jeopardize his chances of making it on time.

For eighty dollars he hired a driver with a horse and a small carriage to accompany him. A friend named Charles Foster agreed to ride along for support.

Then, as Weston recalled, "I bethought myself to devise some means to defray my expenses." He lined up sponsors, a trick he probably learned from the Hutchinsons, but something that was virtually unheard of at the time for what was essentially an endurance contest. He went to New York and convinced the Grover & Baker Sewing Machine Company to pay him one hundred dollars to hand out promotional literature on his walk. A pharmacy, a photographic studio, and a haberdashery also agreed to pay him to hand out circulars. The Rubber Clothing Company furnished him with a waterproof suit. Time and again, Edward Weston would pioneer strategies that have become commonplace in contemporary American sports.

Always eager for publicity, Weston also mailed copies of his itinerary to newspapers along his intended route.

Edward Payson Weston.
ISLINGTON LOCAL HISTORY CENTRE

Late on the cold, gray morning of Friday, February 22, 1861, Weston arrived at the yellow-domed State House on Beacon Hill to commence his long walk. He was dressed in blue wool tights and a white blouse covered with a heavy blue coat with brass buttons. On his feet he wore sturdy boots a few sizes larger than his usual size. A large crowd was waiting to see him off. It seemed an auspicious beginning, but things did not get off to a good start.

Weston had a habit of falling into debt, and when two of his creditors in Boston caught wind of his intended jaunt, they sent constables to the State House to arrest him. One creditor was owed eighty dollars, the other ten dollars. Just minutes before noon, the time he was scheduled to leave, he was hauled off to a police station. Weston was a smooth talker—he was a traveling salesman, after all—and he somehow managed to talk himself out of this embarrassing predicament. He was released after promising to pay his debts as soon as he returned to Boston.

At twelve minutes before one o'clock, Weston finally started his journey. He was already forty-eight minutes behind schedule. Several hundred people accompanied him from the State House, down Beacon Street, followed by the carriage that contained his supplies, his friend Foster, and the fliers he was to hand out along the way. A few friends stayed with him until he reached Newton, five miles down the road, less than an hour later.

At 5:45 that evening he stopped at an inn in Framingham for supper. Afterward he went to the parlor to rest but found "a number of ladies" were waiting there to see him. One of them asked if she could send a kiss to the president. Weston said he "had no objection to receiving the kiss," but "could not promise to deliver it to the president." The lady kissed him anyway, as did the others. Feeling "highly flattered," he resumed his journey—but only after distributing some of his sponsors' handouts, as he would do at every stop along the way.*

On he walked into the night, through snow and ice, pausing occasionally for a glass of milk or water from the carriage. Clouds obscured a nearly full moon. His way was lit only by a dim kerosene lamp. Around midnight he arrived on the outskirts of Worcester, about forty miles west of Boston, where he was greeted by yet another constable. It turned out Weston had an unpaid debt in Worcester, as well.

The previous summer, Weston had lived in a Worcester boarding house owned by a man named E. T. Balcom. "While there," Weston later confessed, "I managed my affairs very injudiciously, and it may be extravagantly, consequently, I was somewhat involved in debt." In fact, he'd skipped town owing the landlord nearly fifty dollars in rent. "I promised to pay him part of the amount the following November," Weston wrote, "but was unable to keep my promise."

The constable escorted Weston to Balcom's boardinghouse, where he was detained for nearly two hours until "two gentlemen, almost entire strangers" agreed to sign a promissory note for him. Weston then went to a friend's house to rest for about an hour

---

* Weston would later report that he distributed some fifty thousand cards advertising Grover & Baker sewing machines during the walk, as well as five thousand packages of other circulars.

before setting out again. It was 3:15 in the morning. Less than a day into his journey he was already nearly three hours behind schedule.

Trudging through snow a foot deep, Weston became deeply discouraged. At one point he directed his team to return to Worcester before abruptly changing his mind. "He seemed to think if he went back *at all* it would be a failure," Weston later wrote, employing two of his favorite literary devices, italics and the third person, "and if he went ahead it would kill him, yet said that he would sooner die on the road than back down." By the time he reached East Brookfield, Massachusetts, about fifteen miles west of Worcester, it was 8:40 AM.

The proprietor of a hotel in East Brookfield prepared a hearty breakfast for Weston and offered him a bed. Weston slept for two hours and upon arising declared himself "much refreshed." At noon he hit the road again, reaching Palmer, Massachusetts, at 6:20 that evening. Upon reaching Palmer, Weston was surprised to find a large crowd had been waiting for hours in the cold to see him arrive. Word of his undertaking had, to put it in modern terms, gone viral. Telegraph operators along the route were sharing reports on Weston's progress, and newspapers were publishing updates.

On he trudged, south through Connecticut—Hartford, Wallingford, New Haven, Norwalk, Greenwich. In the last town, a six-year-old boy presented him with a gold medal depicting Lincoln, unmindful, apparently, that Weston had bet on the president-elect to lose. In each town the crowds greeting him grew larger.

Walking from Boston to Washington was no picnic in 1861. Roadmaps were unreliable, signage was practically nonexistent, and the state of America's roads at the time was deplorable. Yet Weston kept going, through cold and wind, rain and snow, sleeping just three or four hours a night in roadside inns or the homes of sympathetic strangers. Along the way, "people would come to the road-side and offer him refreshments, and not unfrequently he would partake of milk, also molasses and water." Dogs were his constant nemesis. Weston was deathly afraid of the animals and was often forced to take long detours to avoid them. Shortly after leaving Hartford, he sprained his left ankle trying to fend off a mutt that was chasing him.

At 9:45 on the morning of Wednesday, February 27, five days after leaving Boston, Weston walked across the Harlem Bridge and entered Manhattan. His first stop was the offices of Grover & Baker, the sewing machine company that was his main sponsor. There he curled up on a table and took a nap. At five o'clock that evening he rode a ferry across the Hudson to Jersey City, New Jersey—his only respite from bipedal locomotion since setting out.

By now Weston's walk was attracting considerable attention up and down the East Coast, and when he arrived in Newark the crowd that greeted him was so large and unruly that several policemen had to be called out to maintain order.

Weston captivated the country because the nation empathized with him. America was a walking nation in 1861. The overwhelming majority of people traveled primarily, if not exclusively, by foot. Only the wealthy could afford a carriage—or even a horse; a good one would set you back more than one hundred dollars, at a time when the typical laborer was lucky to earn a dollar a day. More than 80 percent of the population lived in rural areas, where public transportation was practically nonexistent. To put it in contemporary terms, the 1 percent sat when they traveled; the other 99 percent walked. Virtually everyone had, like Weston, trudged many miles over dreadful roads in harsh conditions, whether to attend services at a distant church or to fetch a doctor in the middle of the night.

In 2010, a study published in the journal *Medicine & Science in Sports & Exercise* found that American adults, on average, take 5,117 steps each day. That works out to about 2.5 miles—and that's counting every single step, from the first one out of bed in the morning to the last one before climbing back in at night. To maintain good health, doctors generally recommend people walk at least ten thousand steps a day—about five miles. A person who takes fewer than five thousand steps a day is usually considered sedentary. The study's authors concluded that "low levels of ambulatory physical activity are contributing to the high prevalence of adult obesity in the United States." America is no longer a walking nation.

It's impossible to say just how many steps the average American took each day in the nineteenth century, but it's safe to assume it was many more than 5,117. For example, the historian Steven Mintz has cited an 1886 survey that found a typical housewife in North Carolina walked nearly a half mile a day—just carrying water.

Weston's walk resonated for another reason. The winter of 1860–61 was one of the darkest in American history. On December 20, South Carolina became the first state to leave the Union. Over the next six weeks, six more states seceded, and on February 4, 1861, just eighteen days before Weston left Boston, the Confederate States of America was formed. A civil war was now inevitable. America was desperate for diversions, especially unifying diversions. By walking south across the Mason-Dixon Line from New England to Washington, Weston represented a rare and welcome symbol of unity in a nation about to be violently fractured.

The walk also resonated for a less lofty reason: gambling. In saloons and pool halls up and down the East Coast, wagers large and small were placed on whether Weston would reach Washington in time to see Lincoln's inauguration. With so much money riding on the outcome, interest in the walk was naturally piqued. Even children were eager for a piece of the action. In Massachusetts, Weston was approached by a boy who urged him to reach Washington "on time," for the lad had wagered on Weston's success. Weston promised to do his best, "but at the same time expressed his regret, that any one should have bet upon his performance of a feat, such as he had never before attempted."

On the morning of Friday, March 1, Weston arrived in Trenton, New Jersey. "Weston, the pedestrian, arrived here about 9 o'clock to-day and attracted a crowd of spectators," the *New York Times* reported. "He made a short speech to the crowd, and said he was well and felt confident that he would accomplish his feat." However, between his battles with creditors and the unforgiving weather, Weston had fallen far behind schedule. Then, early the next day, just south of Philadelphia, he got lost. He walked twelve miles down the wrong road before realizing his mistake. Now there was no hope that he would make it to Washington on time.

Weston finally touched the white marble columns of the United States Capitol, its dome still under construction, at 5:00 PM on Inauguration Day, Monday, March 4, 1861—five hours too late to witness Lincoln taking the oath. The walk had taken him 10 days, 4 hours, and 12 minutes. He had failed to pay off his bet but had won widespread admiration.

Capitalizing on his newfound celebrity, Weston finagled an invitation to one of Lincoln's inaugural events, where he was introduced to the new president. Lincoln did not begrudge Weston for having bet on him to lose. In fact, he offered to pay his train fare home. But Weston demurred, insisting he would walk back to Boston. Evidently, Weston did not deliver to Lincoln the kiss he had received from the young woman in Framingham.

Weston planned to begin walking back to Boston on April 23, but on April 12, Confederate forces attacked Fort Sumter, beginning the Civil War. "I thought proper to forego that task for some future occasion," he wrote, "and to use my pedestrian abilities in serving our government."

Weston volunteered as a messenger for the Union army. Disguised as a "Susquehanna Raftsman" "on a bender," he carried letters sewn into the lining of his jacket through a rebel stronghold in Maryland to a Union fort in Baltimore. When he arrived at the fort he was mistaken for a Confederate spy and briefly imprisoned.

In 1862 Weston published an overwrought, third-person account of his walk from Boston to Washington, as well as his exploits behind Confederate lines. In the book, Weston was careful to thank each and every one of his sponsors by name, like a NASCAR driver interviewed after a race. He also thanked "Messrs Brooks, Brothers, clothing dealers, corner of Broadway and Broome St., New York" for furnishing his messenger disguise. Weston ended the book by declaring that he hoped "soon to enter a more laudable business than pedestrianism."

After the war, Weston once again found himself in arrears. "In the winter of 1866," he wrote, "I became somewhat involved in debt by entrusting money to other parties. Eventually I lost all I had and some thousands of dollars which kind friends had loaned me." When a friend suggested he walk for money, Weston decided to "turn pro." He contacted George Goodwin, a prominent New York gambler, who agreed to back Weston in a wager with a gambler named T. F. Wilcox. Weston bet Wilcox $10,000 that he could walk the 1,200 miles from Portland, Maine, to Chicago in thirty consecutive days, excluding Sundays (after his famous 1861 walk, Weston had promised his mother that he would never again walk competitively on the Sabbath). It was, of course, a fantastic sum, though Weston was coy about his stake: "I need only say that should I win, I receive an amount sufficient to pay my indebtedness and to reinstate myself in business."

He left Portland at noon on Tuesday, October 29, 1867. Weston wore a black jacket and red leggings. He also wore a specially designed pair of boots equipped with tubes into which he occasionally poured whiskey to "keep his feet from chafing or swelling." Four witnesses, two each for Goodwin and Wilcox, followed him in a carriage pulled by two horses. According to an agreement signed by the two gamblers, "If at any time or under any circumstances, the said Weston enters any vehicle or mounts any animal, or conveyance, for the purpose of riding, or does ride one foot of the distance to be walked, then this wager is forfeited against the said Weston and his backer."

Again the nation was captivated by Weston the Walker. In Buffalo, a detachment of twenty-four police officers escorted him through the city. "The police formed a hollow square with Weston in the center," a reporter for the *Buffalo Express* wrote.

> Before, behind and around them were people on foot and on horseback, in wagons, in wood racks, elegant coaches and rheumatic buggies, running, walking, pushing, crowding, a wild throng inextricably tangled. . . .
>
> Through Genesee street the scene was animated in the extreme. Every available place of lookout was occupied, the windows, the doorways and the housetops.

"The excitement here over the matter is really extraordinary," wrote a reporter in Erie, Pennsylvania. "Everybody is discussing it, and all eager for the latest rumor concerning the pedestrian hero."

"Congress meets in a week or so," noted the *Erie Dispatch*. "Nobody talks about Congress. It's all Weston, Weston, the walkist—Weston, the pedestrian. He's the man."

Weston faced many of the same obstacles he'd faced on his first walk—nasty weather, miserable roads, unfriendly dogs—but, with so much money riding on the outcome, the stakes were much higher this time. Weston was fearful—even paranoid—that gamblers who'd wagered against him would attempt to sabotage the walk.

To avoid being poisoned, he ordered that "no particle of food or drops of beverage is to be given to me unless prepared under the immediate supervision of Mr. Grinnell." (John Grinnell was one of the witnesses on the walk for Weston backer George Goodwin.) The *Buffalo Courier* reported that Weston also insisted on being surrounded by a no-go zone when he walked: "Weston is morbidly sensitive of being approached closely while walking, probably fearful that some one, with a pecuniary interest in the result of his undertaking, will tread on his feet and disable him.

He walks in a clear space of some ten feet in diameter, preceded and followed by a person whose duty it is to see that the charmed circle is not intruded upon."

Weston won the wager with a day to spare. He reached the Chicago city limits at 9:07 AM on Thursday, November 28—Thanksgiving Day, a holiday, incidentally, that had been formally proclaimed for the first time by the late President Lincoln just four years earlier. More than fifty thousand people—nearly a fifth of the city's population—lined the streets to cheer Weston as he walked to the Sherman House hotel.* He was surrounded by a phalanx of fifty police officers. A thirty-piece marching band led the way. That day Weston delivered two lectures at Crosby's Opera House. Admission was $1.50—not cheap—but both sold out. "This walk," *Harper's Weekly* would later say, "made Weston's name a household word."

A few days later, Weston was sitting in the lobby of the Sherman House when he was approached by an "enthusiastic individual" who, quite unexpectedly, presented Weston with a gift: a puppy. A reporter for the *Chicago Republican* witnessed the event: "Weston viewed the dog a moment, laughed heartily, and desired the man to put him down, which he did, and left. Hardly had the door closed upon the donor of the dog when Weston got up, grasped the pup by the nape of the neck, and threw him through an open window into the street, remarking as he did so, "D**n the dogs; they are my bane."

His contempt for puppies notwithstanding, the victorious Weston was feted from coast to coast. A Cleveland music publisher hurriedly released a new composition: "Weston's March to Chicago." The *Chicago Tribune* urged Weston to run for vice president on a ticket with George Francis Train, a business magnate and

---

* The Sherman House, along with much of the rest of Chicago, would be destroyed in the Great Fire four years later. And, like most of the city, it would be rebuilt.

political gadfly. (Train, at least, took the suggestion seriously, running for president as an independent in 1872. He received no electoral votes.)

Another paper hailed Weston as the most famous man in America—even more famous than General Grant. Advertisements invoking Weston's name popped up in newspapers all over the country, ads like this one in the *Janesville (Wisconsin) Gazette*:

Weston is said to have made a good thing out of his recent walk, but people would do still better if they would walk to the West Side Jewelry Store to purchase their Jewelry, Watches and other Holiday goods.

The acclaim was not universal, however. "Sherman's march from Chattanooga to the sea was a slight affair when compared with Weston's march from Portland to Chicago," the *Milwaukee Semi-Weekly Wisconsin* sarcastically opined. "Seriously, we ask what has Weston achieved that justifies all the fuss made over him? Has he exhibited any more noble, admirable, or praiseworthy qualities than the horse that performs an extraordinary feat of pedestrianism? Is the display of muscle any more honorable because [it was] shown by one of the supposed higher order of creation? We say not." Grudgingly, however, the paper did concede that the walk might prove beneficial in one respect. "If it shall have the effect to popularize among Americans that much neglected species of exercise, pedestrianism, it will be a wholesome sanitary result."

Weston would indeed popularize pedestrianism, and in ways that could hardly be imagined.

2

WALKING FEVER

or

PERHAPS A FOREIGNER COULD DO IT

BEFORE THE CIVIL WAR, SPECTATOR SPORTS barely existed in the United States. A diffuse rural population, arduous travel conditions, negligible disposable income, a dearth of time for recreation, and a lack of suitable venues made it difficult to attend, much less organize, athletic events. Besides, frivolities like sports were anathema to the prevailing antebellum ethos. "The American work ethic," wrote the historian Elliott Gorn, "with its roots in republican producer culture, evangelical Christianity, and new capitalist imperatives of growth and profit, impeded the development of all recreations." Horse races, foot races, and boat races were staged occasionally, but these events rarely proved profitable or noteworthy.

The only spectator sports that prospered in the years before the war were the blood sports: cockfighting, dogfighting, and bare-knuckle boxing. Not exactly wholesome family entertainment, these violent sports were closely associated with gambling, and they operated on the margins of society.

Boxing—antebellum America's most popular sport—was universally banned. In New Jersey, aiding, abetting, or participating in the "degrading practice of prize fighting" was punishable by up to two years' imprisonment and a $1,000 fine. In Massachusetts, the penalty was ten years and $5,000. In New York, even spectators were liable to prosecution. As a result, matches were organized surreptitiously. Fights were staged in the back rooms of saloons, in rural areas where jurisdiction was ambiguous, on remote islands—even on barges.

An 1849 bout between Tom Hyer and James "Yankee" Sullivan was scheduled to take place on Pooles Island, a desolate speck in Chesapeake Bay.* But on the eve of the match, the Baltimore County sheriff caught wind of the plan and sent a posse to the island to arrest the fighters. Hyer, Sullivan, and their backers narrowly escaped by boat. They decamped to a village on Maryland's Eastern Shore, where a ring was hastily erected using rope from the boat's rigging. The next day, before at least two hundred excited onlookers, Hyer and Sullivan pummeled each other for fifteen bloody rounds. In the sixteenth, according to one eyewitness, Sullivan "was found to be entirely exhausted . . . and staggered backward toward the ropes. The fight was done." Hyer took home the $10,000 purse and was declared the "Champion of America."

Back in his hometown of Philadelphia, Hyer was feted with an impromptu parade down Chestnut Street, a display that dismayed the local prosecutor, who said the fight had excited "the worst passions of the community." Hyer was arrested and briefly detained, though authorities back in Maryland declined to press charges.

Another generation would pass before boxing finally emerged from the shadows to win public acceptance.

During the Civil War, the first seeds of modern spectator sports were planted by Union soldiers from New York, who exported

---

* Today, Pooles Island is the site of Maryland's oldest lighthouse, but don't try to visit; it is strictly off limits to the public. For much of the twentieth century the military used the island as a bombing range, and it is littered with unexploded ordnance.

This lithograph depicts Union prisoners playing baseball in a Confederate prison camp in Salisbury, North Carolina, in 1863. COURTESY OF LIBRARY OF CONGRESS

their favorite pastime to the rest of the country. Before the war, baseball, which is believed to be descended from a British game called rounders, was popular among "gentlemen" in New York City. The first recorded game took place in 1846 at Elysian Fields in Hoboken, New Jersey. The New York Nine defeated the New York Knickerbockers, 23–1.

By the 1850s, several teams were based at Elysian Fields. Some of the rules, which were devised by the founder of the Knickerbockers, Alexander Cartwright, differed considerably from today's game. Batters could choose where they wanted the pitcher to throw the ball. Overhand pitching was not allowed. Runners could not steal bases. Nonetheless, a modern fan watching a game played under Cartwright's rules would have no trouble recognizing it as baseball.

During the war, troops from New York played baseball at every available opportunity, often with improvised equipment, usually before audiences composed of their fellow soldiers. The game was even played by Union soldiers in Confederate prison camps, exposing countless Southerners to the pastime for the first time.

Military leaders on both sides of the conflict encouraged the game as a way to build morale and improve conditioning. "The parade ground has been a busy place for a week or so past," Private Alpheris B. Parker of the Tenth Massachusetts wrote in a letter home, "ball-playing having become a mania in camp. Officer and men forget, for a time, the differences in rank and indulge in the invigorating sport with a schoolboy's ardor."

By the end of the war, baseball had been transformed from a gentleman's game into a more democratic enterprise in which talent, not class or rank, conferred status. And, in stark contrast to the blood sports, baseball was well regarded, as it was thought to impart such seemingly traditional American values as teamwork and shared sacrifice.

Yet, despite its newfound popularity, baseball did not immediately emerge as a popular spectator sport after the Civil War. For one thing, it required sprawling outdoor spaces, which were becoming increasingly scarce—and prohibitively expensive—in the rapidly industrializing urban centers. As a team sport, baseball also required a sophisticated organizational structure to oversee the formation and regulation of teams and leagues, as well as scheduling, rule making, and the like. It would take another two decades and the efforts of visionary entrepreneurs before baseball would truly become America's national pastime.

———•◆•———

The Second Industrial Revolution, spurred by Henry Bessemer's invention of a process for mass-producing steel from molten pig iron, profoundly altered America. As the nation industrialized in the decades after the war, cities grew rapidly, public transportation improved vastly, and many workers now had a little extra money in their pockets and some free time on their hands. Now the time was ripe for the development of spectator sports.

Attitudes were changing too. Between 1836 and 1914, more than thirty million Europeans migrated to the United States, largely from Ireland and Germany. These immigrants not only brought with them a fondness for games, but many also saw sports as a vehicle for upward mobility and expressing ethnic pride. No longer were sports anathema.

Another important development was architectural. Before the war, what the historian Steven A. Riess has described as "enclosed semipublic facilities" were practically nonexistent in the United States. This, of course, made it difficult to stage sporting events for paying customers. But as urban populations exploded after the war, cities found it necessary to construct large buildings to accommodate public events, including everything from political rallies to religious revivals and livestock shows. These venues, often called agricultural halls or exposition buildings, would become America's first big sports arenas.

Also important to the development of spectator sports, however, was the humble roller-skating rink.

In the winter of 1860–61, a thirty-two-year-old New York businessman named James Leonard Plimpton fell ill. His doctor prescribed ice skating, believing the exercise and fresh air would improve his health. It worked. Plimpton began to feel better, but as winter waned, he needed to find a new regimen. So he invented something he called "guidable parlor skates," which he patented in 1863. Plimpton's invention, now recognized as the first "quad skate," was a roller skate with four small wheels on two axles. The skate also featured a revolutionary pivoting mechanism that allowed users to make turns simply by leaning to one side or the other. These are the familiar skates that would make roller derby possible in the following century.

Roller skating had been around for more than a hundred years, but before Plimpton's invention, the skates were dangerously unwieldy—imagine a ski with two large wheels attached at each end—so the sport was reserved for daredevils and the foolhardy.

This illustration from *Frank Leslie's Illustrated Newspaper* depicts a "fashionable roller-skating rink" in Washington, DC, in 1880. COURTESY OF LIBRARY OF CONGRESS

The quad skate was infinitely safer and more maneuverable, and it proved wildly popular; roller skating became one of America's first postbellum fads. (William Tecumseh Sherman was said to be a fan.)

But this new fad required large flat surfaces, so Plimpton began building roller-skating rinks. The first was in fashionable Newport, Rhode Island, so as to woo the in crowd. His idea was copied, and, almost overnight, roller rinks began popping up in cities and towns across the country.

Edward Payson Weston instantly recognized the profit potential of the new roller rinks, and in 1870 he began touring the country, performing walking exhibitions in rinks from Goshen, Indiana, to New York City. It was certainly more comfortable than walking outside in the elements. It was lucrative too. He charged up to fifty cents for the pleasure of watching him circumambulate for hours on makeshift dirt tracks—and thousands of people gladly paid. He usually walked against time, such as attempting to cover one hundred miles in twenty-four hours. In some rinks, the tracks were so tiny that it took as many as fifty laps to traverse a single mile. To relieve the tedium, Weston often hired a band to entertain the audience, with Weston himself occasionally playing a cornet while he walked. He wore ruffled shirts, and he always carried a riding crop or a cane, an affectation that would become his trademark. Weston understood intuitively that the event was about entertainment as much as it was about athletics.

At a roller rink in Manhattan in 1870, Weston attempted to walk one hundred miles in less than twenty-two hours to win a $2,500 wager. He succeeded with twenty minutes to spare. A crowd of five thousand squeezed into the rink to cheer him on for the final miles. In the same rink the following year, he walked four hundred miles in five days, earning more accolades—and a cool $5,000 in wagers and gate receipts.[*]

Much was made of Weston's peculiar stride. He swung his hips with each step, not unlike a modern racewalker. One reporter wrote that Weston walked with "a splendid sweeping stride that carries him over the road like the wind." Others, however, were less complimentary, saying his gait was "wobbly." One observer said Weston's legs were "put on like two toothpicks stuck in opposite sides of a potato."

Many years later, a New Yorker named Alfred Meyer, who as a boy attended one of Weston's walks around this time, recalled Weston's form. "As he strode around the track," Meyer wrote, "I noticed that Weston accentuated each third step, visibly accelerating his speed by so doing. This method brought the extra effort alternately on the left and right foot, with a respite between, since

---

* More than $100,000 in today's dollars.

Weston walking at a roller rink in New York City in May 1874. His idiosyncratic stride was sometimes described as "wobbly." Courtesy of Library of Congress

the acceleration fell on the fourth, seventh and tenth step and so on. He also carried in his hand a little whip with which he occasionally switched his sturdy little legs."

"To boys of my generation," Meyer added, "Weston was a hero."

At a rink in Newark, New Jersey, in December 1874, Weston attempted to walk a mind-boggling five hundred miles in six days—an average of more than eighty-three miles a day. So much money was wagered on the outcome that the mayor of Newark, fearing for Weston's safety, threatened to call out the National Guard, and one gambler was arrested for attempting to sabotage Weston by pouring a chemical on the track. Weston succeeded with less than half an hour to spare: he completed his 500th mile in 5 days, 23 hours, 34 minutes, and 15 seconds (25 minutes and 45 seconds less than six days).

The *New York Times* called Weston's feat "the most remarkable on record," but the sporting press was mostly unimpressed.

At the time, periodicals that specialized in sports were aimed at upper-class readers who enjoyed posh pursuits like yachting and prized amateurism above all else in athletics, and Weston's crass commercialization rankled them. The *Spirit of the Times* dismissed Weston as a "humbug" fleecing a gullible public, and the *New York Sportsman* huffed that "any displays with which Weston is connected will be understood by anybody possessed of sense enough to seek shelter when it rains to be mere mercenary exhibitions, and no tests of real merit." Weston was accused of inventing bogus records to set. His bona fides as an athlete were questioned, and his hubris clearly rubbed some people the wrong way. "That fellow is a fraud," the *Sportsman* concluded.

Nonetheless, Weston's exploits captivated the masses, and soon the nation was infected with what the papers called "walking fever." All over America, would-be Edward Payson Westons began walking in circles. Pedestrianism seemed to offer the promise of easy riches, as it appeared to require no unusual talent—only the ability to walk.

In towns large and small, races were held in roller rinks for local pedestrians and itinerant professionals. Hopefuls took out classified ads in newspapers seeking challengers: "I will walk any amateur that works for his daily bread at mechanical or any kind of manual labor six days a week, a twenty-four hour race for a $50 gold medal."

Companies organized pedestrian teams. The best in New York City's department store league was said to be Lord & Taylor's. In Saint Louis, the city's six major newspapers competed in a four-hour race. The winner was James Boyle of the *Globe-Democrat*, who completed more than twenty-four miles and took home a "handsome gold watch" for his efforts.

Retailers wasted no time cashing in on the craze. Tiffany peddled a "remarkable" new invention called a pedometer. A cobbler named John Welsher devised a new "walking shoe" with built-in springs. As Walter Bernstein wrote in the *Virginia Quarterly Review*, "It seemed as though the muscles of the nation were making one final, vast, collective effort before being replaced by the internal combustion machine."

Celebrities caught the bug. *New York Herald* publisher James Gordon Bennett Jr., whose father had inadvertently helped Weston discover his "great locomotive powers" when he retrieved that wayward parcel, became one of pedestrianism's most ardent advocates. Bennett competed too, winning a 10-mile race against a fellow member of the Union Club named John Whipple.

Even Mark Twain was infected with walking fever. In November 1874 he and a friend attempted to walk the one hundred miles from Hartford to Boston. They gave up after just ten miles and took a train the rest of the way. "There was no intention on our part to excite anybody's envy or make Mr. Weston feel badly," Twain told a reporter afterward, "for we were not preparing for a big walk so much as for a delightful walk."

Dan O'Leary.
COURTESY OF LIBRARY OF CONGRESS

Pedestrians seeking fame devised all sorts of gimmicks to attract attention. One walked eight miles under water (presumably with the benefit of a snorkel). Another sought notoriety by walking around Boston Common carrying a beer keg. There were one-legged walking matches and backward-walking matches.

The walking mania also inspired more serious challengers to Edward Payson Weston. Foremost among them was a skinny, mustachioed Irishman named Daniel O'Leary.

Dan O'Leary did not enter the world at a propitious time and place. He was born in 1846, in his family's thatch-roofed cottage near Clonakilty, a tiny village in County

Cork on the southern coast of Ireland. It was the eve of the Great Famine. In the first six years of O'Leary's life, Ireland was ravaged by a potato blight that decimated the population.

The response of the British government, which ruled the island, was inadequate, to say the least. Sir Charles Trevelyan, the British official overseeing famine relief, believed that, since "the judgement of God sent the calamity to teach the Irish a lesson, that calamity must not be too much mitigated." By 1852, an estimated one million people had died from disease or starvation. Another million had emigrated. Ireland's population had fallen by as much as 25 percent.

Young Dan O'Leary must have witnessed unimaginable suffering, but his childhood was not devoid of pleasure. He enjoyed traditional Gaelic games like hurling (imagine a cross between baseball and soccer, if you can), and he was an avid rower. But the catastrophic famine had ruined his homeland's economy, so when he was twenty, O'Leary joined the Celtic exodus and sailed for America.

He landed in New York on April 4, 1866, arriving, like so many immigrants, alone and nearly penniless. He made his way to Chicago, where he found a job in a lumberyard. When winter came, he headed south to Mississippi, where he picked cotton on plantations until the spring of 1868, when he returned to Chicago and, like his future rival Edward Payson Weston, became a door-to-door bookseller.

O'Leary managed to make a decent living selling gilded editions of the Holy Bible and *Webster's Unabridged Dictionary* on payment plans to the city's burgeoning middle class, until his life was turned upside down by another catastrophe: the Great Fire of 1871, which killed hundreds, left thousands homeless, and leveled more than three square miles of Chicago. In a sign of the anti-Irish sentiment that permeated the city at the time, the cause of the conflagration was initially attributed to another O'Leary—an Irish immigrant named Catherine O'Leary, whose cow was said to have started the blaze by knocking over a lantern while she was milking it in a barn. Catherine O'Leary was a scapegoat. Theories abound, but the true cause of the fire remains a mystery. The Chicago City Council formally absolved Mrs. O'Leary of all blame—in 1997.

The Great Fire nearly ruined Dan O'Leary. Customers who owed him hundreds of dollars simply vanished. And, with the city reduced to cinders, the demand for gilt-edged books vanished too. To eke out a living, O'Leary was forced to walk many miles out to the suburbs and back each day. It was wearying, but the exercise would serve him well.

In the fall of 1873, O'Leary was shopping in a large dry goods store on Wabash Avenue when he overheard a small group of men discussing one of Edward Payson Weston's attempts to walk one hundred miles in twenty-four hours.

"None but a Yankee can place on record such a gigantic performance," one of the men said.

"Hold on—not so fast," interjected O'Leary in his brogue, "perhaps a foreigner could do it."

"He won't be an Irishman, though," said another man.

"Ireland has sent forth good men," O'Leary replied.

"Yes, wonderful fellows, indeed; they can accomplish almost anything with their tongues," another man replied sarcastically.

When O'Leary attempted to defend his countrymen, the first man cut him off.

"Bully fellow, hire a hall, and get your name up," he said, provoking laughter among his companions.

"Yes, one in which to walk rather than talk," said O'Leary. Flushed with rage, he stormed out of the store, determined to prove an Irishman's worth in pedestrianism. Presently, he rented a roller rink on the West Side of Chicago and announced his intention to walk 100 miles in 24 hours. He began the attempt at 8:30 PM on July 14, 1874. His only refreshments were ice water and brandy, the latter of which he much preferred. The heat inside the rink was stifling and the track was rickety, but O'Leary met his goal with forty-three minutes remaining. A month later, he rented the rink again, and this time walked 105 miles in 23 hours and 38 minutes.

Emboldened by these successes, O'Leary challenged Edward Payson Weston to a 250-mile walking match, a challenge that Weston laughed off, telling the Irishman, "Make a good record first and meet me after."

Infuriated, O'Leary set out to do just that. At a rink in Philadelphia in April 1875, he broke Weston's twenty-four-hour record of 115 miles by walking 116 miles

This biography of Dan O'Leary was published in 1878. COURTESY OF LIBRARY OF CONGRESS

in 23 hours, 12 minutes, and 53 seconds. "Weston will have to look to his laurels," said the *Philadelphia Times*, "for all of a sudden, in the height of his fame, a competitor springs up who bids fair to throw his best feats into the shade. This wonder bears the common enough name of Daniel O'Leary."

Back at the rink on the West Side of Chicago a month later, O'Leary bested Weston's most cherished record by walking 500 miles in 5 days, 21 hours, 31 minutes, and 50 seconds (2 hours, 28 minutes, and 10 seconds less than six days). That was more than two hours faster than Weston had walked the same distance in Newark the year before. Over five thousand people crammed into the ramshackle building to witness the close of the historic walk. "He showed signs of fatigue," one eyewitness reported, "but was by no means exhausted at the close and walked the last hours at the rate of one mile in twelve minutes and thirty-two seconds."

Afterward, a group of proud Chicagoans presented O'Leary with a gold medal proclaiming him CHAMPION PEDESTRIAN OF AMERICA. Irish immigrants throughout the country exalted in O'Leary's achievement. Bad poetry being a staple of the times, O'Leary was commemorated in a poem that soon became popular in Irish neighborhoods in New York:

> Attend, you loyal Irishmen, of every rank and station,
> I pray draw near and lend an ear here in a distant nation;
> With right good will I take my quill, and never shall get
>   weary
> To sing the praise of that noble youth—brave Dan O'Leary.

There was now no doubt that O'Leary had made a good record, and in the summer of 1875, Weston finally agreed to a match. The country's two most famous pedestrians would meet in a 500-mile race.

Although both men were once booksellers, Weston and O'Leary had little else in common. Weston was a teetotaler, a proud Yankee, and a notorious attention seeker. O'Leary was a hard-drinking Irish immigrant, almost reserved, but not immune to the coarser charms of the Wicked City, as Chicago was then known. (By the end of the century, for reasons still unclear, that bawdy nickname would be replaced by one more benign: the Windy City.)

The first great rivalry in the annals of American sports was born. Weston and O'Leary would become the Frazier and Ali of their age.

3

THE EXPO

or

NOT AN ABSORBINGLY ENTRANCING SPORT

BILLED AS "THE GREAT WALKING MATCH for the Championship of the World," the 500-mile race between Weston and O'Leary in 1875 attracted such intense interest that the two pedestrians agreed to hold the match in the largest venue possible: Chicago's mammoth Interstate Exposition Building.

Of all the grand public buildings constructed in the decade following the Civil War, the Italianate-style Expo on Michigan Avenue was, by far, the grandest: a metal-and-glass palace topped with three massive domes. The central dome soared 165 feet into the sky, serving as a beacon to ships on Lake Michigan. The main floor covered some 240,000 square feet—more than five acres. The Expo was the largest enclosed public meeting space in the United States. Rising from the ashes of the Great Fire of 1871, its construction two years later was an emphatic civic statement

The three domes of the Interstate Exposition Building in Chicago can be seen in this image. The view is looking south on South Michigan Avenue. The Expo was built in ninety days in 1873, just two years after the city's Great Fire. It was demolished in 1892. The Art Institute of Chicago now stands on the site. CHICAGO HISTORY MUSEUM, *CHICAGO DAILY NEWS* NEGATIVES COLLECTION, DN-0078572

that Chicago would not merely rebuild but would prosper.* In fact, some saw the Expo as a symbol of not only Chicago's progress but America's. At the building's grand opening, one of the speakers was Illinois senator (and past and future governor) Richard James Oglesby. "The Senator warned Europe to be on her guard," a reporter who was there noted, "for Young America, full of blood, full of power, full of pride, will not stop until she eclipses the world. Europe, said he, with her countless stores, must beware the ambition and the impudence of Young America."

---

* The Expo would serve as an Illinois National Guard armory and the first home of the Chicago Symphony Orchestra. It was also the site of the 1880 Republican and 1884 Democratic and Republican national conventions. The building was razed in 1892 to make way for the Art Institute of Chicago, which still stands on the site.

The Expo was an awe-inspiring building. "Entering at either one of the grand doors," one sightseer observed, "the visitor is first impressed with the immensity of the structure. What struck him as enormous as contemplated from the outside now seems to grow and expand wonderfully before his gaze. Unimpeded as it was by the details of the exterior, his eyes wander from floor to ceiling, to the concave summit of the central dome, from side to side and from end to end of the structure, in almost stupefying amazement."

By staging the race in Chicago, O'Leary would enjoy a home-field advantage, of course, but Weston was mollified by an offer he couldn't refuse: $500 and half the gate receipts. Besides, the city still regarded Weston highly for his walk from Portland eight years earlier, and holding the event in the gigantic Expo would maximize profits.

Weston and O'Leary were reported to be in training in the weeks leading up to the race, though exactly how they trained is a bit of a mystery. Pedestrians, like other athletes at the time, considered their training methods trade secrets, and they were notoriously circumspect when it came to discussing them. Weston, for his part, would only admit to eating "plain food" and abstaining from "stimulating liquors" when he was preparing for an event. In *Lore of Running*, a history of track and field, Tim Noakes wrote that other nineteenth-century pedestrians were known to train for races by "walking and running for 6 to 8 hours a day," and by adhering to diets that consisted of "roast beef, roast and boiled mutton or chicken, and limited vegetables and stale crusty bread, all washed down with bitter ale."

The race was scheduled to begin just after midnight on Monday, November 15, 1875. As the day drew closer, hype began to build. "This approaching trial of physical endurance has excited a considerable interest," the *Chicago Tribune* noted on the eve of the match, "and its result will be watched with interest by thousands."

The rules for the race were codified in articles of agreement approved by Weston and O'Leary. A team of judges and scorekeepers would be appointed from a list of prominent Chicagoans acceptable to both pedestrians. Admission to the event would be fifty cents. Weston and O'Leary would each be assigned a room in the Expo for resting. The first man to walk 500 miles would be declared the winner. Under no circumstances, however, could the race continue beyond midnight the following Saturday night. This was not merely due to Weston's self-imposed ban on Sunday ambulation; at the time, Chicago, like nearly every other city in the United States (and the United Kingdom, for that matter), had so-called blue laws that prohibited "public amusements" on the Christian Sabbath. Six days was as long as any athletic event could last.

The articles of agreement also stipulated that both competitors must go "fair heel and toe": each was required to keep one foot in contact with the ground at all times. Running was explicitly banned. This was an important distinction. At the time, "pedestrianism" was an ambiguous term that applied to any footrace, whether walking or running. But from then on—in the United States at least—the term would define competitive walking matches exclusively.

The truth was, neither Weston nor O'Leary was an especially gifted runner. Their talents lay in endurance rather than speed. But in time, the true definition of pedestrianism—even the definition of walking itself—would generate great controversy in the sport.

Weston arrived in Chicago on November 11, four days before the race. "He travels in style," the *Chicago Evening Journal* noted, "being attended by two negro servants." He checked into a suite at the Gardner House, a hotel across the street from the Expo. By now Weston was married with three children, but his family did not accompany him. Like his own father, Weston was frequently absent from his family.

Inside the cavernous Expo, two concentric tracks were laid. The inside track measured ⅐ of a mile, the outside track ⅙. The measurements were certified by Chicago's city surveyor. The tracks were made of pressed mulch, more commonly known at the time

The main floor of the Expo covered more than five acres. This photograph depicts the building as it was decorated for the opening of the Republican National Convention on June 2, 1880. COURTESY OF LIBRARY OF CONGRESS

as tanbark. To a generation of Americans, "the tanbark" would become synonymous with pedestrianism, just as "the gridiron" is synonymous with football today.

The doors to the Expo opened at 11:00 PM on Sunday, November 14, 1875. Despite the late hour, between three hundred and four hundred people came to watch the start of the race in the dim light of the building's hissing gas lamps. At precisely midnight, Weston and O'Leary approached the judges' table. Weston wore a black velvet suit with black boots. A silk sash was draped diagonally across his chest. In his right hand he carried a riding crop.

O'Leary was dressed more conventionally for an athletic event: white tights, a striped tank top, a brown knitted jacket. He wore "light walking shoes," and in each hand he held a pine stick— because, he believed, they "absorb the perspiration and keep the hands from swelling." Throughout his career, O'Leary would habitually clutch something in his hands when he walked: wooden sticks, corn cobs, pieces of ivory. It became an affectation as familiar as Weston's crops and canes.

Shortly after midnight, Chicago mayor Harvey Doolittle Colvin addressed the crowd. Noting that "Mr. Weston comes to Chicago to go into a contest with a citizen of Chicago," Colvin urged those in attendance to "see that he [Weston] has fair play."

It was a measure of the event's magnitude that the mayor had been invited to start the race, though he was a bit bemused by the circumstances.

"It seems out of place to be here," he said, "a little after 12 o'clock at night, to transact any sort of business."

"As we understand it," the mayor continued, "the man who has walked 500 miles, he has nothing further to do; he is safe to take a rest."

Lots had been drawn to determine track position. Weston would walk on the inside track, O'Leary on the outside. They took their places on the starting line in front of the judges' table. The mayor turned to face them.

"Are you ready, Mr. O'Leary?"

"Yes."

"Are you ready, Mr. Weston?"

"Yes."

"One! Two! Three!" shouted the mayor. The crowd roared. The time on the massive clock in the Expo, reporters covering the event carefully noted, was precisely 8 minutes and 19 seconds after midnight.*

---

* The direction they walked is unrecorded. Sometimes competitors in walking matches moved clockwise, sometimes counterclockwise. In some matches, competitors were permitted to walk in either direction, or even switch directions, which surely must have caused much confusion. I leave it to the reader to imagine the direction in which the competitors in any given match were moving.

The week before the match, O'Leary had announced his intention to cover 100 miles in the first 18 hours of the match, a pace of better than 5.5 miles per hour, and faster than anyone had ever walked that distance. He was probably just trying to psych out his opponent. Shortly before the race began, O'Leary confided to a reporter that he had "given up the idea . . . and would simply aim to beat Weston."

If it was gamesmanship on O'Leary's part, it worked. Weston became convinced that O'Leary would get "fagged out" before the race ended. Weston's strategy was simple: slow and steady, he believed, would win the race. It would be a tortoise-and-hare affair, with Weston as the tortoise.

From the start, it was clear that O'Leary, seven years younger than Weston, was the faster walker. He immediately shot out into the lead, completing his first mile in 11 minutes and 3 seconds. It took Weston more than a minute longer to complete his own first mile.

The two pedestrians had gaits that were as different as their attire. According to one observer, O'Leary walked with a "straight form, quick stride, and bent arms," while Weston seemed "rather to drag than throw his feet." O'Leary held his head up and looked straight ahead, while Weston appeared "to carry his head on his breast and to see nothing but the dirt before him."

By Monday evening, the Expo was crowded with spectators. No grandstands had been erected for the event, so the audience pressed close to the tracks, jockeying for position. Some spectators even crossed the tracks to view the action from within the concentric ovals, much to the chagrin of the competitors. "The irresistible attraction which draws people into places where they have no sort of business to be was never better shown than in the gaping faces which calmly stood in the paths of the men," a *Chicago Tribune* reporter noted. On several occasions police were called in to clear the way for the pedestrians.

A large chalkboard served as a scoreboard, with each competitor's score updated after each mile. A band had been hired to entertain the audience, and the musicians "discoursed rather doleful . . . music at intervals, such as the wind of the performers dictated."

Some in attendance complained that the music was much too loud. A vendor roasting peanuts over charcoal at one end of the arena did a booming business and filled the space with a pleasing aroma.

The audience, it was noted, was kind to both contestants, with one notable exception: at one point on that first day, a spectator said something "insulting" to Weston as he passed. Weston immediately left the track and demanded that the culprit be "cast forth," which he promptly was.

At the end of the first day, Weston trailed O'Leary by nineteen miles (110 to 91) but seemed unconcerned. He was still convinced O'Leary would wear himself out.

Throughout the contest, the competitors slept just three to five hours a night in the small rooms assigned to them in the Expo, though Weston returned to his hotel to sleep at least one night. Occasionally the two men stopped for meals, but more often they took their nourishment as they walked. Weston was partial to rare beefsteak. O'Leary preferred mutton and sipped either hot tea or champagne.

Although he was behind, Weston was in good spirits, and on Tuesday evening his flair for theatrics was on full display. His "gestures, scraps of song, mimicry of actors, and other recreations, were greatly enjoyed by the audience, and seemingly by the actor," according to one account. Weston told a reporter that evening that "he never felt better," and he predicted he would "be on the track feeling like a bird Saturday night." O'Leary, the more taciturn competitor, seems to have declined to speak with reporters during the race.

When the two pedestrians retired on Tuesday night, O'Leary had added three miles to his lead. By the end of Wednesday night, he had stretched his advantage to twenty-six miles: 273 miles to

247. It was now clear that O'Leary would not wear out as Weston had expected. But Weston was too proud and too stubborn to alter his strategy, or his deliberate, plodding gait, which, after all, had brought him such success.

Just as O'Leary's lead increased as the week progressed, so too did the number of people flocking to the Expo. On Friday night, the *Tribune* reported, the crowd was "simply immense." In the audience were scores of Irish immigrants, bursting with pride, shouting themselves hoarse, their brogues unmistakable as they cheered for their compatriot O'Leary. Those unable to afford the fifty-cent admission resorted to other means of gaining entrance to the Expo. Some volunteered to guard the building's marble statues in exchange for free admittance.

By Saturday morning, the outcome was no longer in doubt: O'Leary was ahead, 425 miles to 395. The foregone conclusion, however, did not deter Chicagoans from flocking to the Expo for the final day of the match, and by three o'clock that afternoon there was a long queue for tickets. That the competitors were by now utterly exhausted, practically dead on their feet, only added to the attraction.

At 7:00 PM "commenced a rush almost unparalleled," according to the *Tribune*. The Expo was "surrounded by a surging mass of humanity, eager to procure tickets. Excitement could not have reached a higher pitch, it would seem, for appearances indicated almost a wild delirium of the throng that besieged the building."

By eight o'clock the crowd inside the building numbered five thousand.

"The crowd was dense; sweeping hither and thither; shouting, yelling, or cheering," the *Tribune* reported. "The crowd was motley, but largely respectable; it represented wealth, standing, and brains, and thieves, gamblers, and roughs. Ladies were there in large numbers, some with husbands and some with lovers, but all had a terribly hard time of it in the ceaselessly moving and noisy throng." Pickpockets and thieves "plied their nefarious vocations." The police had trouble controlling the crowd and on several occasions were overwhelmed, "the mob taking possession of the tracks."

By nine o'clock the crowd numbered six thousand, including many "workingmen, many of whom brought their wives and children with them." Small boys crawled through the forest of adult legs to get close to the action. Older, more adventurous lads clambered up the Expo's trusses and took seats on the beams near the roof, more than one hundred feet above the arena floor.

As O'Leary neared his goal with each passing mile, the throng grew more frenzied. Around 10:15 he completed his 495th mile. Using megaphones—electrical amplification was still fifty years off—announcers informed the crowd that O'Leary had decided to continue walking until midnight, even though he would reach his goal of 500 miles well before that hour.

Weston, meanwhile, plodded on, looking "weary and dejected."

While O'Leary was walking his 497th mile, the crowd once again overwhelmed the tracks. The competitors were unable to move. The trespassing spectators were "driven back [by police] with the greatest difficulty."

O'Leary completed his 500th mile around 11:15 PM. The Expo erupted in delirious cheering. Men threw their hats in the air in exultation. The band played celebratory music. O'Leary's wife greeted him at the finish line in front of the judges' stand with a large basket of flowers, eliciting even more cheers. After a brief respite, O'Leary continued walking, and when the hands on the big clock in the Expo reached midnight, he had completed 503 miles and 2 laps (1/3 of a mile). Weston had completed 451 miles and 4 laps (4/7 of a mile).

Completely drained, the two foes greeted each other warmly and slowly walked several valedictory laps together, a gesture of sportsmanship that drew appreciative applause. Afterward, O'Leary was presented with a massive gold medal proclaiming him CHAMPION OF THE WORLD. Then everybody went home.

O'Leary's victory was weighted with great symbolic importance. Just four years after his namesake, Catherine O'Leary, had been made the scapegoat for the Great Fire that nearly destroyed Chicago, Dan O'Leary, another Irish immigrant, had unified the city in an unprecedented way. He'd only wanted to prove an Irishman's worth in pedestrianism, but O'Leary accomplished much more than that. As the newspapers noted at the time, his triumph was celebrated by every class, from the businessman to the bootblack. O'Leary was the first Irish immigrant since the fire to be embraced by Chicago's "native" population as a favorite son.

As it so often does, sports proved to be a great equalizer. It might be presumptuous to compare Dan O'Leary with Jackie Robinson, who broke baseball's long-standing "color line" some seventy-two years after O'Leary's victory over Weston in Chicago. But just as Robinson opened doors for African Americans, not only in baseball but throughout society, Dan O'Leary opened doors for Irish immigrants, especially in Chicago. He helped the Irish gain acceptance, if not equality, in the city.

Chicago was less kind to Edward Payson Weston. Lionized in the city just seven years earlier, Weston was now ridiculed as a pompous failure. His folly, the *Tribune* editorialized, was "supposing that, after dilly-dallying along for three or four days, and allowing his competitor to get 30 or 40 miles ahead of him, he could make up the difference on the last day and come out ahead. . . . He has only his own overconfidence in himself to blame for his defeat."

Although the *Tribune* covered the race breathlessly, the paper was at a loss to explain its popularity. "Walking," the *Tribune* observed, "is at best not an absorbingly entrancing sport." What the *Tribune* (and others mystified by pedestrianism's appeal) failed to appreciate was the public's hunger for entertainment at the time. It's hard to fathom now, in an age of infinite electronic diversions, but in the 1870s, America suffered from an entertainment deficit. Though urban industrialization had made leisure time possible for millions of working families for the first time, the opportunities for recreation were scant. For most, home entertainment was still limited to reading and storytelling, often by candlelight. Live entertainment outside the home—a play, perhaps, or a musical performance—was still too expensive to be anything more than an occasional treat. (In Chicago, a theater ticket usually cost a dollar, twice the price of a ticket to the great walking match at the Expo.)

In short, the public was so desperate for entertainment, especially affordable entertainment, that watching half-dead men stagger in circles for days on end was, if not absorbingly entrancing, at least an unobjectionable way to kill time. Whatever its attraction, the success of the O'Leary-Weston match was indisputable. After expenses were paid and the promoters took their cut, Weston walked away with $5,000, O'Leary, $4,500.* The match proved pedestrianism was a viable spectator sport.

Like too many vanquished champions, Edward Payson Weston was less than gracious in defeat. In interviews after the race, he complained that the charcoal fumes from the peanut vendor's cart "got into my head" and "made me nervous and worried me." He also said some spectators in the Expo had intimidated him, and he intimated that he'd received death threats, saying he would have been "riddled" (with bullets, presumably) if he'd won the race, and he didn't want to end up a "human cullender" (i.e., colander).

These charges, never proven, were vigorously refuted by O'Leary in a letter to a newspaper. "That he did not wish to leave the track a 'human cullender' is an undeserved insult to the citizens of Chicago," O'Leary wrote, adding that Weston's claim that he would have been riddled with bullets was "one of the most untruthful assertions his empty head or narrow mind could well afford to manufacture." In a parting shot, O'Leary challenged

---

* Roughly $98,000 and $88,000 today.

Weston to a rematch. "If you are not anxious for the match," O'Leary concluded, "please drop my name from your lips and 'champion pedestrian of America' from your cognomen."

Whatever comity had existed between O'Leary and Weston was now shattered. The *Spirit of the Times*, the New York paper that covered sports, flatly refused to take Weston's charges seriously. "To the many hard names which have assailed Weston during his peripatetic career," the paper said, "there is one word of four letters which we desire to add. It is simply L, I, A, R."

It seemed Weston's reign as America's most famous walker had come to an inglorious end. Defeated and chagrined, he sought a new start. He packed up his velvet jackets and silk sashes and, with his wife and children in tow, set sail for England.

4

COCA

or

NATURE SHOULD NOT BE OUTRAGED

AT 12:40 AM ON THURSDAY, JUNE 1, 1809, a twenty-nine-year-old Scottish aristocrat named Robert Barclay Allardice emerged from a small apartment he was renting in Newmarket, a village seventy miles north of London. Captain Barclay, as he was known, was descended from Scottish kings, and descendants of one of his cousins would found Barclays Bank.* But on this night his pedigree counted for nothing; only his stamina mattered, for Captain Barclay was about to embark on what was being called "the greatest human feat ever attempted."

It was a chilly night, and Barclay was wrapped in a blue flannel jacket. He also wore leather breeches, lamb's wool stockings, and "thick-soled shoes." Always impeccably dressed, Barclay completed his outfit with a silk cravat and a top hat. Despite the late

---

* When Barclay's father, also named Robert Barclay, married Sarah Ann Allardice, he agreed to assume her surname in exchange for the land she brought to the marriage. Technically he became Robert Barclay Allardice, though, in reality, both father and son continued to be known simply as Robert Barclay.

hour, a handful of villagers had gathered outside his door, and they gave him three cheers as he stepped out.

Barclay acknowledged them with a tip of his hat. Then he began making his way up the village's main road, a hard, dirt ribbon that connected Newmarket to the village of Fordham five miles to the north. "He walked," one observer noted, "in a sort of lounging gait . . . scarcely raising his feet more than two or three inches above the ground." His route was illuminated by seven gas streetlights, spaced about a hundred yards apart. They had been erected specially for the occasion.

After walking for ten minutes or so, Barclay came upon a white stake that had been driven into the road the previous day. The stake marked the spot exactly half a mile from the door of his apartment. Barclay walked around the stake and headed back for home, completing the mile-long roundtrip shortly before one o'clock. The small crowd outside his door cheered his return.

Back inside his candlelit apartment, Barclay removed his jacket and reclined on a sofa. His faithful servant, William Cross, fetched him a glass of porter. Barclay downed the drink in a gulp. He had walked the first mile without incident.

Now he only needed to walk 999 more.

The previous autumn, Captain Barclay had made a wager with an acquaintance named James Webster: if Barclay walked one mile every hour for one thousand consecutive hours—more than forty-one days, just eight hours less than six weeks—Webster would pay him 1,000 guineas. However, if Barclay failed, he would be liable to Webster for that fantastic sum. At the time, a typical worker in Britain earned about a guinea a week.

It was widely considered an impossible challenge, far beyond the limits of human endurance, but Barclay was undaunted. He'd been born into Scotland's abiding athletic tradition, now embodied in the Highland games—wrestling, lifting heavy stones, throwing a blacksmith's hammer—and at an early age he'd developed what he called a "staunch partiality . . . for general athletic exercises."

Barclay devised an ingenuous strategy for accomplishing the walk. He decided to walk one mile at the end of one hour and the next mile immediately after the beginning of the following hour. That way he could rest for more than an hour before setting out again. This satisfied the condition in his agreement with Webster that he walk the miles in "consecutive hours." But it was an extremely risky strategy: Barclay's timing had to be impeccable. If he failed to return from the first mile before the top of the hour, he would lose the wager.

Webster would come to consider the tactic rather ungentlemanly, though gamesmanship was allowed—even encouraged—when it came to such bets at the time. The Earl of March once wagered that he could "convey a letter 50 miles in less than an hour." This seemed utterly impossible when even the fastest horse going over the best road could cover no more than thirty miles an hour. But the earl won the bet. He enclosed a letter inside a cricket ball and had twenty cricketers stand in a circle measuring a half mile around. They threw the ball around the circle one hundred times, easily conveying the letter fifty miles in less than sixty minutes.

Heavy rains began to fall on the tenth day of the walk, turning the route into a quagmire. By the twelfth day Barclay was complaining of intense pain in his neck and shoulders. He also discovered what succeeding generations of pedestrians and other endurance athletes have come to know all too well: the crippling effects of too little sleep.

It's no wonder that sleep deprivation is considered a highly effective form of torture. It can impair speech and vision, and cause nausea, hallucinations—even death. Most of us are monophasic sleepers: we sleep once a day. Some, however, are biphasic sleepers, who sleep two times a day. People renowned for needing just a few hours' sleep each night are often biphasic sleepers who also sleep during the day. (Margaret Thatcher, who was famous for sleeping just four hours a night, often napped each afternoon.) And a small minority are polyphasic sleepers, who sleep in thirty- to ninety-minute increments four or more times a day. This is the sleep pattern adopted by sailors in long-distance solo boat races today. It was also the sleep pattern used by many successful long-distance pedestrians, including, it seems, Captain Barclay.

On the twenty-sixth day, at the start of his 607th mile, Barclay fell asleep standing up at the starting line. William Cross, his servant, was forced to strike his master several times with a walking stick to arouse him. Barclay's risky strategy of walking successive miles immediately before and after the top of the hour nearly backfired too. On some occasions, he completed one mile with less than thirty seconds to spare before he had to set off again.

It's impossible to know how many people poured into Newmarket to witness the final days of Barclay's walk. Thousands came, perhaps even tens of thousands. In any event, by July 11, the forty-first and penultimate day of the walk, the crowds had grown so large that "not a bed" could be procured within twenty miles of the village. Tents were erected to shelter the masses, and Barclay's course had to be roped off to keep them at bay. The village was so crowded that many in the audience were unable to get close enough to even catch a glimpse of the celebrated pedestrian. Not that it mattered. "Just being there was enough," wrote Peter Radford in his biography of Captain Barclay. "Just being able to tell people when you got back home that you were there at the finish. Just being able to tell your children and your grandchildren that you had been there and been part of it."

At 3:37 PM the following day, July 12, 1809, Barclay successfully completed his thousandth mile. Newmarket was bedlam. Church bells pealed in his honor. Barclay had lost thirty-two pounds, and "the spasmodic affectations in his legs were particularly distressing." He laid down for his first uninterrupted sleep in nearly forty-two days. After eight hours he awoke for a meal, then slept another nine hours. On July 17—just five days after completing the walk—Barclay was said to be "as well as before he started."

Barclay's feat spawned a competitive-walking craze in Britain, much like that which would grip the United States later in the century. In 1815 an Englishman named George Wilson attempted to walk fifty miles a day for twenty days at Blackheath, England. So thick were the crowds that escorts armed with whips had to clear a path for him. Fearing a riot, magistrates arrested Wilson, prematurely ending his walk on the sixteenth day.

Later that year, another Englishman, Josiah Eaton, bested Barclay by walking 1,100 miles in 1,100 consecutive hours. Then, in 1818, Eaton walked a quarter mile every fifteen minutes for six weeks. Pedestrians began competing against each other in races lasting hours or even days. Huge sums were wagered on these events. Newspapers began listing the results of matches, often under the simple heading PEDESTRIANISM, giving rise to the world's first sports pages.

———

Though the craze had waned by the time Edward Payson Weston arrived in London early in 1876, the British still considered their pedestrians the best in the world, and they regarded Weston as an unworthy interloper. Indeed, Weston embodied much that the British disliked about Americans: he was proud, boastful, flashy, vain. Weston did nothing to dispel this notion when, almost the moment he arrived in London, he challenged England's best young pedestrian, William Perkins, to a twenty-four-hour race. Perkins, who was in his early twenties, had recently come to fame for walking eight miles in less than an hour. It was an impressive feat, and it earned him the title "Champion Pedestrian of England," but he had never before competed in a race as long as twenty-four hours.

Weston had much to prove in Britain, where accounts of his famous walks in the United States were regarded with suspicion or outright disbelief. Papers scoffed at his claim to have walked five hundred miles in six days. "It is not wonderful [i.e., surprising] that the accounts published of Mr. Weston's performances by American newspapers have been received in this country with hesitation or even incredulity," said London's *Saturday Review,* "because it is difficult to feel sure that times and distances have been accurately taken."

But there were deeper reasons for the skepticism: an undercurrent of international rivalry. As 1876 began, America was preparing to celebrate, rather ostentatiously, the centennial of its independence from Britain, complete with an elaborate international exposition in Philadelphia, the city where the Declaration of Independence was signed. The British were in no mood to cede superiority to the Americans in any endeavor, much less pedestrianism, a sport the British believed they had invented.

The British medical journal the *Lancet* flatly stated that the United States produced inferior athletes. Americans, the journal said, were "far beyond other nations in their hygienic unwholesomeness. Living habitually in their close, stove-heated rooms, bolting their food at railway speed . . . year by year Americans grow thinner, lighter, and shorter lived." Newspaper advertisements touted the twenty-four-hour match between Weston and Perkins as a test of the "relative pedestrian powers of England and America."

Proving his critics wrong was one of Weston's main motivations. According to the sporting journal *Bell's Life,* Weston said his only interest in undertaking exhibitions in London was to "convince the sceptical portion of the English sporting press that the accounts of his doings which have appeared from time to time in American sporting journals were correct."

———◆◆◆———

The Weston-Perkins match would take place in February 1876 at the Royal Agricultural Hall in the Islington neighborhood of London. The Aggie, as it was known to generations of Londoners, was originally built for livestock shows. Cattle had been traded in an open market in the nearby neighborhood of Smithfield since the eighteenth century, but as London rapidly expanded through the first half of the nineteenth, a more suitable (and sanitary) venue was needed.

As Alec Forshaw explains in *The Building That Lived Twice*, his history of the Aggie, the Smithfield Club, a group of "well-connected and wealthy gentlemen" whose "main purpose was the promotion of improvements in farming," raised £50,000 to build a new hall for exhibitions of "livestock, farming products and agricultural machinery." Designed by a little-known architect named Frederick Peck, the building was colossal: 384 feet long and 217 feet wide. It was a relatively simple structure, a brick box with two slender, ninety-five-foot towers flanking the main entrance on Liverpool Road. Most impressive was the arched roof, an iron-and-glass canopy over the main hall that allowed sunlight to stream in. At night the interior was illuminated by four thousand gaslights, augmented by seven massive chandeliers that hung from the ceiling, each equipped with forty-eight gaslights.

The Aggie opened on December 8, 1862. The first event was a weeklong livestock show, which attracted 134,669 visitors, including the Prince of Wales, as well as royalty from Belgium and Prussia. The Aggie was, as one London paper noted with understatement, "well entitled to a place among the prominent features and institutions of the Metropolis."

The Aggie, however, was not without its faults. London's toxic fogs, which contained unhealthy levels of sulfur dioxide from coal smoke, frequently permeated the building. During a livestock show in December 1874, one of these "pea soupers" killed many cattle. Most sheep and pigs, however, survived; those animals were closer to the ground, where the smog was less noxious. Killer fogs notwithstanding, the Aggie became London's premier public venue, hosting (in addition to livestock shows) circuses, minstrel shows, religious programs, dog shows, grand cotillions, military tattoos—even bullfights.

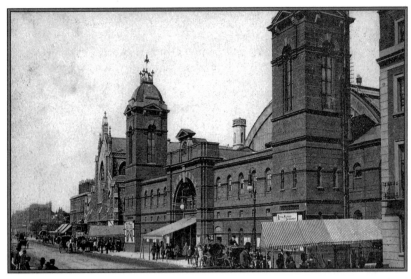

London's Royal Agricultural Hall, better known as the Aggie, photographed around 1906. Islington Local History Centre

Though not nearly as grand as Chicago's Interstate Exposition Building, the Aggie proved infinitely more durable. It remained one of Britain's largest indoor arenas until World War II, when it was converted into a postal sorting facility. Abandoned by the Royal Mail in 1970, the building was left vacant and began to succumb to the elements. The iron-and-glass canopy started to collapse, "shards of glass . . . falling from the roof and impaling like javelins in the wooden block flooring of the Main Hall," as Aggie historian Alec Forshaw, who toured the derelict structure, remembered. The interior became an urban forest of weeds, trees, and debris.

Slated for demolition, the Aggie was saved by Sam Morris, a Londoner who'd made a fortune designing inexpensive display cases for retailers and dabbling in real estate. Morris had attended events at the Aggie as a child. In May 1981, his son Jack noticed an advertisement in a trade publication for property developers. "It was a very small ad," Jack told Alec Forshaw. "'For sale—The Royal

The Aggie (now known as the Business Design Centre) in 2012. Photo by author

Agricultural Hall'—as if it was some semi-detached house." Sam and Jack went to inspect the place. "It was the most phenomenal experience," Jack recalled. "It was a time warp, very eerie."

Sam Morris was enchanted, and he became determined to save the Aggie. He raised £10 million to purchase the decrepit building and convert it into a convention center and office space. The renovated Aggie—rechristened the Business Design Centre—opened on October 6, 1986. The exterior still looks much as it did when the Aggie first opened more than 150 years ago. The Business Design Centre, now one of London's most successful convention centers, stands a short walk from the Angel tube station on the Bank branch of the Northern Line, just around the corner from a Burger King. It is the only major nineteenth-century pedestrian venue still in existence.

The venerable and capacious Aggie was the only logical venue for Weston's British debut, his twenty-four-hour race against Perkins.

Before the match, Weston was approached by Frederick William Pavy, a prominent physician who was a lecturer on physiology at Guy's Hospital in London. The workings of the human body enthralled Pavy. With small eyes and a beak-like nose, Pavy was an elfin figure with a brilliant mind. "He was quiet and reserved," a friend recalled, "but his face lit up and became suffused with a smile of pleasure if he talked about any research in which he was at the time interested." Pavy dedicated much of his career to studying diabetes, and his 1862 paper "Researches on the Nature and Treatment of Diabetes" was the definitive guide to the disease for many years. But he was also interested in the physiology of athletes, and, in addition to his groundbreaking work on diabetes, Pavy would become one of the earliest practitioners of the specialty now known as sports medicine.

Pavy told Weston he was interested in "investigating the effects of prolonged muscular exercise upon the system," and he asked the pedestrian to be his guinea pig. Pavy wanted to study Weston while he competed. Weston agreed. Pavy was delighted. "Mr. Weston enters with as much enthusiasm into the spirit of these researches as into his walk, and has placed every facility at my disposal," Pavy wrote at the time. "It is only a just tribute to him to say that science is indebted to him for his desire to aid its advance."

Tuesday, February 8, 1876, was a propitious day in London. Queen Victoria, still mourning the death of her beloved consort Albert fifteen years earlier, made a rare public appearance to open the third session of the ninth Parliament of her reign. (It was during this session that members of Parliament, led by Prime Minister Benjamin Disraeli, passed the Royal Titles Act of 1876, which formally recognized Victoria as "Empress of India.") But as day turned to night, London's attention turned from Westminster to Islington, where the famed American pedestrian Edward

Payson Weston would make his British debut at the Aggie against England's preeminent pedestrian, William Perkins.

An estimated five thousand curious Londoners paid a shilling each to watch the start of the race. Two concentric tracks had been laid to each pedestrian's specifications. Weston's was on the inside, a 1/7-mile oval covered with gravel and loam, a mixture of wet clay and sand. Perkins's 1/6.5-mile track on the outside was bare: he would walk on the wooden floor of the arena.

Around 9:00 PM Weston made his entrance wearing a pea jacket over a black "close-fitting guernsey" (a wool shirt), black knickerbockers, black leather leggings held in place with elastic bands, and "thick-soled but light boots with a shallow heel, laced up in front and reaching above the ankle." In his right hand he carried his ever-present riding crop. Perkins wore an "ordinary athletic costume": a "white guernsey with black drawers to the knees" and "thin slipper-shoes."

The race began at 9:25. Weston adopted his usual strategy of slow but steady, and quickly fell behind. By 3:00 AM he trailed Perkins by four miles, 32 to 28. It was a "foggy, oppressive" night, and Weston complained the atmosphere inside the Aggie was making him "distressed." But he marched on, at one point throwing off his pea jacket.

Perkins (left) and Weston in their twenty-four-hour match at the Aggie. COURTESY OF PETER RADFORD

At 3:45 AM Perkins took a break. He ate a meal consisting of "a large loin mutton-chop and a pint of Burton ale," all of which he promptly regurgitated. His feet were badly swollen and blistering, so he changed into canvas shoes. But when he resumed walking, he grew "more and more footsore," and at 8:45 AM he had to stop for more than an hour to recuperate. By then Weston was just a mile behind. At twenty minutes before noon, Perkins finally surrendered, having completed just 65 miles.

Dr. Pavy examined Perkins and noted that his pulse was "feeble and irregular," and he was running a fever of 100.6 degrees. His feet were caked with blood, and removing his socks was excruciating. Another doctor who examined Perkins said that, due to "the swollen and bleeding condition of his feet and manifest nervous exhaustion, he could not have continued any longer on the track." Perkins explained his failure by saying he had "never assayed a long distance match before."

By the time Perkins withdrew from the race, Weston was already five miles ahead. On he merrily plodded, and when the twenty-four hours were up at 9:25 PM on February 9, he'd completed 109 miles—short of his goal of 115, but more than enough to prove his superiority to England's champion pedestrian. Weston had proved his critics wrong. Amid tumultuous applause, he was triumphantly hoisted onto the shoulders of enthusiastic spectators and paraded around the Aggie. "This is certainly one of the greatest pedestrian feats on record," the *London Sporting Times* said, "and shows that our American cousins are 'spry' in other matters besides the manufacture of cocktails and wooden nutmegs."*

Less than three months after his crushing loss to Daniel O'Leary in Chicago, Weston had made a remarkable comeback.

Throughout the race, Dr. Pavy, notebook in hand, meticulously recorded Weston's every move, like an ornithologist studying a rare bird. "The food taken by Weston during the walk was mainly of a

---

* "Wooden nutmeg" meant a fraud. Legend has it that unscrupulous American merchants sometimes sold the British counterfeit "nutmegs" made of wood.

liquid nature," Pavy noted, "consisting of beef-tea made from Liebig's extract [a popular brand of bullion cube at the time], yolks of eggs, jelly, sea-moss farina (an American preparation), coffee, tea, milk, sugar, and toward the end of the walk a little champagne, and brandy much diluted with water. To economise time he did not stop to take it, but consumed it whilst walking on the track in small quantities at a time and frequently." (Though nominally a teetotaler, Weston occasionally consumed alcohol for "medicinal purposes.") After the race, Pavy noted that Weston "appeared but little muscularly tired." His pulse was "steady and firm" and his temperature was 97.6. He passed 113.4 cubic centimeters of urine (about four ounces), which Pavy dutifully collected.

Weston was now the talk of London, and he wasted little time capitalizing on his newfound renown. A week after the Perkins race, Weston undertook to walk 180 miles in forty-eight hours at the Aggie. This time his foil was Alexander Clark, a twenty-six-year-old novice pedestrian who "underwent no preparation for the arduous task he engaged in." The result, unsurprisingly, was a rout. The race began at 9:45 PM on Tuesday, February 15. Clark withdrew less than twelve hours later, after completing 55 miles. Weston continued walking, completing 100 miles in the first twenty-four hours. On Wednesday night he slept for about four hours in a small room in the hall, returning to the track at 3:27 Thursday morning. He kept walking straight through until the night.

Although the outcome of the match was hardly in doubt, thousands still streamed into the Aggie to watch its conclusion. Weston was clearly in his element, and he hammed it up for the crowd, at one point playing "God Save the Queen" on his cornet while he walked. He completed his 180th mile at 9:25, with twenty minutes to spare. Afterward Weston addressed the audience, saying he "had never had fairer play than he had been shown in this country."

By now, Weston must have been feeling invincible, for immediately after the race he announced his intention to walk 275 miles in seventy-five hours in the Aggie beginning the following Tuesday night. This time his opponent would be Charles Rowell, a twenty-three-year-old who had gained fame as a rower at Cambridge. Though he was not a pedestrian by training, Rowell was regarded as one of Britain's best up-and-coming athletes. "[He] is a very muscular and powerfully-built man," one London paper said of Rowell, "regarded as likely at any rate to make some semblance of a struggle." Rowell still lived near Cambridge, and when he had an appointment in London, he thought nothing of jogging to the capital and back—a 120-mile roundtrip.

Raising the stakes, Weston announced that, while he would walk, his young rival would be allowed to—gasp!—run.

In all great movements, especially international movements, there are schisms, and pedestrianism was no exception. In the case of pedestrianism, the breach stemmed from a simple question: What is the definition of walking?

American pedestrians, Weston and O'Leary foremost among them, largely held to the traditional definition: one part of the foot must always be in contact with the ground, or "fair heel and toe," as it was usually codified in the articles of agreement that governed races.

In British pedestrianism, however, competitors were often permitted to "go as you please," meaning they could walk, trot, jog, run, sprint, or crawl. It didn't matter.

By the middle of the nineteenth century, "go as you please" races were more popular than "fair heel and toe" matches in Britain. That the Americans seemed to prefer competitive walking to running struck the British as perplexing, even a tad daft. "Formerly settlers in what were then the Western States were necessarily great pedestrians," London's *Saturday Review* noted. "But in America, as with us, the necessity for long walks has almost disappeared. . . . The fact that in England in the last century there were almost no hard roads was not unfavourable to pedestrianism, and as a good walker could travel as fast as any cheap conveyance, the habit of walking must have been largely developed. . . . All this, however, belongs to a bygone world, and we might have thought the change of habit, which has been great among ourselves, would be even greater in America."

Maybe the British were just more pragmatic. Peter Radford, a historian who won four track medals for the UK at the 1960 Olympics, said the British have long preferred sports that were easy to officiate. In cricket, if the bowler knocks a pin off the wicket, the batter is out. In baseball, it is left to an umpire to determine whether a pitch is a ball or a strike. "We preferred simple rules that the crowd would accept," Radford said. "This prevented disputes. And walking is much harder to officiate than running."

Even today, disputes often arise during competitive racewalking events. The rules of the International Association of Athletics Federations (IAAF) stipulate that a racewalker must maintain contact with the ground, "so that no visible (to the human eye) loss of contact occurs." The rules also stipulate that "the advancing leg shall be straightened (i.e. not bent at the knee) from the moment of first contact with the ground until the vertical upright position." It's all rather complicated, and it requires a small army of judges to ensure compliance. Yet disputes are not uncommon. A competitor may have both feet off the ground for a fraction of a second, which may be visible to one human's eyes but not another's.

This problem could be solved quite easily with an electronic system like the one used in fencing. When the tip of one fencer's weapon touches a point-scoring part of the other fencer's body, an electrical circuit is completed, which triggers an alarm. A racewalker could be equipped with shoes that trigger an alarm when continuous contact with the track is broken. But the IAAF has repeatedly rejected this seemingly sensible suggestion, citing the high cost of implementing such a system. So modern racewalking is judged the same way nineteenth-century "fair heel and toe" races were judged: by old-fashioned human beings.

———•••••———

In 1876, Americans may have been superior walkers, but the British believed they were better runners—and they were pinning their hopes on Charles Rowell to put Edward Payson Weston in his place. For his part, Weston, who professed to disdain running, relished the opportunity to prove the superiority of his preferred mode of locomotion.

The seventy-five-hour race began at 8:30 PM on Tuesday, February 22, 1876. Once again, the Aggie was packed. As expected, Rowell sprinted into the lead, while Weston wobbled along in his distinctive gait. At 11:45 PM Rowell was ahead by four miles, 23 to 19. But the "jolly young waterman" in the running costume soon tired. Rowell was forced to take a three-hour break early Wednesday morning and a two-hour break around midday. By Friday he was so "footsore" that he was off the track for nearly twelve hours.

Meanwhile, Weston, clad in a black velvet jacket and white kid gloves, walked for nineteen hours straight before taking a break. At 8:30 Wednesday night, twenty-four hours into the race, Weston had completed 104 miles and was nearly ten miles in front of Rowell. By ten o'clock the next morning, Weston had increased his lead to twenty-eight miles.

By Friday night, the outcome was no longer in question, yet the Aggie was packed once again. Alone on the track for much of the evening, Weston entertained the crowd by playing the cornet as he walked. "It is a pity that so fine a performance should have been accompanied by so much rhodomontade," the *Sporting Times* would harrumph. "The cornet playing and the kid gloves might well have been left out of the programme."

When the race ended at 11:30 PM, Weston had completed 275 miles—nearly a hundred more than Rowell, who finished with 176. "The astounding American walker is no chicken," one London newspaper said of Weston. But Charles Rowell, the

Cambridge rower defeated by Weston, would ultimately prove to be no chicken either.

It seemed Edward Payson Weston had little left to prove in London. "The only difficulty about making any more matches seems to be that there can be no opponents except time, who is but dull company," said the *Saturday Review*. But it was time, precisely, that Weston wanted to beat. He now set his sights on reclaiming his most cherished record: the 500-mile record that O'Leary had snatched from him a year earlier by covering that distance in 5 days, 21 hours, 31 minutes, and 50 seconds. (2 hours, 28 minutes, and 10 seconds less than six days).

On February 26, the day after the race ended, Frederick William Pavy published the first of what would become a series of articles about Weston in the prestigious medical journal the *Lancet*. In the series, entitled "The Effect of Prolonged Muscular Exercise on the System," Pavy listed in stupefying detail everything Weston ate and drank during his competitions:

The first twenty-four hours of Weston's seventy-five hours' walk. Distance walked 104 miles. Food consumed: 4 oz. meat (lean from 1 chop); 2¼ oz. bread made into dried toast; 1¼ oz. Liebig's extract of meat; 1 6 oz. tin (by measure) of Brand's essence of beef; 2 oz. oatmeal made into gruel; 2 pints 14½ oz. jelly; 3¾ oz. mixed tea; 2½ oz. coffee; 8½ oz. sugar; 1 lemon; 10 yolks of eggs; 4 oz. grapes; 4 oz. prunes, for making prune-tea; 18 oz. (by measure) sea-moss farina blanc-mange; 5 milk biscuits (Peek, Frean, and Co.); 2½ pints of milk.

Pavy also published the results of his analyses of samples of Weston's urine collected before, during, and after competitions: "Amber colour, and clear. Microscopic characters: A few crystals of uric acid." The point of Pavy's meticulousness was explained in an editorial that appeared in the *Lancet*. The journal predicted his research would prove valuable "in reference to the food best adapted for armies on long march, and others engaged in arduous labor."

"These feats of Weston," the *Lancet* said, "may be looked upon as affording an invaluable opportunity of investigating the chemical phenomena concerned in muscular action."

Shortly after midnight on Monday, March 6, just ten days after completing his seventy-five-hour race against Rowell, Weston began his attempt to break the 500-mile record in a six-day walk at the Aggie. Over the previous four weeks he had already walked more than five hundred miles over three races. It was a grueling schedule, and it had taken its toll. He had a sprained knee and was suffering from a bad cold. He coughed constantly as he walked around the gravel and loam track inside the damp Aggie. By the middle of the week he was running a fever. Dr. Pavy offered to issue him a "certificate of temporary unfitness," but Weston refused and, as the *Lancet* put it, "with characteristic pluck and perseverance he went at his great task."

At the end of the sixth day Weston had walked "just" 450 miles, far short of his goal. Yet, even in failure, Weston won the admiration of London, for, as the *Islington Gazette* put it, "from the first mile to the last he never wavered in his steady tramp, and never seemed to lose heart." Yes, Weston was a vainglorious American—but he also had guts.

Weston had now walked before some two hundred thousand paying customers in London. The indefatigable American had rejuvenated the sport of pedestrianism in Britain and had become something of a cult hero in the process. At the end of his six-day at the Aggie, he thanked his rapturous audience, saying, "God bless every man, woman, and child in this grand old England."

———

One man in grand old England who was closely following Weston's exploits in London was a medical student named John Ashburton Thompson. Thompson would go on to become a leading authority on the plague and leprosy, but in 1876 he was just a twenty-nine-year-old employee of the Great Northern Railway Company and still two years from earning his medical degree.

Thompson had attended nearly all of Weston's exhibitions at the Aggie, taking notes while he watched. After reading Frederick William Pavy's first article in the *Lancet,* Thompson wrote a letter to the *British Medical Journal,* a rival publication, in which he postulated an explanation for Edward Payson Weston's seemingly superhuman stamina. It was simple, really: Weston was doping.

"At intervals," Thompson wrote, "as he persistently pursues his route, Weston may be seen to go through the action of chewing; and a brown stain upon his lips, which the observant spectator may notice at the same time, lead to the suspicion that he is refreshing himself with tobacco. Yet it is well known that both during a walk, and for some time previous to it, Weston renounces tobacco; and, on these occasions, he is masticating a substance, which, although credited with some of the properties of tobacco, is the most serviceable of its class for use under exertion. That substance is the dried leaf of the *Erythroxylon coca.*"

Europeans discovered the wondrous effects of the coca leaf the same way they discovered so many other wondrous things: by conquest. In the sixteenth century, Spanish conquistadors in Peru noticed that the locals chewed the leaves for religious, medicinal, and (less frequently) recreational purposes. In fact, the indigenous population of western South America had been chewing coca leaves for millennia before Europeans caught them in the act. In 2005, the *Journal of Psychoactive Drugs* reported that traces of coca leaves had been found in a three-thousand-year-old mummy discovered in northern Chile.

Later South American colonists noted that miners who chewed the leaf "every three hours with only a handful of maize [could] perform for twelve long hours the severe work of the mine such as no Europeans could effect."

The earliest account of coca leaves in Europe was published in Seville in 1569 by a Dr. Monardes. "The use of it amongst the Indians," he wrote, "is a thing general for many things, for when they travel by the way for neede, and for content when they are in their houses." Three hundred years later, the properties of the coca leaf were still not fully understood, but its effects certainly were. "All accounts, without exception, agree in attributing great and marvellous powers of endurance to its use," wrote a British researcher in 1876, the same year Weston was performing his great and marvelous feats in London.

John Ashburton Thompson's article ignited a controversy reminiscent of more recent allegations of steroid use in baseball. Stimulants were not unknown in pedestrianism, of course; nearly every pedestrian consumed coffee or tea during competitions, not to mention alcohol, which was considered a stimulant at the time. But the coca leaf was a different animal entirely, favored by "savages," disreputable.

Thompson was tipped off to Weston's use of coca leaves by "a fellow-townsman of Mr. Weston's." Thompson said he asked Weston about his use of the leaves twice, on March 7 and March 11. Both times Weston declined to address the matter directly, though on the latter occasion, Thompson later wrote, Weston begged Thompson to "say nothing about coca in connection with his performances 'outside.'" But by then it was too late: Thompson's letter had already been submitted to the *British Medical Journal* and would be published that very day.

The allegation not only threatened to besmirch Weston's reputation; it also threatened Dr. Pavy's, for he had made no mention of coca leaves in his exceedingly thorough account of Weston's diet. How could Pavy not have known Weston was ingesting coca leaves when he weighed every grape the pedestrian ate? On March 12, Pavy, no doubt furious, confronted Weston at the Aggie and asked him directly if he had chewed the leaf during his walks. According to Thompson, who was present, Weston assured Pavy that "he had not seen a coca leaf since his first walk."

Weston subsequently addressed the controversy in a letter to the *Lancet* that was published on March 18:

Sir,

So much has been said of late in the public press regarding my use of the South American "Coca leaves," that I deem it my duty to contradict an impression which is erroneous.

During my first trial in London on the 9th of February, while walking from the sixty-fifth to the seventy-fifth mile, I chewed the coca leaves freely, acting under the advice of my medical adviser in America. I found that they did not have the effect expected; that is, they would not keep me awake or in the least stimulate my efforts, but, on the contrary, they acted as an opiate, and forced me to sleep; which was mainly the cause of my being absent from the track for forty-five minutes after the seventy-eighth mile on that occasion.

Previous experience in America, taken together with this later experiment with coca leaves here, lead me to the belief that, far from being any assistance in any trial of physical endurance, the use of the leaves in question would prove a great detriment; hence I abandoned them, *and have not even tasted them since my first trial in London, which closed on the evening of February 9th* [emphasis in original]. I deem it my duty to thus make public this explanation, in view of the fact that I daily receive scores of letters asking me if I believe in the efficacy of coca leaves; and also in justice to the efforts of Dr. Pavy, whose investigations would have been somewhat disturbed had I allowed myself the use of any false stimulant.

In conclusion, permit me to add that, after an experience of upwards of eight years in public life, during which time I have walked *over* 14,000 *miles* [emphasis in original], experience has taught me that Nature should not be outraged by the use of artificial stimulants in any protracted trial.

I am, Sir, with sentiments of respect and esteem,
Faithfully yours,
Edward Payson Weston

What a bizarre letter. Weston admits to having used coca leaves, not only in his "first trial in London," but also before that, in America. But he also says the leaves proved to be a great detriment because they forced him to sleep. This was a bit of linguistic legerdemain; Weston told Thompson not that the leaves made him tired immediately, but that, when he retired after chewing them, he slept more deeply than usual. Then he concludes by saying, "Nature should not be outraged by the use of artificial stimulants in any protracted trial." In sum, Weston chewed coca leaves in competition on more than one occasion, and he did not wish that fact to be known, yet he saw no harm in the practice. This sounds much like the rationale embraced by modern professional athletes who have been caught using performance-enhancing drugs.

It's obvious Weston hid his use of coca leaves from Pavy. For the doctor to have known Weston was ingesting the leaves and not reported it in the *Lancet* would have been an unforgivable breach of ethics. Pavy, esteemed as he was, was unlikely to risk his reputation to protect Weston. (Pavy, in any event, escaped the scandal with his reputation intact. When he passed away in 1911, he was hailed as one of England's "brightest ornaments.") It's also clear that Weston believed his own reputation would suffer if it came to be known that he chewed the leaves. All that is certain, however, is that Weston chewed coca leaves during his first walk in London. Whether he chewed them on subsequent walks is unknown.

The controversy, however, failed to dampen enthusiasm for Weston in Britain. In April 1876, the satirical magazine *Judy* published a poem about the pedestrian:

"Walker!"
A footprint on the sands of time
Most men essay to trace on;
There's one will surely leave his mark—
That's Weston, Edward Pace-on (Payson)!

5

REMATCH

or

NOT SILLY LITTLE FEMALE CIGARETTES EITHER

WHILE EDWARD PAYSON WESTON was wowing the Brits, Dan O'Leary—now officially America's "champion pedestrian"—spent most of 1876 touring the United States. In March he took a train from Chicago to San Francisco, where, after a bit of sightseeing—Chinatown, Yosemite—he attempted to break his own 500-mile record by walking that distance in less than 140 hours (5 days and 20 hours)—the record that Weston so coveted. The walk took place in the city's Horticultural Hall. It began at 4:00 AM on Tuesday, April 4, and, according to one eyewitness, "from start to finish the building was crowded with spectators, among whom were many of San Francisco's most respected citizens."

On Wednesday night, while O'Leary was walking at the Horticultural Hall, another event took place in San Francisco that galvanized the city in a way that even the champion pedestrian could not. At Union Hall, twenty-five thousand people attended a rally on the "Chinese question." Labeled a "Protest Against the Mongolian [sic] Invasion," the rally was a response to the rapid influx of Chinese immigrants into California, particularly the Bay Area.

At the beginning of 1849, there were fewer than one hundred Chinese in California. But after word spread that gold had been discovered at Sutter's Mill in the small northern California town of Coloma, Chinese immigration surged, and by 1876, there were more than one hundred thousand Chinese in the state. This was hardly surprising; after all, before completion of the first transcontinental railroad or the canal across Panama, it was easier to get to California from China than from the East Coast. But the sudden increase in the Chinese population alarmed many of California's Caucasian inhabitants, who blamed the "coolies" for high unemployment after the mining boom waned in the mid-1850s.

"The cry was raised that the large number of Chinese in the country tended to injure the interests of the working classes and to degrade labor," historian Henry K. Norton wrote. "It was claimed that they deprived white men of positions by taking lower wages and that they sent their savings back to China; that thus they were human leeches sucking the very life-blood of this country."

California's anti-Chinese movement enjoyed broad popular support. One of the speakers at the Union Hall rally that Wednesday night was California governor William Irwin, who told the audience,

> Your minds will recognize in what I say a fundamental truth when I declare that, in the continued emigration of the Chinese to this country, is involved the subversion of everything that characterizes distinctly the Anglo-Saxon; ay, more, everything that characterizes distinctly European civilization. [Great applause.] It is not, then, fellow-citizens, a question merely of morals, of social conditions, of political economy. It is all these; it is everything that goes to make up American civilization.

When the rally against the "Mongol" invasion broke up late that Wednesday night, at least a few attendees undoubtedly headed over to the Horticultural Hall to watch Dan O'Leary's attempt to walk 500 miles in less than 140 hours. The irony of San Franciscans castigating Chinese immigrants while simultaneously paying fifty cents apiece to watch an Irish immigrant walk in circles for days on end seems to have been lost on the citizenry.

O'Leary ended up completing his 500th mile with 52 minutes to spare, lowering his record to 5 days, 19 hours, and 8 minutes. A crowd of three thousand cheered the Irishman on for the final miles, including an unusually large number of women waving their handkerchiefs at the lithe, mustachioed pedestrian in the tight-fitting athletic costume as he passed by. At the end of the walk, the crowd carried the triumphant O'Leary from the track on their shoulders. He was lifted onto the judges' stand, where he was presented with a gold watch and chain, which he would carry proudly for many years.

In August, O'Leary went to New York. At a roller rink in Manhattan, he once again attempted to walk 500 miles in less than 140 hours. The heat was stifling, and O'Leary drank more champagne than usual attempting to stay cool. He was also suffering from a cold. He completed 500 miles, but it took him 5 days, 22 hours, 27 minutes, and 25 seconds (142 hours, 27 minutes, and 25 seconds), considerably longer than his record time. He considered his performance disappointing, but New Yorkers didn't. By eight o'clock on the final night of the walk, the *New York Times* reported, "there were about 7,000 persons in the building, and they became perfectly wild with excitement." The paper noted that O'Leary had "accomplished one of the greatest feats ever witnessed by a New-York public."

Several days after the walk, a letter signed "Frank Clarke" was sent to several New York papers. The letter claimed that O'Leary's ⅛-mile track was "short," and that the pedestrian actually walked only 300 miles, not 500. O'Leary dismissed the charge as a crude attempt at blackmail, saying he was approached during the walk by a man who demanded twenty dollars to keep from accusing O'Leary of "having perpetrated a fraud upon the public." O'Leary hired two surveyors to measure the track, but by then it had already been dismantled. The five men who acted as judges for the walk all signed an open letter saying the accusation was "entirely without foundation."

The city of New York seemed satisfied that the walk was legit. At a banquet on the evening of Tuesday, August 29, 1876, city officials presented O'Leary with a $500 gold medal specially designed by Tiffany. The medal proclaimed O'Leary CHAMPION WALKER OF AMERICA.

Four days later, on Saturday, September 2, O'Leary sailed for England on the steamer *Idaho*. He was eager for a rematch with his old foe Edward Payson Weston in London, where Weston wouldn't be able to complain about O'Leary's supposed home-field advantage as he had after their first race in Chicago.

Eleven years earlier, Dan O'Leary had crossed the Atlantic in steerage, a penniless immigrant. Now he crossed it in first class, as a champion.

As soon as he stepped off the *Idaho* in England, O'Leary challenged Weston to a six-day race. In early January 1877, Weston finally agreed to the rematch, and the two men signed articles of agreement:

> Memorandum of Agreement made and entered into this 3rd day of January between Daniel O'Leary and Edward Payson Weston, whereby they agree to engage in a six days' walking match, for Five Hundred Pounds aside; the race to take place in a covered building or ground (to be mutually agreed upon by both parties) within a radius of five miles of Charing Cross, at Eastertide, starting at five minutes past

twelve a.m. on Monday, the second day of April, and terminating Saturday, the seventh day of April, 1877, at ten minutes to twelve o'clock in the evening (143¾ hours from the start), each man to walk upon a separate track, to be laid down according to his own directions, and surveyed by a competent authority in the presence of the judges appointed. The measurement of each track to be made eighteen inches from the inside border frame. Each man must walk fair—the judges appointed to be sole judges of fair and unfair walking—and any lap adjudged to have been traversed unfairly to be disallowed and cancelled in the record book. Each man must walk alone, and no attendant to be allowed to go more than twenty-five yards at a time with either competitor, and then only for the purpose of handing refreshments. The Stakes and two-thirds of the "gate" money (after all expenses have been deducted) to be handed over to the winner, and the loser to take one third. The Editor of the Sporting Life is appointed Stakeholder, and the whole of the Stakes must be deposited at the Sporting Life Office one calendar month before the time appointed for the commencement of the race. The said parties (Weston and O'Leary) to appoint the four judges at the time of the last deposit, and in case they cannot agree in making these appointments, the Editor of the Sporting Life is hereby empowered to make such appointments; also, if the men cannot agree in selecting a building or ground for the decision of the match, the Editor of the Sporting Life to have the power of naming where the race is to be decided. The judges to be four in number and to have full control over the race from the time the men start; the decision of the majority of the judges to be final and conclusive under any circumstances. Two bands to be in attendance, and play from five a.m. till twelve p.m.; the bands to be under the direction of both men in alternate hours, and to discontinue playing whilst either man is absent for the purpose of sleeping. In the event of any question arising which may not be provided for in these articles, the judges jointly to have full power to decide such question, and their decision to be final and conclusive. The Stakeholder shall in each and every case be exonerated from all responsibility upon obeying the direction of the judges. Either party failing to comply with any of these articles to forfeit the whole of the Stakes.

(signed) Daniel O'Leary

(signed) Edward Payson Weston

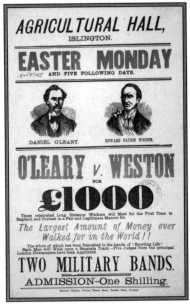

A broadside advertising the six-day race between Weston and O'Leary at the Aggie, April 2–7, 1877. ISLINGTON LOCAL HISTORY CENTRE

The "covered building or ground" chosen for the race was, naturally, the Royal Agricultural Hall in Islington. Soon, broadsides promoting the event were posted all over London.

In the days leading up to the race, a dispute arose as to the meaning of walking "fair," as stipulated in the articles of agreement. Weston's hip-swinging, wobbly stride had long been controversial. "Weston's gait when walking was very peculiar," one fan remembered, "hardly fair heel and toe perhaps." The judges appointed by Weston and O'Leary released a joint statement clarifying their definition of walking: "a succession of steps in which it is essential that some part of one foot must always touch the ground."

On Easter Sunday, two concentric tracks of loam covered with sawdust were laid on the floor of the Aggie. Weston would walk the ¹⁄₇-mile inner track, O'Leary the ¹⁄₆.₅-mile outer one. Each competitor was furnished a tent for resting in privacy. At five minutes after midnight on Monday, April 2—right on schedule— the race began. Again, the differences between the two walkers were readily apparent. The *Islington Gazette* described O'Leary's stride as "statuesque," while Weston's was "jerky . . . the reverse of graceful."

"In point of speed also there is no comparison," the *Gazette* added. "O'Leary is much faster than his opponent."

The walkers continued to exhibit markedly different personalities on the track too. Weston worked the crowd, joking with spectators as he walked. He basked in the attention and seemed to appreciate and enjoy his role as an entertainer as well as an athlete. O'Leary, on the other hand, was what sports commentators today would call "intensely focused." He evinced no interest whatsoever in the audience and instead concentrated entirely on the task at hand.

Surprisingly, Weston jumped out to an early lead, and after twenty-four hours he led O'Leary by three miles, 116 to 113. By noon on Tuesday, however, O'Leary had overtaken Weston, and by the end of that day the Irishman led Weston by fourteen miles, 208 to 194. By 4:30 on Wednesday afternoon, O'Leary had stretched his lead to twenty-one miles, 266 to 245.

Weston's backers urged him to close the widening gap by taking fewer breaks, but he refused. Weston had calculated that it would take exactly 506 miles to win the race, and he had formulated a precise schedule to reach that number, a schedule from which he would not deviate. As a friend later noted, Weston "rested according to his table, feeling quite certain . . . that his opponent would overdo himself and come back to him." It was the same strategy Weston had employed in his first race with O'Leary seventeen months earlier at the Expo in Chicago.

O'Leary (left) and Weston on the track at the Aggie, April 1877.
Courtesy of Peter Radford

All week long, huge crowds descended on the Aggie to watch the race, including thousands of London's Irish immigrants, who rooted vociferously for their compatriot O'Leary.

The race illuminated a messy bit of geopolitics. Britain (the island comprising England, Scotland, and Wales) and the whole of the island of Ireland together made up the United Kingdom.* The Irish, of course, were not pleased with this arrangement. They

---

* Today the UK comprises Britain and Northern Ireland. And while we're on the subject, Northern Ireland comprises only six of the nine counties in the historic Irish province of Ulster. The other three are in the Republic of Ireland, parts of which, incidentally, are actually north of Northern Ireland.

blamed the British—and the English specifically—for the hunger, disease, and poverty that had forced millions of them to flee their homeland. Many, like O'Leary, ended up in the United States. Others took the short trip across the Irish Sea to, as they saw it, the land of their oppressors. Of London's five million inhabitants at the time, one in five was Irish. They comprised the lowest class in a rigidly hierarchical society. Rare were the opportunities for them to express national pride. The great pedestrian match at the Aggie was one of those opportunities, and they relished it. O'Leary carried the hopes and dreams of his countrymen with every step he took.

The race also attracted a sizable number of spectators from the opposite end of the social spectrum. Numerous members of Parliament were spotted in the Aggie during the race, including one with a special interest in the outcome. He was Lieutenant-Colonel Sir John Dugdale Astley, Third Baronet, a Conservative member of Parliament and Britain's leading sportsman. With his white hair and bushy white beard, and a huge cigar perpetually clenched between his teeth, Astley was one of the most recognizable figures in British sports.

Born into a wealthy family in 1828, Astley was fourteen when he was shipped off to Eton, where his love of sports blossomed. He played football and cricket and was an avid rower and hunter. "I may say there was very little in the shape of sport that I did not take to," he later wrote. In the autumn of 1846 he matriculated at Oxford, where, by his own admission, his time was "most wasted." He frequently shirked chapel and cut classes. When he was caught harboring a stray dog he named Pepper in his apartment, he was denied breakfast privileges for a fortnight.

"I at once made up my mind that it would never do to go without breakfast, so that I had better go and fetch it myself," he remembered. "I watched my opportunity, darted into the kitchen, seized half a chicken and hurried off to my rooms with my prize, and it was thus that I discovered that I possessed a fair turn of

Sir John Astley. COURTESY OF LIBRARY OF CONGRESS

speed; for, though two men cooks (both young and active fellows) raced after me, I easily left them behind and gained my rooms, where I devoured my breakfast in peace."

After a year at Oxford, one of his advisors told him, "You are doing no good up here, and I really should advise you to go down."

"I am entirely of your opinion, sir," Astley replied, "and will readily support any statement to that effect that you may think proper to send to my father." When Astley returned to Oxford that fall to "settle up matters," he "ran a race over hurdles with H. Blundell, at Bullingdon." Astley won.

In 1848, when he was twenty, Astley joined the Scots Fusiliers Guards. He would see action in the Crimean War, but became best known as his battalion's fastest runner. Over the next ten years, Astley ran seven races for money, over distances ranging from 100 yards to ¼ mile. He won them all.

In 1858, Astley, now thirty, married twenty-year-old Eleanor Blanche Mary Corbett, "the only child of a well-to-do and well-born squire," and settled into a comfortable semiretirement. He was elected to Parliament in 1874, but sports, not politics, remained his true passion. Affectionately known as the Mate, Astley became legendary for wagering huge sums on horse races and boxing matches, with mixed results. In 1876, Astley became transfixed by Edward Payson Weston's walking exploits in Britain, and he was convinced Weston would whip Dan O'Leary in their match at the Aggie—so convinced, in fact, that he wagered a remarkable £20,000 on Weston to win.

Even from a distance removed, Americans followed the race closely, through the miracle of the transatlantic cable. Just a dozen years earlier, news from the Old World reached the New only as fast as a steamship could carry it across the Atlantic: about eight days. Then, in 1866, the first fully functional telegraph cable was laid on the ocean floor from western Ireland to Newfoundland. (A cable laid eight years earlier had failed after just three weeks.) This was an almost inconceivable technological leap: now Britain and the United States could communicate (via Morse code) almost instantaneously. "The Atlantic Telegraph," the *Times of London* wrote, "has half undone the declaration of 1776 and has gone far to make us once again, in spite of ourselves, one people." This "lightning beneath the sea" made it possible for newspapers in the United States to publish stories about events in the Weston-O'Leary race on the very same day they occurred.

By 3:00 PM on Friday, the fifth and penultimate day of the race, Weston, adhering to his strict schedule, had managed to whittle O'Leary's lead down to sixteen miles (424 to 408). "As thus slowly Weston decreased O'Leary's lead," a London newspaper reported, "the excitement in the hall increased, and the impression seemed to gain ground that Weston would, after all, prove his words true, which prophesied that O'Leary would lead up to the last two days, when he (Weston) would gradually gain and ultimately win." But it was not to be, for by now Weston was clearly spent. He sometimes staggered around the track, and it took him more than 20 minutes to complete his 440th mile.

On Saturday morning, Weston, realizing all hope was lost, retreated into his tent. Sir John Astley, who had a fortune riding on Weston, understandably didn't want him to surrender, and he went to fetch him.

"When I tried to get him out of bed he went soft," Astley later recounted, "and on my telling him I should chuck some cold water over him, he burst out crying, and that settled the matter: for you can do nothing at any game with a party who pipes his eye."

After 97 minutes, Weston finally returned to the track.

Meanwhile, O'Leary, although "evidently suffering from giddiness," soldiered on. At 2:05 on Saturday afternoon he completed his 500th mile, a milestone that sent the Irishmen in attendance into ecstasy. Several even joined him on the track as he walked, like the fans who accompanied Hank Aaron around the bases when he hit the home run that broke Babe Ruth's career record

These illustrations of the six-day race between Weston and O'Leary at the Aggie appeared on the front page of London's *Penny Illustrated Paper and Illustrated Times* on April 14, 1877. COURTESY OF BRITISH LIBRARY NEWSPAPERS

in 1974. "Ladies waved their handkerchiefs and gentlemen threw their hats in the air," the *Chicago Tribune*'s correspondent in London reported via the transatlantic cable, "while the cheering was perfectly deafening."

O'Leary kept on walking. His lead was now insurmountable, but the public's interest in the match was insatiable. By six o'clock on Saturday night there were ten thousand people in the Aggie, with more streaming in every minute. Hurriedly, the promoters more than doubled the price of admission, from a shilling (one-twentieth of a pound) to a half crown (one-eighth of a pound)— and still the crowds kept coming. No less than twenty thousand people were in the massive hall at nine o'clock, when Weston formally conceded the race.

O'Leary, the weary victor, was showered with applause and bouquets. Then he returned to his tent and practically collapsed into his bed. Weston, though vanquished, remained on the track for two more hours, entertaining the audience by "doing all sorts of hanky-panky tricks, and in one of his laps rolling a light garden-roller before him." When he finally quit at 11:00 PM, Weston received a thunderous ovation. "To have made a good fight against a walker so infinitely his superior speaks volumes for his pluck," one paper noted. O'Leary then emerged from his tent to deliver a short speech in which, according to the *London Standard,*

> he first thanked those present for the perfect fairness and impartiality that he had been shown, and afterwards said that he also thanked Mr. Weston, his late opponent, for had it not been for him, he should never have known his own powers. This ended the great match, and the hall soon emptied.

Officially, O'Leary finished with 519 miles, setting the standard for six-day races. Weston finished with 510—four more than he'd thought he'd need, and by far his best performance over six days—but still not enough.

Total attendance for the race approached eighty thousand. O'Leary collected a check drawn on the Bank of London for $14,000 (roughly $280,000 today). "It was a good week's work," said O'Leary years later, "and I would not mind repeating it."

But the race took its toll on O'Leary. Afterward he was too weak to climb into the carriage that carried him back to his hotel. His friends had to lift him into it. Astley wrote that "poor Daniel, the winner, was all wrong for some days after" the race.

To Astley's amazement, however, Weston was "as fresh as a kitten" after the race, and even accompanied Astley to church the next day.

Astley lost his wager, but the match left him spellbound. He almost never left the Aggie for the whole six days, sleeping just two or three hours a night. "I never was more excited over any performance," he later wrote, "and the number of cigars I got through was a record—not silly little female cigarettes either."

The popularity of the event took many Londoners by surprise. "The walking of 500 miles in six days shows wonderful powers of endurance," editorialized the *Holloway Press*, a London newspaper, "we only fail to understand how it is interesting enough to attract about eighty thousand to see it at its various stages."

The news of Dan O'Leary's second victory over Weston was received rapturously in Ireland. The pedestrian was inundated with letters and telegrams of congratulations from every corner of the island, as well as from the Irish quarters of Paris, Glasgow, San Francisco, Philadelphia, Chicago, and New York, all paying tribute to the "world's champion."

On Wednesday, April 25, the Irish members of the British Parliament held a lavish banquet in O'Leary's honor at the Westminster Palace Hotel in London. The contrast between the hosts and the guest of honor could not have been more stark. Most of the members of Parliament were Protestant landowners; among those present that night was Charles Stewart Parnell, who, despite his aristocratic background, would become a leader in the home rule movement, which advocated Irish self-government within the United Kingdom. Dan O'Leary, on the other hand, was a proud product of Ireland's Roman Catholic peasantry. Yet the MPs took as much pride in O'Leary's accomplishments as the Irish expatriates who had packed the Aggie to cheer him on.

Much in the same way he had united Chicago's many factions, O'Leary brought together Ireland's. According to the *Weekly Irish Times*, Patrick Keyes O'Clery, MP, the master of ceremonies for the banquet, introduced O'Leary to the 130 assembled guests as "a champion whose endurance, fearlessness, and courage were the same as those which had ever characterised the Irish race, and made its prodigies recognized as belonging to the highest types of the human family."

Mr. O'Leary, who was warmly cheered, thanked the company for the honor they had conferred upon him. He did not think he was deserving of it. He knew there were thousands of his countrymen in Ireland who could do the same as he had done. If he could only talk as well as he could walk he might express to them his thanks in eloquent language, but he would only say there was no man who could feel prouder of an honour shown to him than he did that evening.

Some London papers found the affair comical. "Certainly undignified, but then no one expects dignity in an Irish member of Parliament!" the *Sporting Times* wrote condescendingly. "Still, the spectacle afforded on Wednesday night of Hibernian M.P.'s entertaining the pedestrian O'Leary at dinner was amusing, and in its way a recognition of pluck."

The following month, May 1877, O'Leary crossed the Irish Sea and lived what must be every immigrant's dream: he returned home triumphant, a hero. It had been eleven years since O'Leary left Clonakilty, destitute and anonymous. Now he was wealthy beyond his wildest dreams and, at that moment anyway, the most famous Irishman in all the world.

When O'Leary's train pulled into the tiny depot in Clonakilty—back then Ireland had a comprehensive rail network; Clonakilty was served by the West Cork Railway—O'Leary must have been agog at the crowds that awaited him on the platform. The village had shut down for the day in O'Leary's honor. A proclamation was read in which the commissioners of Clonakilty offered O'Leary their heartiest welcome:

> In the Agricultural Hall, London, where the last feat of your wondrous prowess was displayed before the eyes of admiring thousands, you surpassed all your previous efforts, having succeeded in accomplishing a distance of some hundreds of miles within a short and stated period, which no man of any age or in any country has heretofore accomplished. Thus you have an immortal praise reflected on the Irish nation and on the Irish nation alone, the honor due to the fortune of your birth, having succeeded in performing a feat unparalleled in the annals of physical endurance.

O'Leary responded with a short speech. Public speaking always made him uncomfortable; he never enjoyed being in the spotlight the way Weston did. O'Leary simply said he was "sincerely pleased that he had gained to such an extent the good will of his fellow-townsmen, and he assured them that he valued their mark of approbation far more than if kings or senates were to lay at his feet the tribute of their admiration." For one so reticent, it was a touchingly heartfelt response.

O'Leary's time in Clonakilty was brief—probably less than a day. It was also bittersweet. Much had changed in the years since he'd left the village, as his biographer John Tansey noted:

The fields looked more green, and the wild birds' song appeared far more sweet than when he had last seen or listened to them; but where was the old, old home, beneath the thatched roof of which he drew his first breath, at whose once cheerful hearth he so often heard the "fireside tradition" of his plundered country repeated? It was numbered with the homesteads of the past, eviction's hand having wiped away every trace of it. Where now were the companions of his youth, with whom he had so often skipped along the verdant plains of his native village? Some were on foreign shores, the green turf of fatherland was waving over many of them, and but few were left to welcome him back to the early scenes of his childhood.

On May 12, 1877, Dan O'Leary, world champion pedestrian, departed his homeland on the steamer *Wisconsin*, bound once again for the New World.

6

THE ASTLEY BELT

or

MORE TALKED ABOUT THAN CONSTANTINOPLE

IN EARLY 1878, SIR JOHN ASTLEY, now utterly besotted with pedestrianism, announced that he would sponsor a series of six-day races to determine the "Long Distance Champion of the World." The first race would take place in March at the Aggie. It was open to any experienced pedestrian willing to put up a stake of ten pounds. The winner would receive £500 (roughly £44,000, or $67,000, today), the second-place finisher would receive one hundred pounds, and third would get fifty pounds. Astley also promised that each competitor who covered more than 450 miles would receive his ten-pound stake back, as well as a ten-pound bonus. In all, Astley guaranteed at least £750 in prize money, the richest purse ever offered in a pedestrian match.

In addition to the prize money, the winner of the race would also take possession of a bejeweled, five-pound, four-foot-long, silver-and-gold belt, commissioned by Sir John himself. Astley stipulated that the holder of the belt must defend his title within three months of any bona fide challenge, but was free to choose the site of the match. The first pedestrian to win the belt three times in a row could keep it forever. Valued at one hundred pounds, the Astley Belt would come to represent the pinnacle of pedestrianism, akin to the British Open's Claret Jug, which had been awarded to the winner of that golf tournament for the first time just four years before.

Astley, however, imposed some conditions on the races for his belt. First and foremost among them was the stipulation that the races be "go as you please" affairs. Entrants could, in Astley's words, "walk, trot, run, mix, lift or introduce a new style of pedestrianism if clever enough." Astley claimed he implemented the rule only because "the wobbling gait of Weston was open to objection as not being fair heel-and-toe walking." Dan O'Leary, however, had another theory. Since Americans had clearly demonstrated their superiority to the British in long-distance walking matches, O'Leary believed Astley "deemed [it] necessary to invent a style of progression which would place the legitimate champions at a decided disadvantage."

In any event, it seemed as if the cards had been stacked against the Americans, and only two agreed to compete in the first Astley Belt race: Weston (the proud Yankee) and O'Leary (the Irishman who was now a naturalized citizen of the United States).

Once again, two concentric tracks were laid out on the floor of the Aggie. The outer ⅙-mile track was for the British pedestrians, and the inner ⅐-mile track was for the two Yanks. At the last minute, however, Weston pulled out of the race. He claimed he was too ill to compete, "so seriously indisposed as to render his starting practically useless." What had made him ill, some joked, was the prospect of losing to O'Leary for a third time. In the *New York Times*, the story about Weston's abrupt withdrawal was headlined IS WESTON AFRAID OF O'LEARY?

Weston may have been afraid to race O'Leary again, but the real reason he pulled out of the race wasn't psychological, it was

The interior of the Aggie as it appeared for a livestock show in 1862 (left) and for a business conference 150 years later in 2012. COURTESY OF LIBRARY OF CONGRESS; COURTESY OF HENRY POTTS

financial: he was broke. Incredibly, even though he'd earned a fortune in Britain over the previous two years, Weston couldn't come up with the ten-pound stake to enter the first Astley Belt race. In fact, he was so destitute that he was stranded in Britain, unable to afford a ticket home. He'd probably squandered his fortune on fancy clothes and expensive hotels. Weston always had a knack for spending at least 10 percent more than he earned, whatever his income. In October 1878, Weston would file for bankruptcy. Identifying himself as a "gentleman" in documents filed in a British court, he listed £1,300 in liabilities. A few of the snarkier papers reveled in Weston's misfortune. "[Weston] has been for another walking match," said one, "one through the Bankruptcy Court."

Weston's liabilities, however, became O'Leary's asset: Weston's withdrawal left O'Leary as the lone American in the race, meaning he would have the inside track all to himself, while the sixteen British pedestrians entered in the race would have to share the outside track. This would give O'Leary an unexpected advantage, though he, theretofore strictly a "fair heel and toe" pedestrian, would still be competing against "go as you please" racers. And the Brits were no pushovers. They had also been studying very carefully the Americans' training methods and race strategies when they competed in Britain.

As was the case in America, the best pedestrians in Britain were often workingmen who had demonstrated unusual stamina and were willing to push themselves to extremes in the pursuit of fame and fortune. Among the sixteen Brits competing against O'Leary in the first Astley Belt race at the Aggie were the following three men.

Henry Vaughan, a carpenter by trade, was, Astley recalled, "a real clean-made and thoroughly respectable man." Like O'Leary, Vaughan preferred walking to running; Astley called him "perhaps, the finest walker I ever saw." Even his opponents admired him for his "long-striding giant-like" step, his steady pace, and his pleasant temperament. In late 1876, Vaughan had covered 100 miles in 18 hours, 51 minutes, and 35 seconds, and 120 miles in 23 hours, 45 minutes, and 0 seconds, both believed to be British records at the time.

Henry "Blower" Brown was a brickmaker who "had early distinguished himself by the rapid manner he trundled his barrow of bricks to the kiln, and back again for another load," Astley wrote, "and, like all brick-makers (I have ever heard of), he was wonderfully fond of beer." His trainer, an old-time pedestrian named John Smith, would exhort his protégé: "Yes! Blower shall have a barrel of beer all to himself if he wins; go it, Blower!" Once, in the middle of a race, Brown showed signs of "shutting up," so Astley and Smith took him to Astley's nearby apartment and gave him a hot bath—"quite a new sensation for him," Astley remembered—while two chops were ordered up. After the bath, Astley was helping Brown back into his track suit when he noticed Smith "busily employed gobbling up all the best parts of the chops, leaving only the bone, gristle, and fat." When Astley chastised Smith for his gluttony, the trainer laughed. "Bless yer, Colonel!" Smith said. "Blower has never had the chance of eating the inside, he likes the outside." Sure enough, Astley wrote, "the brick-maker cleaned up the dish." The source of Blower's nickname is a mystery. He claimed he'd had it since childhood but did not recall its origin. Other sources said it was because he'd once worked the bellows in a blacksmith shop, that he had a habit of puffing his cheeks when he ran, that he liked to blow his own horn. The last theory is the least likely. Brown was not much of a talker. "The pedestrian himself, when asked the reason [for his nickname], gave no response," the *New York Sun* reported, "but stared blankly at the reporter." Another reporter who once attempted to interview Brown flatly declared that the pedestrian "had no ideas worth communicating to the public."

William Gentleman, who competed under the name "Corkey," was both older (forty-six) and smaller (five feet four, 114 pounds) than most of his competitors, and he moved "ungracefully and with a sad look on his face." "He didn't look a bit like staying," Astley wrote of Corkey, "was as thin as a rail, and stuttered very funnily," but "he had won a lot of running matches in his time." Corkey's secret weapon was his wife. "She never left him day or night [during a race]," Astley recalled, "and was always ready to hand her sweetheart a basin of delicious and greasy eel-broth, that he loved so well, and which evidently agreed so famously with him."

Before the race, London bookmakers made Vaughan the favorite to win. Brown and Corkey were the favorites for second place, along with O'Leary.

———⊕•×•⊕———

The race began early on the morning of Monday, March 18, 1878. The Aggie was nearly empty; it wouldn't be opened to the public until later that morning. In the dim gaslight of the cavernous arena were gathered the official scorekeepers and judges, newspaper reporters, the pedestrians and their trainers, and a few special guests invited by Astley, including a number of Americans, recognizable by their "soft hats."

It was an uncanny, almost spectral scene. "The great wide space of benches, set apart for spectators, looked chill and dirty," the *New York Times* London correspondent noted. "The light of a charcoal fire in a brazier fell mysteriously upon the small encampment of the pedestrians near the entrance doors. One tent stood alone near the foreigners' track." (Each of the British competitors was assigned a tent at one end of the hall, while O'Leary was assigned one inside the tracks.)

Astley called the pedestrians to gather round him. Their expressions ranged from apprehensive to indifferent. Some tugged nervously at their uniforms. "You are about to enter on a trying match, in which running and walking and physical pluck and endurance are necessary to compete," Sir John told them. "Every possible arrangement has been made to have a fair, straight fight, and I hope the best man will win, no matter what his nationality or where he comes from."

The seventeen competitors took their places on the starting line: the sixteen Brits on the outside track, O'Leary alone on the inside.

"Now, lads, are you ready?" Astley asked. "A fair, honest, manly race, and the best man wins. Ready? Then away you go!"

The time was 1:03 AM.*

Some of the competitors took off running like hounds unleashed on an unlucky fox. Others jogged at a leisurely pace. Still others walked, hoping to conserve energy for the long haul. One reporter described the men as going "round and round something like a school of herrings in the Brighton Aquarium, round and round, in groups, in twos and threes, in ones and twos, in threes and fours, round, and round and round."

Corkey and Brown, the runners, immediately shot out into the lead, while Vaughan and O'Leary, the walkers, struggled to keep up. O'Leary occasionally tried running to keep up with the leaders, but it hurt the tendons in his legs and made him feel dizzy and nauseated. By 4:00 AM, he had stopped trying to run altogether, and for the rest of the race he would stick to his preferred mode

---

* Six-day races were not always exactly six days long: they often started around one o'clock Monday morning and ended around eleven o'clock the following Saturday night.

of locomotion. At 5:00 PM on that first day, Corkey was in the lead with 87 miles. O'Leary was second with 83 miles, Brown third with 78, and Vaughan fourth with 77. At eleven that night, Corkey, Brown, and Vaughan retired for a few hours of rest, but O'Leary, who was said to possess a "morbid dread" of not being in first place, stayed on the track until 2:44 AM on Tuesday, by which time he had accumulated 124 miles, enough to retire with the lead.

Corkey recaptured the lead later Tuesday morning, but the effects of his prolonged running were beginning to show. Even his wife's "greasy eel-broth" failed to perk him up, and at seven o'clock that night, Corkey's legs were so sore that he was forced to rest for several hours. By then O'Leary had pulled even with him at 174 miles—the equivalent of completing more than six marathons—in 42 hours. And the race still had more than four days to go. The advantage that the runners were expected to enjoy in this "go as you please" race was not as great as many had expected. By Wednesday most of them were so fagged out they could barely even walk, much less run.

By one o'clock Thursday morning—after three days, the halfway point of the race—O'Leary led with 288 miles. Vaughan and Brown were tied for second with 270 miles each. Corkey had faded to fourth place and was all but finished. Around this time it was reported that a "well-known sporting man"—probably Astley himself—had promised Brown a £500 bonus if he "saved the championship to his country." It had become more than a footrace. It was a matter of national pride. Patriotism was rampant in Britain at the time because the country was preparing to go to war. In Afghanistan.

———— ·•·•· ————

Just a few weeks before the race, a treaty ending a war between Russia and the Ottoman Empire had been signed at a house in San Stefano, near Constantinople. This triggered a chain of events resulting in Russia sending a diplomatic mission to Kabul to establish an embassy there—a provocative move, since Afghanistan was the buffer between the Russian Empire to the north and British-ruled India to the south. The British had long feared Russia would attempt to seize India, and they were deeply suspicious of Russian motives in Afghanistan. In fact, Britain's foreign policy, known as the Great Game, was to minimize Russian influence in Central Asia, and Russia and Britain had gone to war in Afghanistan forty years before.

Nominally, Afghanistan was an independent state and neutral in the dispute between Britain and Russia. But its ruler, an emir named Sher Ali Khan, was weak and vacillating, and the newly arrived Russians in Kabul began to pressure him. When Britain sent its own envoy to Kabul in August 1878, he was turned away at the border by Afghan troops. This the British government could not countenance, so, on November 21, 1878, some forty thousand British and Indian troops invaded Afghanistan, launching the Second Anglo-Afghan War.*

The Afghan government asked Russia for military support, but the Russians declined to get involved, so it was left to the Afghans alone to repel the invaders. As often seems to be the case with wars in Afghanistan, the results were muddled. Unable to secure an outright victory against the country's innumerable tribes, Britain negotiated a treaty in 1880 that installed a new emir, Abdur Rahman Khan, who promised to conduct the country's foreign relations in accordance with the "wishes and advice" of the British government.†

So, in the late winter and early spring of 1878, Britain felt its empire was under threat, not just from the machinations of Russia

---

* The most famous veteran of the Second Anglo-Afghan War was fictional. In the Arthur Conan Doyle stories, Dr. Watson, Sherlock Holmes's friend and assistant, was a surgeon in the British Army who was wounded in the war.

† Britain has since invaded Afghanistan two more times, in the Third Anglo-Afghan War in 1919 and in the War in Afghanistan in 2001.

in Afghanistan, but also from the nascent home rule movement in Ireland and America's exponentially expanding economic and diplomatic influence. It was in this charged atmosphere that the first Astley Belt race took place in London. Britain's superiority was at stake, and it was unthinkable that not one of the sixteen entrants racing under the Union Jack could defeat the lone American in the race—an American born in Ireland, no less.

—•••—

While Sir John Astley was disappointed that the American was in the lead, he couldn't have been happier with the reports from the box office. Indisputably, the race was a hit. Attendance exceeded all expectations, averaging about six thousand for each of the first three days. Shrewd promoter that he was, Astley sold tickets in a range of prices, from a shilling for general admission seats on the floor of the arena, to ten times that—a half sovereign, or ten shillings—for a reserved seat in a box in the balcony overlooking the tracks. This effectively segregated the rabble—particularly the Irishmen boisterously exhorting their erstwhile countryman O'Leary—from the swells.

This might help explain the event's popularity among the upper crust. "Scores and hundreds of people came in just to have a peep, and were so fascinated that they stayed for hours, returning day after day," Astley wrote. "Amongst them were many refined men of letters." A long line of broughmans, the most luxurious of carriages, queued along Liverpool Road in front of the Aggie each night, depositing well-heeled gentlemen and ladies who enjoyed the great walking match from the comfort of the balcony.

The race was the most talked-about topic in London that week. "For a time," the *Irish Times* correspondent in London wrote, "Islington was more talked about than Constantinople, and the Agricultural Hall than Ignatieff's house at San Stefano, where the treaty was signed." Even the stodgy *Times of London* was taken aback by how popular the event was. "The large attendance on each day would alone testify to this," the paper wrote,

Vaughan, O'Leary, and Brown (left to right) competing in the first Astley Belt race at the Aggie, March 18–23, 1878. COURTESY OF PETER RADFORD

"but the way in which the walk has been made a topic of conversation among those who have not journeyed to Islington is surprising."

"From the large attendances . . . at the Agricultural hall," the *Islington Gazette* noted, "it would appear that the interest taken in long-distance performances is by no means on the wane."

It may be worth pondering again the peculiar appeal of pedestrianism, an appeal that transcended the boundaries of social class, gender, and nationality at a time when such boundaries were rigid, particularly in Britain. Watching half-dead men stagger in circles for days on end might strike the reader as monotonous, if not outright boring. Yet, judging by the attendance at the first Astley Belt race at least, there was obviously something alluring about the sport. Perhaps it was the electric atmosphere inside the vast arena, with brass bands blaring and a packed house shouting itself hoarse. Perhaps it was the quirky personalities of the competitors: the genial, giant-striding Henry Vaughan; the brick-making, beer-swilling, bone-chewing Blower Brown; the impish, stuttering, eel-broth-loving William "Corkey" Gentleman. Perhaps it was the bitter rivalries the competitors embodied: O'Leary, the lone Irishman, pitted against the overwhelming forces of British pedestrianism—a metaphor for the Irish struggle for independence from imperialist Britain. Of the handful of spontaneous utterances of the audience that were recorded, nearly all express a degree of nationalism: "Vaughan, step out for England!" "O'Leary, hump it, and lick the Britisher!"

But there was something else about it, something oddly captivating. It was like watching a NASCAR race in super-slow motion: hypnotic, mesmerizing, with the promise of imminent catastrophe. "[A] brilliant poet," Astley wrote (without naming names, unfortunately), "confided to me one morning, in the small hours at the Agricultural Hall, that he had never been so interested in any show in his life."

On Friday, March 22, the penultimate day of the race, there were still thirteen men moving in circles on the floor of the Aggie, but only the top three stood any chance of winning. At 6:00 PM the score was O'Leary, 433 miles; Vaughan, 421; Brown, 395. The rest of the field was in bad shape. "Several were in a very pitiable plight as regards their feet," a reporter for the *London Observer* wrote, "and it seemed positively cruel to encourage them to keep on their legs, struggling against nature, and perhaps doing themselves a permanent injury."

O'Leary, the leader, wasn't in much better shape. By Saturday morning, the final day of the race, he was struggling to maintain his advantage. His condition was deteriorating, and he seemed on the verge of collapsing. His feet were aching, and his legs were stiff and sore. He was suffering from sleep deprivation, of course, and he was dehydrated and malnourished. Earlier in the week he'd drunk some bad port, which had made him sick and destroyed his appetite. "Why, I didn't eat anything for six days," O'Leary would tell a reporter after the race. "No, sir, except an orange now and then. I lived on tea, coffee, and milk." He was also experiencing tunnel vision. "At one time he was so dazed he could not see the edge of the track," Astley recalled, "until some fresh white sawdust was brought and laid round near the edge."

"It was a sorry sight the last few hours of the week's walk," the *New York Times* correspondent wrote. "Haggard, dazed, staggering O'Leary, his arms no longer knitted in pedestrian form and braced with muscular strength, were limp and almost helpless. His legs were swollen. He went his miserable round in evident pain."

Yet, somehow, O'Leary still managed to keep walking, managed to keep the lead. It was as if his body were on autopilot. One spectator said he "seemed more like a machine than a man." It was a remarkable exhibition of endurance, but it was painful to watch.

On Saturday night, the Aggie was "besieged by a multitude," according to the *Irish Times*. "Turnstiles were stormed by the impatient throng, and reserved seats and enclosures were swamped by the rush." By one estimate, the attendance that night was twenty-five thousand. Around 7:30 PM, Henry Vaughan, still in second place and nineteen miles behind O'Leary, finished his 500th mile and retired, conceding the race. But O'Leary kept walking while the band played "See the Conquering Hero Comes," and the vast crowd cheered so loudly it seemed the Aggie's glass roof might crack. O'Leary completed one more mile to finish with 520, a mile farther than he'd walked in his race against Weston a year earlier, and a new six-day record. Blower Brown finished third with 477 miles. Corkey, the early leader, finished in sixth place with 332 miles.

Unsteadily, O'Leary managed to walk two victory laps before collapsing into the arms of his attendants and being "half led, half carried" out of the hall to a room at a nearby hotel. Astley shook his hand as he left, as did two Catholic priests in attendance. The Irishman-cum-American had won, defeating all sixteen of his British challengers. O'Leary was "indomitable," the *Irish Times* reported. His "marvellous staying power and unyielding spirit excited the unqualified admiration of all present."

Well, maybe not all. In an interview two months later, O'Leary was asked if anything "unpleasant" had occurred during the race. "I was treated fairly well," he answered diplomatically, "but Englishmen don't admire Irishmen. That is sure." When O'Leary took possession of the Astley Belt after the race, he noticed that, engraved on one side of the buckle was an image of a man running, and on the other side was a man walking. The runner was on the left. "They put the runner ahead," his wife told him, "because they wanted him to win."

Some British papers pooh-poohed O'Leary's record-breaking performance. "The fact of his being allowed a separate track is in itself a great advantage," the *Times of London* huffed. "It gave O'Leary an incalculable advantage." Other papers complained that O'Leary's tent was close to the track and "commodious," while the British competitors were relegated to "hovels."

The American press saw things a little differently. AMERICA BEATS THE WORLD, read a headline on the front page of the *Boston Globe* the day after the race ended. "Chicago is ahead again," bragged the *Tribune* in O'Leary's adoptive hometown. "It has been a great time for the United States and for Chicago and 'a great day for Ireland.'"

The *Logansport (Indiana) Daily Journal* compared O'Leary to the yacht *America*, which had defeated fifteen British yachts in a race around the Isle of Wight in 1851, winning the silver trophy that now bears its name: the America's Cup. Like the *America*, the paper said, O'Leary had "demonstrated that . . . the new world is more than a match for the old."

"With this triumph," crowed *Harper's Weekly*, "the effeteness of monarchical institutions becomes more evident to many minds."

That O'Leary was born in Ireland seemed not to matter in claiming his victory as America's. As a Pennsylvania paper pointed out, "In this International Match he entered the lists as an American, represented America, and if he had been beaten it would have been considered an American defeat."

———◦••◦———

On his way back to America, O'Leary once again visited the Emerald Isle. By defeating sixteen Brits in a race to determine the "Long Distance Champion of the World," O'Leary had become a proxy in Ireland's fight for independence, whether he liked it or not, and he was received rapturously. "Ireland is in a very sunburst of excitement over the achievements of her favorite son," the *Chicago Tribune* reported, "who . . . beat the 'blarsted Britisher' on his own soil."

O'Leary, however, was much more interested in profits than politics. In Dublin he rented a hall and attempted to walk 220 miles in 60 hours. He beat the clock, but the financial results were disappointing. As O'Leary discovered, Dublin at that time was practically an English city. "There are five Englishmen in Dublin to one Irishman," he said after the walk. "If I had been an Italian or a Bohemian I would have done better." He claimed to have lost £300 on the venture.

On May 5, O'Leary, Astley Belt in tow, sailed for America on the steamer *Idaho*, arriving in New York nine days later. He then embarked on a punishing series of exhibitions: 220 miles in 60 hours in Cincinnati in June, a 75-hour race in Chicago in July, 400 miles in 125 hours in Boston in August, and 275 miles in 75 hours in Providence in September. Everywhere he went, large crowds turned out to watch the champion pedestrian, and to see for themselves the now-famous silver-and-gold belt, which was displayed in a glass case.

Then, in October, O'Leary defended his Astley Belt title for the first time. The challenger was a fellow Irish immigrant named John Hughes.

The leading British pedestrians, including Henry Vaughan, Blower Brown, and William "Corkey" Gentleman, had all wanted another crack at O'Leary, but he would only defend his title on American soil. John Hughes was a relatively unknown pedestrian from New York, and, when Hughes challenged O'Leary, the reigning champion initially dismissed him as a mere "speculator," unworthy of competing for the prestigious belt. But Hughes persisted, and Sir John Astley eventually ruled that O'Leary must race Hughes or surrender the belt.

Hughes had been itching to race O'Leary for years, and there was bad blood between the two Irishmen. When O'Leary first went East to walk in 1875, Hughes had wanted to race him but could find no backers. If he only had the money, Hughes told anybody who'd listen, he could "easily defeat O'Leary at any distance."

These protestations annoyed O'Leary terrifically. When O'Leary stopped in New York on his way to the first Astley Belt race in London, Hughes tracked him down and told him he would "go to England and beat him but he had no money." O'Leary responded sarcastically, "I'll build you a bridge." This infuriated Hughes, who became more determined than ever to vanquish "the rapscallion [who] told me he'd build me a bridge."

As soon as he learned of O'Leary's victory in London, Hughes frantically began searching for a backer to underwrite his challenge. He finally found one in Harry Hill, who promoted illicit boxing matches in New York and operated a dancehall that was a popular hangout for the city's sporting fraternity. Hill agreed to pay Hughes's entrance fee and underwrite his training costs.

The site of the second Astley Belt race was Gilmore's Garden in New York.

Four years earlier, in 1874, Phineas T. Barnum had erected an arena on the site of an abandoned train terminal between Fourth (later Park) and Madison Avenues and Twenty-Sixth and Twenty-Seventh Streets. He leased the land from the New York and Harlem Railroad, which was owned by Cornelius Vanderbilt.

In his understated way, Barnum named the new arena the Grand Roman Hippodrome and declared it the "largest amusement

Phineas T. Barnum's Grand Roman Hippodrome in New York, pictured shortly
after it opened in 1874. Before a permanent roof was installed, Barnum occasionally covered the open-air arena with one of his circus tents. Milstein Division
of United States History, Local History & Genealogy, The New York Public Library, Astor,
Lenox and Tilden Foundations

building ever constructed." Despite Barnum's ballyhoo, however,
the Hippodrome was a rather simple structure: an elongated dirt
oval surrounded by wooden bleachers. Balconies that hung low
over the main floor were later installed, bringing the venue's
capacity to ten thousand. The Hippodrome was enclosed by a
three-story brick wall, but originally had no roof. Seventeen huge
furnaces warmed the space in the winter. Occasionally Barnum
would cover the arena with one of the canvas tents from his traveling circus—in a way, it was the first stadium with a retractable roof
in the United States.* A permanent roof was finally added around
1876.

---

* But not in the world: The Colosseum in Rome—the original Grand
Roman Hippodrome— was equipped with a retractable canvas awning.

The Hippodrome officially opened on April 27, 1874, and for the next two years, Barnum's three-ring circus was the building's primary tenant. "To behold the wonders inside," wrote Joseph Durso in his history of the arena, "all you had to do was pay Barnum the significant sum of one American dollar."

"In return," Durso wrote, "the great man rewarded the senses."

Chariots with lady drivers raced over the turf. Japanese acrobats tumbled through the air. Cowboys chased Indians, and Indians chased cowboys. Freaks devoured fire or exhibited their tattooed bodies. Actors portrayed the many lives and many wives of Bluebeard the ogre. The flags of the Congress of Nations flapped in the breeze. Arabian horses pranced and elephants waltzed to the music.

In 1876, for reasons that are unclear, Barnum did not renew his lease with the railroad. Perhaps he found a traveling circus to be more lucrative than a stationary one. In any event, the lease was auctioned off, and the winner was a bandleader named Patrick Gilmore.

———

Born in County Galway on Christmas Day 1829, Gilmore emigrated to Boston in 1848 and embarked on a career in music. An accomplished cornetist, he formed a band comprising two woodwinds to each brass instrument—the same arrangement used in concert bands today. During the Civil War, Gilmore's Band served in the Massachusetts Twenty-Fourth Regiment. It was during the war that Gilmore was inspired to write a song called "When Johnny Comes Marching Home," which was based on an old Irish folk tune and became a hopeful anthem for both sides in the conflict.

The song made Gilmore's name, and after the war his band became the most famous in the country. Gilmore bought Barnum's Hippodrome to give the band a permanent home. He renamed the arena Gilmore's Garden, and, in addition to his band, began booking everything from religious revivals to beauty pageants. In May 1877, he rented the arena to the Westminster Kennel Club for its first dog show, which has been held annually in New York ever since.

———•••••———

Patrick Gilmore had heard about the lucrative walking matches at the Aggie in London, and he was eager for a piece of the pedestrianism pie. He offered Dan O'Leary very favorable terms for hosting the second Astley Belt race. Gilmore and O'Leary would divide the gross receipts equally, but Gilmore agreed to pay all expenses out of his share. John Hughes would be paid one-third of O'Leary's share, meaning Hughes would receive one-sixth of the gate and O'Leary one-third.

Concentric tracks, each 30 inches wide, were laid out: ⅛ mile on the outside, ⅑ on the inside. O'Leary won a coin toss and chose to walk the outside track. For the race, O'Leary would wear a special pair of custom-made leather shoes that wrapped around his feet as tightly as tourniquets. For obvious reasons, pedestrians were very particular about their footwear. It was not uncommon for them to lose toenails during races due to ill-fitting shoes.

"He picked up one of his shoes," a reporter who met with O'Leary shortly before the race recounted, "and began to point out its beauties."

> The sole was very wide, so that the foot could not, by any possibility, spread out wider than the shoe. Its greatest peculiarity was the heel, only about half an inch high. "I had that put on in London," said O'Leary, tapping a little extra piece that had been put on across the bottom of the heel. "It is to make the heel elastic. When I walk fast, I walk almost entirely upon my heels, and this springiness prevents any jar and is a great convenience." The elasticity in the back of

the heel is due partly to the extra piece not being fastened at that point, and partly to its being slightly wrinkled in the putting on, the effect being that when it strikes the floor it acts like a spring, trying to straighten itself out, with scarcely a sound.

The second Astley Belt race began at 1:00 AM on Monday, September 30, 1878. O'Leary and Hughes were the only entrants. Hughes sprinted out to an early lead, covering the first five miles in a blistering 35 minutes and 41 seconds. It took O'Leary 53 minutes and 14 seconds to cover the same distance. But by the end of that first day, O'Leary, going fair heel and toe, had caught Hughes, and by Tuesday afternoon O'Leary was twenty miles ahead.

It turned out Hughes was not nearly as talented as he'd thought. By the third day he was so far behind that many spectators "did not hesitate . . . to denounce him as a fraud." Two Catholic priests who visited Hughes advised him to "drink nothing but champagne in small quantities." Hughes took their advice, sort of. He began consuming the bubbly by the magnum. Awakening from a nap, he demanded a bottle and downed it all. "Ah," he said. "That's the stuff to make one walk! Open me another bottle." By the fourth day, according to the *New York Times*, "he was so used up that he could scarcely crawl along; and in the last 48 hours of the match he did not average a mile to the hour."

O'Leary barely had to break a sweat to win his second consecutive Astley Belt race. The final tally was 403 miles to 310.

After the race ended, O'Leary was presented with "a handsome gold medal," which was pinned to his chest by the city's commissioner of charities and correction, Thomas "Big Tom" Brennan. O'Leary was sheepish. "Had I had a better competitor," he said, "I could have made many more miles; but, from the start, I was convinced that it was a walk-over. I would have been better satisfied, and so would my friends, if Hughes had shown better powers of endurance and better speed."

Despite the lopsided result, the match was a financial success. Attendance on the final night was seven thousand. O'Leary took home $5,000 and Hughes pocketed $2,500. Gilmore was so pleased that he immediately offered O'Leary favorable terms for hosting the next Astley Belt race in the Garden. O'Leary agreed— and if he won the race, the belt would be his to keep forever.

7

PEDESTRIENNES

or

PIONEERS

IN THE WINTER OF 1878–79, just two months after the second Astley Belt race, New York was captivated by another amazing walking feat: a pedestrian was attempting to walk a mind-boggling 2,700 quarter miles in 2,700 consecutive quarter hours—more than twenty-eight days. But this pedestrian wore revealing dresses and colorful bows in her hair. Her name was Ada Anderson.

Ada Anderson was born in London in 1843, but her maiden name is lost to history. Her parents were "tradespeople of the humbler class." She once said her father was a "Cockney Jew," and her mother was said to be either English or German. When she was sixteen, Ada left home to join a traveling theater company in which she "played subordinate parts and sang acceptably, and was the favorite of the troupe, owing to her sweet voice and agreeable person." At twenty-two she married a man named Anderson and took his name. He died just three years later.

While in Wales in early 1877, Anderson was introduced to a pedestrian named William Gale. Anderson had always "indulged in physical culture," and her meeting with Gale piqued her interest in pedestrianism. Anderson, who was undoubtedly aware of Edward Payson Weston's phenomenally successful exhibitions at the Aggie in London the year before, decided to pursue her own career on the tanbark, and she hired Gale to train her.

Gale was a diminutive Cardiff native who specialized in Captain Barclay–type feats of endurance (and sleep deprivation). In the summer of 1877, he walked 1½ miles every hour for one thousand consecutive hours. That autumn, he walked four thousand quarter miles in four thousand consecutive periods of ten minutes (nearly twenty-eight days), a performance that allowed him to rest no more than six minutes at a time. "The amount of perseverance and abnegation requisite naturally excites admiration," the *Times of London* noted of the latter event. "It seems incredible that a man should be able to forego the demands of nature for so long a time." (However, as the paper also pointed out, "The entire absence of competition rendered the affair monotonous in the extreme.") Broadsides advertising his exhibitions depicted Gale being stalked by the Grim Reaper.

Anderson underwent "a thorough course of training" under Gale's tutelage. "The result," the *Brooklyn Daily Eagle* later reported, "was that Gale gave her every encouragement to continue in the business—advice which she avers had a decisive influence on her."

In September 1877, Anderson made her professional walking debut in Newport, Wales. Madame Anderson, as she now billed herself, successfully walked one thousand half miles in one thousand consecutive half hours. Two months later in Plymouth, England, she walked 1¼ miles every hour for one thousand straight hours, likely becoming the first woman to outdo Captain Barclay's celebrated walk. The following April in Leeds she bettered that record again, covering 1,500 miles in one thousand hours.

Like Edward Payson Weston, Anderson considered herself an entertainer as well as an athlete. She punctuated her performances with singing, oratory, and occasional pranks (applying black greasepaint to the faces of sleeping spectators was a favorite). Her performances were quite popular, especially among women, an audience theretofore ignored by sports promoters. During a walk in King's Lynn, England, Anderson addressed the women in attendance. "She was a Londoner herself," the local paper reported her saying, "and had often seen the seamstresses . . . go to their daily toil and often sit up all night with a small piece of candle and only bread and butter to eat. Though she had to stay up all night, she was only too thankful that she was well fed and well taken care of."

By the autumn of 1878 Madame Anderson had performed at least nine successful walks in venues throughout England and Wales. She had acquired an agent—and a second husband, a man named W. H. Paley.* She was Britain's most celebrated female pedestrian. Now it was time to take her act abroad. She boarded a White Star steamer and sailed for New York.

This illustration of Madame Anderson appeared in *Frank Leslie's Illustrated Newspaper,* February 1, 1879. Courtesy of Library of Congress

For her American debut, Anderson rented Mozart Garden, a newly opened music hall on the corner of Fulton and Smith Streets in Brooklyn. Styled after the music halls then popular in London, Mozart Garden was, despite its highfalutin name, a simple brick building with a large stage at one end and a balcony reserved for

---

* Some sources say her second husband's surname was Wood.

ladies at the other. ("No gentlemen admitted to balcony without ladies," patrons were warned.) Beneath the balcony was a large bar. Wooden folding chairs on the main floor provided seating for eight hundred people. While spartan, the venue was not without its charms. "Indeed," the *Brooklyn Daily Eagle* reported shortly after it opened, "the general effect of the interior is extremely refreshing in its simplicity and freedom from meretricious effect."

What Madame Anderson would attempt inside Mozart Garden had never been attempted before in the United States by a pedestrian of either sex: she would endeavor to walk a quarter mile every fifteen minutes for one thousand consecutive quarter hours—more than twenty-eight days. It would be, by far, the most challenging walk she had ever undertaken.

A three-foot-wide tanbark track was laid on the main floor of Mozart Garden. Owing to the relatively small size of the venue, the oval track measured less than 189 feet around—$\frac{1}{28}$ of a mile—meaning Anderson would have to walk seven laps to make a quarter mile. Chairs were arranged rather haphazardly both inside and outside the oval. A small dressing room on the ground floor of the building was provided for her use during the walk.

Teams of judges and scorekeepers were recruited to oversee the event. The *New York Herald*, a newspaper that heavily promoted pedestrianism, agreed to certify the results. To ensure fairness—and, undoubtedly, also to increase attendance—a one-hundred-dollar reward was offered to "any one who would discover that she failed, night or day, to carry out her agreement to the letter."

The price of admission was twenty-five cents for adults, fifteen cents for children, and five dollars for a "season pass." Anderson was eager to project an aura of respectability, and the management of the venue promised to maintain the "strictest decorum" and that "ladies and children shall have a good opportunity of viewing this exhibition of human pluck and endurance."

The walk commenced on the evening of December 17, 1878. At 7:45, Mozart Garden's manager, Alexander Samuells, mounted the stage to introduce Madame Anderson. He said she "undertook the task not so much for pecuniary remuneration as she did to promote physical health, and encourage ladies and children to indulge in the healthful exercise." He concluded by saying he had no doubt that "Madame Anderson would easily accomplish the feat she had undertaken."

Anderson then addressed the audience in a "clear, resonant voice," according to one eyewitness. "In the course of her brief remarks," the *Eagle* reported, "she expressed the hope that more of her lady friends would attend to encourage her in her arduous feat. . . . It was always pleasant to her to see a large representation of her own sex at her exhibition, and it would greatly encourage her on her long journey."

Several hundred people were in attendance, including "a number of ladies" and several Brooklyn aldermen. (At the time, Brooklyn was an independent city; it would not become part of New York City for another twenty years.)

As it was throughout her career, Madame Anderson's physical appearance was much discussed in the press. The *Eagle* described her as "robust, rosy and hearty." "Her face, although of a slightly masculine type, is bright and prepossessing; her eyes are expressive and her entire appearance very agreeable." Her "costume," the paper reported, consisted of "black velvet knee breeches, and a loose flowing robe of blue and scarlet cloth, embroidered with white, descending just far enough to allow the free exercise of the body. On her feet were stout, loose leather shoes, topped by stockings of flaming scarlet. Her rounded limbs were inclosed in silver tights." Her hair was worn in a long braid, and "crowned by a jaunty little cap of blue and white." The wardrobes of male pedestrians were rarely so dissected.

At precisely eight o'clock, a small bell was rung to signal the start of the walk. On the stage, the band struck up a lively march. The crowd cheered as Madame Anderson began her long journey. One paper analyzed her gait as assiduously as a batting champion's swing is analyzed today:

She walked with an easy, graceful and yet dignified movement. She carried her head erect, her shoulders well squared, her chest expanded, and as she moved rapidly over the tan bark [*sic*] with toes pointed outward, she swung her arms to and fro in consonance with the motion of her limbs. So lightly did she step that she scarcely seemed to touch the track. Every muscle was brought into full play.

She circled the track seven times, completing her first quarter mile in four minutes. Then she retired to her dressing room. Eleven minutes later, at 8:15, the bell rang again, summoning her back to the track. It was time to walk her second quarter mile.

A few minutes after midnight, after she had completed her 17th quarter mile, the *Eagle* correspondent interviewed Madame Anderson as she rested in her dressing room. She was wearing a fur robe and reclined on a couch. Beef broth bubbled in a kettle on a gas stove in a corner of the room. "Madame Anderson looked somewhat flushed after the last quarter," the reporter noted. "She was, however, cheerful and communicative."

Anderson asked the reporter what he thought of her style of walking. When he expressed his admiration, she replied, "Well, I try to please. You know that some of the professional pedestrians walk with a stride that is positively painful. Take Weston for instance. Why it seems as if he was suffering the greatest tortures. Now I think the public are entitled to something better than that and that the pedestrian should strive to move along as perfectly as possible." Although she could sleep no more than ten or eleven minutes at a time, Anderson said it was only difficult to sleep when her legs hurt. "The pain keeps me awake and sometimes I cannot get to sleep till it is time for me to go on the track again. If my feet remain in good condition I will sleep with ease and comfort." It seems Madame Anderson was a polyphasic sleeper. One newspaper reported that doctors who had studied her concluded that "Madame Anderson . . . has trained her constitution into the habit of accepting the requisite sleep in small doses."

Madame Anderson was not America's first famous female pedestrian. That title belongs to Bertha von Hillern, a German immigrant who was said to be from a "respectable military family." In 1876, von Hillern, who was in her early twenties, competed in a series of six-day races against another female pedestrian, Mary Marshall. The races attracted thousands of spectators and received favorable coverage in newspapers across the country. These pedestriennes, as the newspapers dubbed them, were considered pioneers for women's rights. In an editorial, the *New York Times* noted that the Supreme Court had recently barred women from arguing cases before it. "Today it is the walking match," the paper said, "next it will be the coveted Bar. After that, who shall tell how soon the ballot will come."

From 1876 to 1878, von Hillern performed a series of solo exhibitions—at least twenty-five in thirteen different cities—walking, in at least one case, 144 miles in fifty hours. In Boston, up to ten thousand people a day paid fifty cents apiece to watch her walk in circles at a music hall. Her photograph was sold in department stores, and "von Hillern hats" became fashionable. The *Washington Post* called her "one of the wonders of the nineteenth century." Another paper called her "an apostle of muscular religion . . . a true evangel to her sex."

Bertha von Hillern did not flaunt Victorian conventions. She walked in long petticoats. She attended church regularly and was "conscientious and careful in her devotions." "Her great fear is that in her contact with the public she may be suspected of evil, and she is every way circumspect and guarded," the *Worcester Evening Gazette* reported. "It is this natural modesty which prevents her exhibitions from turning into mere sporting affairs and which commend her to the confidence and good will of the best society." In other words, Bertha von Hillern didn't rock the boat.

But Madame Anderson did. In fact, she capsized it. Muscular, charismatic, masculine-faced, half Jewish, twice married, outspoken, and independent, she was unconventional in an era that prized conformity. A century before Billie Jean King, Anderson proved that women could be athletes as accomplished as men.

In spite of Anderson's nonconformity—or, perhaps, because of it—her exhibition at Mozart Garden proved extraordinarily popular. By the end of December as many as four thousand people were passing through the venue each day to watch her walk. After the New Year, with her mission more than half complete, word of this "plucky little Englishwoman" began to spread beyond Brooklyn. Papers nationwide started carrying updates on her progress. The demand for tickets became so great that the price of admission was raised from twenty-five cents to fifty cents, then to a dollar—two dollars for a reserved seat. Alexander Samuells, the manager of the venue, had a grandstand built on the stage to accommodate more than one hundred people. "This will involve an expenditure of about $3,000," the *Brooklyn Daily Eagle* reported, "but it will amply repay the outlay."

Mozart Garden was packed day and night. "These crowds are largely composed of women, and of these no small portion are ladies," reported the *New York Times* (careful to make the distinction between women and ladies), "for it is now quite the correct thing in Brooklyn to 'drop into Mozart Hall and watch Anderson for an hour or so.'" The women, the paper said, had come to regard Anderson "as one of the most wonderful of their sex."

The *Eagle* described the scene inside Mozart Garden one night during the walk:

> The audience, which almost filled the oval formed by the track, was largely composed of ladies. Many of these represented the best classes of city life—society queens who nestled in fluffy sealskin sacques and rustling silks, on whose heads reposed hats radiant with birds of paradise and long, gracefully flowing plumes. They chatted gaily with their

fashionably dressed escorts during the intervals between quarters. But when the brave Englishwoman stepped upon the tanbark, their demeanor changed. Every voice was hushed. Smiles of encouragement illuminated their faces, their eyes sparkled with enthusiasm and their jeweled fingers waved delicate lace handkerchiefs approvingly.

As was her custom, Madame Anderson occasionally entertained the audience by accompanying herself on the piano as she sang. One of her favorites was a song called "My Sweetheart When a Boy." She also gave speeches and took questions. At one point she addressed her extreme sleep deprivation. "In every twenty-four hours I have fits of sleepiness which are very severe," she said. "While I sleep I suffer. Sometimes I wish I could never sleep, it is so painful to wake up." On more than one occasion, the *Eagle* reported, she was observed "to be in a very sound doze on the track during the first few laps of the quarter." "Oh, she's only taking a nap now," regular attendees would inform newcomers bemused by the somnambulation. "Just wait for half an hour and you'll see her come out here as chipper as a lark."

As she neared her goal, a rumor began to circulate that Anderson had a twin sister who periodically walked in her stead. It was preposterous, of course, but not too farfetched for the *New York Times* to investigate. The paper dutifully reported that it had "established the fact beyond doubt that the rumor has not the slightest foundation in fact."

Anderson was a bit of a clotheshorse, and she liked to change her outfit several times a day. Her favorite ensemble was "a tunic of royal purple trimmed with white ermine fur." At least once she was costumed as the Goddess of Liberty, waving US and British flags as she went. As the walk progressed, her attire seemed to grow more daring, even titillating for the time. In the last week of the walk, the *New York Times* reported, "her shapely and superbly developed limbs" were "visible to the knee."

More controversial than her dress, however, was Madame Anderson's decision to walk on Sundays. This was a brazen violation of the blue laws that prohibited public amusements on the Christian Sabbath, and it infuriated the Woman's Christian Temperance Union and other moral crusaders, who appealed to the city's board of aldermen to stop the exhibition. But the board, several of whose members regularly attended the event, declined to pursue the matter.

On the evening of January 12, 1879, the final day of the walk, Mozart Garden was packed so tightly that it was practically impossible to move. "Many women were seen to faint in the dense crowd," the *Times* reported, "but as they could not be carried out, it is not known what became of them." Worried police halted ticket sales at 9:00 PM. About four thousand people were left to stand outside the hall, waiting eagerly for news from within.

At 10:45 PM, the bell rang to summon the weary Madame Anderson to the track for her final quarter mile. Invigorated by the thunderous ovation she received when she emerged from her dressing room, she completed it in 2 minutes and 37.75 seconds— the fastest of all her 2,700 quarter miles. She was then helped into a chair and handed a glass of port wine. After a few minutes, she rose unsteadily to address the crowd.

"She begged American women to walk more and use the horse cars less," according to the *Times*, "and, above all, she begged ultra-religious women who had refused to witness her performance at any time because she walked on Sundays to be consistent, and not compel horse-car drivers to work on Sundays to carry them to church when they could just as well walk."

Total receipts for the event were said to be $32,000 (roughly $740,000 today), of which Madame Anderson's cut was $7,000 ($162,000).

Her success, athletic and financial, was groundbreaking.

Madame Ada Anderson completing the 2,700th and final quarter mile of her long walk on January 12, 1879. Courtesy of Library of Congress

Anderson turned Victorian conventions upside down. According to sociologist Dahn Shaulis, "Although women were expected to be morally superior to men, they were thought to be physically frail." Yet here was a woman who challenged moral conventions and, clearly, was not frail. "The idea," said the *Brooklyn Daily Eagle*, "as general as it is venerable, that a woman cannot, by reason of her sex, endure as much as a man, is exploded, and to Madame Anderson is due the overthrow of the mistaken notion."

Suddenly, pedestriennes were everywhere. Women attempted to equal or better Anderson's feat in Boston, Chicago, Cincinnati, New York, San Francisco, Washington, and Wheeling. All failed but one: the wonderfully named Exilda La Chapelle, an immigrant from France who walked a jaw-dropping three thousand quarter miles in three thousand consecutive quarter hours before packed houses in Chicago.

Female pedestrians accomplished feats of endurance no less astonishing than those of their male counterparts. They were some of America's first famous female athletes, pioneers in the history of women's sports, the prophets who paved the way for

Title IX. And, like all pioneers, they confronted hardships at seemingly every turn.

In March 1879, a women's six-day race was held at Gilmore's Garden. The prize was $1,000. But no shapely limbs were visible. Anxious to avoid offending Gilded Age sensibilities, the organizers decreed that all competitors must wear full-length dresses—rather cumbersome attire for athletes. Eighteen women began the race. (Madame Anderson, who was staging an exhibition in Pittsburgh at the time, was unable to participate.) Most were young immigrants, though a few were middle aged, and at least two were "society ladies" who entered for "fun and reputation." Some of the competitors were clearly unprepared for the rigors of a six-day. One retired after just one hour on the track; two others were hospitalized during the race, including one who was "said to have lost her mind."

The attendance was good—as high as eight thousand on some days—but it seemed a fair number of the spectators came not to cheer the women, but to mock them.

"Men and women sit at ease in the boxes for hours at a time," reported the *Times*, "making themselves merry at the expense of the walking women, jeering at the gray hairs of this one, and at the limp or pale face of another. They are of the class of people who would revel in a bullfight and gloat over a gladiatorial contest."

Only five of the eighteen starters managed to finish the race. The winner was a German immigrant named Bertha von Berg, who walked 372 miles, a respectable distance, especially considering the attire she was compelled to wear.

The rapid rise of female pedestrianism engendered an equally rapid backlash. It was one thing to watch men "half delirious from want of sleep . . . lollopping along a track with their tongues out," but it was quite another to watch women in such wretched straits. (The generic term for this is "double standard.") The *Times* called the women's six-day "dreary" and "cruel," and posited that the results "show the disastrous effect of such a terrible strain upon

the constitution of the average woman." The *New York World* said
the race was akin to the "public torture of women."

Dr. John Harvey Kellogg, famed proprietor of a Michigan sani-
tarium and later a cereal magnate, wrote, "Nothing could be much
more inhuman than the exhibitions made in satisfying the mania
for female pedestrianism which has recently arisen." A woman,
Kellogg asserted, was "generally less graceful and naturally less
skillful in the use of the extremities than [a] man, and hence less
fitted for athletic sports and feats requiring great dexterity."

A girl throws a stone awkwardly, less from want of practice than from a natural peculiarity of physical structure.
A woman walks less gracefully than a man, owing to the
greater relative breadth of her hips, requiring a motion of
the body together with that of the limbs. In consequence
of this peculiarity, a woman is less fitted for walking long
distances.

Kellogg recalled visiting a hall in Boston where two women
were engaged in a walking match:

The sixty hours for which the walk was to be continued
had nearly expired, and the excitement grew more intense
each moment. One of the walkers, who was a few miles in
advance, strode on at a pace almost marvelous, constantly
stimulated to greater efforts by the coarse shouts of the masculine audience, who evidently took the same sort of interest in the proceeding that they would in a dog race or a
cock fight. The other was pale and spiritless, and it seemed
with difficulty that she dragged herself along to keep upon
the track until the last. At times she seemed to be almost
fainting, as the result of the long-continued excitement and
fatigue; but she managed to keep going until nine minutes
before the slow moving clock had measured off the sixty

hours, when she became too ill to be longer able to stand, and was carried off the track.

The cheers for the winner were as vigorous as though a rebel fort had been captured, a million people emancipated from slavery, or some great and noble deed of honor or daring had been done; but no one thought of the injury which had been done the contestant. We turned away in disgust.

Disgusting it may have been to some, but female pedestrianism was also profitable, and in December 1879 a second women's six-day was held at the Garden. After that race, New York City's board of aldermen considered an ordinance banning "all public exhibitions of female pedestrianism."

It failed to pass, but it was an ominous sign, and not just for the female pedestrians.

TERRIBLE BLOWS

or

A CRACKLING WAS HEARD

WITH DAN O'LEARY NOW JUST ONE VICTORY away from winning the Astley Belt for the third consecutive time—and gaining permanent possession of it—Sir John Astley was determined, even desperate, to see the belt returned to Britain.

In October 1878, Astley staged a six-day "go as you please" race for British pedestrians, hoping to find a worthy challenger for O'Leary. The winner of the race was the wily William "Corkey" Gentleman with 521 miles. Another veteran, Blower Brown, took second with 506 miles. Of course, both had already been defeated by O'Leary in the first Astley Belt race. So Astley turned his attention to the third-place finisher, an up-and-comer who'd racked up an impressive 470 miles. He was Charles Rowell, the Cambridge rower who'd been defeated by Edward Payson Weston in a seventy-five-hour race at the Aggie three years earlier. Since that inauspicious debut, Rowell, now twenty-six, had trained hard and taken part in several long-distance races. Rowell had once worked as Astley's boat boy, and Astley remembered him fondly.

"Rowell . . . took my fancy very much, as he was a very clean-made, muscular young fellow." Astley was convinced that Rowell would make a "great score" in a six-day race, "if properly looked after." Sir John always prided himself on spotting young talent, whatever the sport, and in Rowell he was convinced he'd found a diamond in the rough.

Shortly after O'Leary defeated John Hughes in the second Astley Belt race at Gilmore's Garden in October 1878, Astley formally issued a challenge to O'Leary on Rowell's behalf. O'Leary accepted, and the race was scheduled for the following March at the Garden.

"I bid Rowell get himself fit," Astley wrote in his memoirs, "and I would pay expenses of himself and two friends (to look after him) in the land of Stars and Stripes." Rowell immediately began an intensive training regimen overseen by Astley. "In due time he reported himself in proper fettle for the contest; so I wrote to him to come down to Elsham, and I would see him run four or five hours." Rowell arrived the next day. Astley measured out a track in the garden on his estate and told Rowell to start running.

He ran the first sixteen miles with such ease in two hours that I went away, telling one of the gardeners to score up the laps with a bit of chalk on the garden-wall. In about an hour I returned, and he seemed going easier than when he started; so I let him continue another hour, and when he had covered thirty-two miles—just under the four hours— he had not turned a hair.

After a cold bath and a rubdown, Rowell asked Astley if he could go rabbit hunting on the estate. "[A]nd away he went," Astley remembered. "I was satisfied that he was good enough to send over to try and bring back the champion belt to England." In February 1879, Astley put Rowell and his two friends on a steamer bound for New York. He gave them £250 for expenses—and instructions to bring his belt back home.

Besides Rowell and O'Leary, two other pedestrians were entered in the race: John Ennis, a thirty-six-year-old Irish immigrant from Chicago best known for his feats of endurance ice skating,[*] and Charles Harriman, a long-limbed, twenty-six-year-old Mainer who had never before competed in a six-day race.

The third Astley Belt race was the most anticipated sporting event in the history of New York City, and perhaps all of the country, up to that time. Stoked by patriotic fears that America would lose the Astley Belt to the effete monarchy across the pond, the race was as hyped as a Super Bowl is today. "Such general interest in a match of this kind has never been excited in this or any other city," reported the *New York Times.* Said the *New York Herald,* "[The race] may prove the most exciting and bitterly contested event of its character that ever took place."

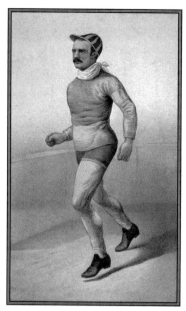

Charles Rowell in his pedestrian costume, circa 1879. Courtesy of Library of Congress

"Each competitor," the paper added, "means to win or 'die on the track.'"

In the days leading up to the race, papers nationwide were filled with reports on the preparations for the "Great Walking Match" at Gilmore's Garden. (Although running was permitted, colloquially

---

[*] Ennis held the American hundred-mile speed skating record for many years, but he deserves to be remembered for another reason: by the time he died in 1929, Ennis had rescued from drowning at least eighteen people who had fallen through thin ice.

the Astley Belt races were still called walking matches.) A single, 10-foot-wide, ⅛-mile track was laid on the floor of the arena. It would be shared by all four competitors. Rowell, a runner, had wanted a hard track. O'Leary, the walker, wanted a soft one. The result was a compromise: The hard dirt on the arena floor was thoroughly spaded, covered with sawdust, and then rolled for several hours. The interior of the oval was covered with new flooring and was "as free from dirt as a country kitchen." A sturdy wooden railing was built along the inside of the track. Wrapping all the way around the outside of the track was a twelve-foot-wide wooden platform to "afford space for a vast number of people." This too was guarded by a "stout rail." Small footbridges were built over the track at each end of the oval, allowing spectators to move freely between the inside and the outside without interfering with the competitors. Four tents were erected inside the track for the competitors, one at each corner of the oval.

On August 8, two days before the race began, lots were drawn to assign the tents. O'Leary was pleased to be assigned the largest tent, as his wife and seven-year-old daughter would be joining him from Chicago. Rowell was just as pleased to be assigned a tent at what was usually the somewhat quieter end of the arena, an area "less liable to invasion by the masses expected to attend." Each tent was identically furnished with a gas stove, a comfortable bed, cooking utensils, and "all other necessary articles for a six days' occupancy" (presumably including a chamber pot). The *Herald* pronounced the tents "as cosy, comfortable, and complete as the most exacting pedestrian could require." An immense blackboard for keeping score was hung at one end of the arena. Western Union set up a small office to relay scores by telegraph to the rest of the country. "Gilmore's Garden . . . never looked to better advantage," the *Herald* declared after the preparations were completed.

Teams of judges and scorekeepers were recruited from the sporting papers and the city's various athletic clubs to work in six-hour shifts around the clock throughout the race.

The doors to the Garden opened on the evening of Sunday, March 9, 1879. By 10:00 PM, three hours before the match was even scheduled to begin, 1,200 spectators were already inside the arena. A band entertained the growing crowd by playing sacred music until midnight, when the Sabbath ended and it switched to more lively tunes, such as "Baby Mine," which was loudly encored. By now between four thousand and five thousand were in attendance, including "many distinguished citizens . . . judges, lawyers, and politicians." Thick clouds of cigar smoke swirled in the dim gaslight.

After midnight, the competitors, who had spent Sunday resting at their respective hotels, began to enter the arena. Rowell was the first to arrive. He wore a blue-and-white striped shirt and lavender tights with blue trim. It was a distinctive costume. One newspaper said he looked like a zebra. A small contingent of British expats in the audience cheered loudly for their countryman as he made his way to his tent. The rest of the crowd was more subdued. After all, Rowell was the enemy.

The United States and Britain now may enjoy what Churchill called a "special relationship," but in the nineteenth century the two nations were bitter rivals. Border disputes between the United States and British-ruled Canada nearly led to wars in 1839 and 1859. According to historian John Moser, the People's Party (also known as the Populists), a political party formed in the late 1880s, "dedicated itself to ridding the country of British influence." The Populists considered England a "monster" that had "seized upon the fresh energy of America and is steadily fixing its fangs into our social life." Politicians of all stripes rode the anti-British bandwagon. "America for Americans," declared Ben Tillman, the inflammatory Democratic senator from Alabama, "and to hell with Britain and her Tories." ("Pitchfork Ben," as he was known, was a notorious racist who also said, in a speech on the floor of the United States Senate, "This is a white man's country and white men must govern it.") This "strong undercurrent of Anglophobia," as historian John Steele Gordon has termed it, would not abate until the Great Rapprochement, an easing of tensions that began at the end of the nineteenth century and culminated with America's entry into the First World War as Britain's ally.

Dan O'Leary, on the other hand, embodied nothing less than the American Dream (a concept that was already well established, though the phrase itself would not be popularized until 1931, when the historian James Truslow Adams coined it for his mammoth tome, *The Epic of America*). O'Leary was the archetypical immigrant who, by dint of hard work, pulls himself up by his bootstraps and finds fame and fortune in the Land of Opportunity. That he was a naturalized citizen and not, as the Constitution puts it, "natural born," seemed not to matter—as long as he was winning, anyway. It was on O'Leary that the audience—and all of the country, really—was pinning its hopes of keeping the Astley Belt out of British hands. When he entered the Garden dressed in a white shirt and black velvet shorts over white tights, O'Leary was showered with applause, though he barely acknowledged the cheers. O'Leary seemed utterly focused on the task before him.

If not for their athletic costumes, the other two entrants, Charles Harriman and John Ennis, probably wouldn't have even been recognized when they entered the arena.

As the starting time of one o'clock drew closer, the arena continued to fill. "The jam was growing worse and worse every minute," the *Herald* reported, "and with the fresh accession of hundreds, the bookmakers shouted their odds in louder tones." The bookies had made O'Leary the favorite to win at odds of 1.5 to 1. Rowell was at 2 to 1. Harriman and Ennis, the lesser-known pedestrians, were the decided underdogs at 5 to 1 and 12 to 1, respectively.

Outside the arena, an entirely different spectacle was unfolding. Thousands of fans were still waiting in long lines, frantic to purchase their fifty-cent tickets and get inside the building in time to see the start of the race. But the ticket-sellers couldn't work fast enough, and, as the minutes ticked by, the crowd grew impatient and agitated and began pressing closer to the ticket windows en masse.

At 12:45 AM, a worried police captain named Alexander Williams ordered the doors to the Garden locked and the box office closed. "This infuriated those who were thus excluded," the *Times* reported the next day, "and their numbers being constantly augmented by fresh arrivals, who, not comprehending the situation, pressed forward until those nearest the building were in danger of being crushed." Seemingly in an instant, the crowd outside the arena had become an angry mob, surging toward the locked doors on Madison Avenue. Fearful screams filled the air. "Bitter curses and yells of pain were heard from every part of the struggling mass of humanity," said the *Times.*

Inside the arena, however, all were oblivious to the panic on Madison Avenue. The pandemonium within the arena was drowning out the pandemonium without. The four pedestrians were on the starting line now, receiving their final instructions. The crowd was frenzied, cheering wildly, men waving their hats in the air, while the band competed to be heard and the bookies shouted themselves hoarse soliciting last-minute wagers. "The spectators seemed almost crazy," one attendee recalled.

Rowell, the Englishman, had never seen anything like it. "A great sight!" he shouted to no one in particular. The next day the *Herald* would say, "It is safe to say that no competition of any other character whatsoever ever created such enthusiasm among the masses as the competition for the Astley belt." Precisely when the hands on the big Garden clock reached one o'clock, the match referee, William B. Curtis of the New York Athletic Club, sent off the pedestrians with the simple command, "Go!" At that instant the crowd inside the Garden let out a great cheer, which "acted upon the mob [outside the building] much as the flaunting of a red flag acts upon an infuriated bull."

Realizing the match had begun, the mob outside the Garden pressed even harder against the locked doors, which finally burst from their hinges under the pressure. The ticketless hordes began pouring into the lobby of the arena.

Captain Alexander Williams ordered his officers to clear the lobby. What ensued was likely the worst episode of civil unrest in New York City since the Civil War draft riots sixteen years before.

Even in a police department rife with brutality and corruption, Alexander Williams stood out. Born in Nova Scotia in 1839, he left home as a boy and traveled the world working as a ship's carpenter. He claimed to have been the first white man to lay the keel of a ship in Japan. He eventually ended up in New York, and, in 1866, he traded in his toolbox for the navy blue uniform of the New York Police Department.

Tall, muscular, and heavily mustachioed, Williams cut an imposing figure, and he quickly distinguished himself as an officer unafraid to use force, justified or not. His first assignment was the dangerous neighborhood around Broadway and Houston Street.

New York City police captain Alexander Williams was nicknamed "Clubber." George Arents Collection, The New York Public Library, Astor, Lenox and Tilden Foundations

Williams immediately sought out the "two toughest characters in the district" and picked a fight with them. It ended when Williams threw both men through a plate glass window.

At the time, New York City police officers were not issued guns; instead each was issued a truncheon, made of the hard wood of a locust tree and measuring twenty-four inches in length and one and three-eighth inches in diameter. It was a formidable weapon, and Williams wielded his with such dexterity—and such frequency—that, by the time he was promoted to captain in 1872, he'd acquired the nickname "Clubber." Williams professed to dislike the nickname, because, he insisted, he never clubbed anybody who didn't deserve it.

By 1872, Williams had also acquired a small fortune through bribes and kickbacks, mainly protection money from gambling houses and brothels. This was not an unusual arrangement at the time, but Williams had turned graft into an art form. In 1876, after serving as commander in several low-rent precincts, Williams was assigned to command the prestigious Twenty-Ninth, a precinct centered around Thirtieth Street and Sixth Avenue that encompassed a large swath of Manhattan, including Gilmore's Garden— and innumerable brothels. It was the center of the city's nightlife, and Williams was eager for a piece of the action. "I like it fine," he told a friend when he learned of his new assignment. "I have had chuck for a long time, and now I am going to eat tenderloin." For generations of New Yorkers thereafter, the neighborhood around Thirtieth and Sixth would be known as the Tenderloin.

In the Tenderloin, Clubber became the czar, ruling with ruthlessness and impunity. When an eager young cop began shutting down houses of prostitution, Williams intervened. Such businesses, he later explained, were "fashionable." Besides, Williams said, closing brothels would only force prostitutes onto the streets. "It's like taking a small-pox patient into the street," he said, "it merely spreads the disease."

In 1879, Alexander "Clubber" Williams was at the very apex of his long, colorful, and corrupt career. Gilmore's Garden was part of his empire, and he would not permit it to be invaded by a mob on the opening day of the prestigious Astley Belt race. When he ordered his men to clear the lobby of the arena, they did not hesitate. With Williams leading the way, the police "rushed into the mob and did terrible execution with their long night clubs," the *Times* reported the next day. "The sound of the heavy blows rained upon the defenseless heads and bodies of the unfortunates who happened to be in the front ranks was sickening." One eyewitness said many "hapless individuals . . . found themselves borne along by the terrible press of the mob until within reach of the clubs of the Police."

Swinging savagely, the police beat the throng back out the broken doors and onto Madison Avenue. Then Williams called in reinforcements to clear the street, and a full-scale riot erupted. Pitched battles broke out between truncheon-wielding police and the "angry thousands still smarting from their recent clubbing." The rioters threw rocks, shattering at least one window in the arena. Some climbed onto the roof of the building. The riot was not merely a manifestation of disappointment at being denied entry to the great walking match. It was also an explicit expression of pent-up rage at the bullying and brutal tactics of the New York Police Department in general—and of Captain Williams in particular.

The riot lasted two hours before the police finally restored order at three o'clock on Monday morning. At least seventy people suffered injuries requiring hospitalization, but, miraculously, no fatalities were reported. There would be no official inquiry into the riot. Public opinion seemed to support the police. "Had the gang of turbulent spirits outside forced their way on the track the walk would have been broken up," said James Kelly, who managed Gilmore's Garden for owner Patrick Gilmore.

The *Times* called the actions of the police "merciless" but "unavoidable." "On many sides, Capt. Williams has been blamed for the charge and subsequent clubbing," the paper said, "but those who were witness to the whole affair agree that under the circumstances nothing else could have been done." Naturally, Williams agreed with that assessment. Of the gatecrashers, he told the *Times*, "[I]f they had not been driven out as they were they not only would have rushed in on the track and stopped the walk, but they would have torn the whole front of the building down." The walking-match riot would be much discussed and well remembered in New York for many years.

At six o'clock on Monday morning, three hours after the riot was quelled, sunlight began peeking through the circular windows that ringed the top of Gilmore's Garden. It was five hours into the race, and all four pedestrians were still on the sawdust track. Rowell was in first with 30 miles, three miles ahead of O'Leary. Ennis was third with 26 miles, Harriman fourth with 25. Rowell had put in many long runs through the night to build his lead. O'Leary occasionally jogged for a lap or so, but otherwise stuck to walking.

Despite the early hour, the arena was surprisingly full. Hundreds of spectators had stayed the night. Some, undoubtedly, had been too frightened to leave due to the rioting outside. A few were still awake in the dawning light, shouting encouragement to the pedestrians as they passed. But most slept soundly in their chairs, chins resting on chests.

This somnolent audience was soon augmented by workingmen who stopped by the arena on the way to their factory jobs. Lunch pails in hand, they enjoyed the race for a spell before their shifts began at seven. Unlike in Britain, pedestrianism in the United States was a truly democratic spectator sport. Everyone paid the same price of admission: fifty cents. The crowds at the Garden, the *Times* noted,

> were composed of all classes of society, from the preacher and the millionaire to the black leg and the tramp, looking so ragged and forlorn that the wonder was how he ever obtained admittance, for he certainly could not have bought a ticket. But the intense interest manifested everywhere was the same, and the wretch who has not money enough to buy himself a meal watches every movement of the contestants, and criticises them as carefully as he who has thousands staked on the result.

As Monday morning progressed, "the character of the crowd grew more aristocratic, and ladies began to fill the seats." In the afternoon, the character of the crowd changed again, as "men of business began to arrive." The band returned too and "enlivened

This illustration depicts the first day of the third Astley Belt race, Monday, March 10, 1879. O'Leary is leading the pack. COURTESY OF LIBRARY OF CONGRESS

matters generally, though one old walker and a good judge of such things said that the 'leader ought to be scolded for playing such music to walk by.'"

At 4:00 PM the arena was already half full, and Rowell's lead over O'Leary had grown to seven miles, 78 to 71. By now the Englishman's strategy for defeating the reigning champion was clear: he would hound and harry him. At every opportunity, Rowell followed right on O'Leary's heels and mimicked his every move. Rowell called the strategy "dogging." When O'Leary walked, Rowell walked. When O'Leary jogged, Rowell jogged. Occasionally Rowell would pull up alongside O'Leary and give him a "patronizing look."

Of O'Leary the *Times* said, "Rowell worries him terribly when they are on the track together by keeping just behind him, and never giving up this position." One of the friends who had accompanied Rowell to New York had given him this advice on beating O'Leary: "Break his 'eart." Today we'd say Rowell was trying to get inside O'Leary's head.

It was an obnoxious strategy, but it seemed to be working. By 8:00 PM, Rowell was in first with 97 miles. Harriman was second with 86. O'Leary had dropped back to third with 84 miles, thirteen miles behind the leader.

Rowell's tactics were not appreciated by the partisan majority in Gilmore's Garden, and the Englishman was loudly jeered whenever he dogged O'Leary. "Rowell was hissed and abused at every step he took," according to one spectator. The band continued to play lively tunes, but the atmosphere inside the arena was tense. And, in the wake of the rioting early that morning, Captain Alexander Williams was taking no chances. Extra police were stationed inside and outside the building. "Monday's crowd," Captain Williams would later say, "required strict management."

By nine o'clock Monday night, Gilmore's Garden was sold out, with some ten thousand people crowded into the big wooden arena. Thousands more, unable to gain admittance, stood patiently outside the Madison Avenue entrance, eagerly awaiting news from inside the building. "Ticket speculators" mingled discreetly among the crowd, offering fifty-cent tickets for seventy-five cents. Also outside, at the back of the arena, industrious young boys put their penknives to good use, methodically carving holes in the massive wooden doors that Barnum had installed for his elephants. Their reward was a peek at utter darkness, but this did not deter the lads from trying again and again, until the doors looked bullet ridden. Older boys, meanwhile, clambered up the side of the building and attempted to gain entrance through the circular windows that ringed the top of the arena. The few who managed to get inside were greeted by a policeman's club.

Throughout the city, regular updates on the race were posted on bulletin boards in city parks, outside post offices, and in the windows of newspaper offices, and each of these drew its own large crowd. The crowd in front of the *Herald* building was said to be as great as it ever was on a presidential election day. Everywhere in New York, it seemed, the talk was of nothing but the great walking match. "Even the weather," the *Herald* said, "that traditional sheet anchor of polite conversation, has snapped its chain cable and temporarily disappeared from view."

"The craze continued to permeate all quarters of the City," the *Times* reported that week, "and little else was talked about by delicate ladies in fashionable parlors, by business men in their offices, and by bar-room loungers, than the chances of the match." Newspapers published extra editions, sometimes hourly, with the latest updates on the front page, which newsboys hawked on street corners day and night. When a fresh bundle of newspapers, still damp from the presses, landed on the sidewalk in front of Gilmore's Garden, the crowd nearly tore it to shreds in their eagerness to unwrap it. "The scene resembled the distribution of loaves to a starving army," said one onlooker.

A mania gripped the city, arousing intense passions. On the first day of the race, Daniel McCarthy and Henry Hughes, two friends who lived in a rooming house on Sixth Street in what is now the East Village, got into an argument with James L. Lamb, their landlord. McCarthy and Hughes were rooting for O'Leary to win. Lamb was backing Rowell. An argument ensued, and Lamb was stabbed, resulting in a nonfatal wound.

The mania was not confined to New York. Through the miracle of telegraphy, updates were instantly transmitted from the Western Union office in Gilmore's Garden to newspapers across the country—and across the ocean. In Boston and Philadelphia, in Dublin and London, and in countless other cities and towns on both sides of the Atlantic, crowds gathered outside telegraph and newspaper offices, awaiting the latest returns on the race. In

Trenton, the *New York Herald* reported, more than five hundred people were gathered in front of a cigar store where updates were posted. In Philadelphia, the *Herald*'s offices were "surrounded by eager inquirers, who scan the bulletin boards with noisy demonstrations of interest."

"One would suppose that the fate of the nation depended upon the result of the walking match," the *Herald* said. The paper tried to make sense of it all in an editorial:

> Philosophers who insist upon cataloguing all human actions under appropriate heads must have been placed hopelessly at sea by the pedestrian furore which, though it broke out long ago, has indulged in such a full blown culmination this week. . . .
>
> The meaning of it all must be sought a little deeper than the philosopher's plummet ever reaches. In spite of the general intellectual development of humanity and the religious idea that the physical man is sorry trash, there is latent in mankind an irresistible sympathy for any one who accomplishes unusual physical feats, particularly if they are such as imply patient, self-denying training of the physique up to its finest possibilities.

At Gilmore's Garden, it was becoming apparent that Dan O'Leary was not himself. Whether or not it was the result of Rowell's "dogging," O'Leary's pace was much slower than in his first Astley Belt race. Several times on Monday he'd retired to his tent for long rests. That night, his attendants announced that O'Leary was suffering from a "disordered stomach" and had vomited several times that day, but that he would persevere. There were whispers that O'Leary, who had always sipped a little bubbly during matches, was overdoing it this time. At one point he was said to have "swallowed 2 large bumpers of champagne." Another time, according to a reporter who was there, "he was not closely watched and got some liquor." One of his attendants confided to another reporter, "His trouble is drink."

Another rumor was that O'Leary had been poisoned. The *Herald* claimed that, the week before the race, "some men" at the St. James Hotel were overheard discussing ways to "fix" O'Leary, and that one of those men—"a fellow townsman of Rowell's"—was spotted near O'Leary's tent at the Garden. The implication was clear: Rowell's people were somehow poisoning O'Leary. This would be O'Leary's explanation for his poor performance.

Later that year, John Tansey, one of O'Leary's closest associates, would publish a biography of the pedestrian in which he claimed that one or more of O'Leary's attendants had been bribed to poison O'Leary during the race. But Tansey never named the perpetrators, nor explained precisely how O'Leary had been poisoned, and O'Leary himself never pursued a criminal or civil case in the matter.

It's unlikely O'Leary was poisoned, or even that he overindulged in alcohol. The simple fact was, O'Leary was spent. Over the previous twelve months, he had walked nearly three thousand miles in eight competitions and exhibitions. It was a murderous schedule, and he was, as one paper put it, "stale." What O'Leary was suffering, one reporter speculated, was "simply that warning which nature was giving that the age had been reached when he could not undergo so much fatigue as he had in the past."

O'Leary refused to give up, but his chances of winning his third consecutive Astley Belt race—and permanent possession of the belt itself—were rapidly vanishing. At one o'clock on Tuesday morning, twenty-four hours into the race, Rowell was leading with 110 miles. O'Leary was seventeen miles behind Rowell and in last place.

Later that morning, Rowell received a telegram from Sir John Astley:

London. March 11, 1879.
To Rowell, Gilmore's Garden, New York:—

Go it my boy. Don't overdo it. Tell Atkinson to put on a
century for me.

Astley.

Tuesday evening "brought the greatest crowd the race has yet
seen," the *World* reported. Many spectators sat in the aisles, making them impassable. Others sat on the wooden railing that ran
along the inside of the track. When a section of the railing gave
way, sending several fans tumbling, laughter and applause filled
the arena. One of the balconies, the *World* noted, "became a black
mass of people, and as it is very flimsily built there was peril of a
grand smash."

The bar in the basement of the building was doing booming
business. "Seven minutes were occupied in the consumption of
each keg of lager," the *World* said. "Multiply this by fifty, the number of spigots in operation at the time, and some notion may be
formed of the flow of the beverage." (Incidentally, the drinking
age in New York at the time was sixteen.)

Business was also brisk for the numerous pickpockets plying
their trade in the teeming arena. At one point, Rowell was star-
tled by two men who rushed across the track just in front of him.
For a moment, Rowell thought the men might attempt to "han-
dle him roughly," but it turned out to be a pickpocket, "who had
abstracted a watch and chain from a gentleman's pocket," being
chased by his victim.

Rowell was still in the lead, and the target of much vitupera-
tion. Around nine o'clock, Captain Williams was patrolling the
arena when he noticed a large and "very boisterous" crowd gathered around Rowell's tent, which, it turned out to Rowell's dis-
may, was not in an area of the arena less liable to invasion by the
masses. Rowell was inside the tent, attempting to rest. Williams
waded into the boisterous crowd and proceeded to break it up in
his usual manner. He struck one of the men near the tent twice
with his club. This drew an immediate reaction from nearby spectators, who serenaded Williams with hisses and epithets. Furious,

Clubber looked up into the hostile audience and, for some reason, zeroed in on one spectator in particular, a thirty-five-year-old potter from Trenton named William Vincent Blake. An Englishman who'd moved to the United States seven years before, Blake was, according to his employer, "a sober, honest, and industrious citizen." Apparently, Williams wanted to make an example of Blake.

According to Blake's account, he was seated when Williams walked up to him and gave him a "violent prod" in the chest with his truncheon. Williams said, "Come out of here you —— —— sneak thief." When Blake stood up, Williams clubbed him on the shoulder. "He then caught hold of me by my coat collar," Blake recounted, "and said, 'Come out of here, you —— loafer,' and pulling me in a very rough manner to the edge of the gallery, forced me over and caused me to jump down into the arena, not allowing me to walk down the stairs." Williams jumped down after Blake. "If you will show me the way out I will go out," Blake pleaded. Williams kicked and shoved him "with great violence" toward an exit, then clubbed him across his shoulder one more time for good measure. The final blow caused Blake to "reel and stagger like an intoxicated man."

"At least twenty persons saw the occurrence," the *World* reported. "No one interfered and the citizen hobbled off."

"Bet you five he don't make a complaint," one of the eyewitnesses said to a friend.

"Bet you ten, if he does, it never sees daylight," the friend replied.

Blake said Williams gave him no explanation for clubbing him and forcibly ejecting him from the Garden, and made no attempt to arrest him. Blake wandered around outside the building in a daze for several minutes before finally regaining his senses. Then he bought another ticket and went back into the building to watch more of the race. He was molested by Captain Williams no further.

At three o'clock on Wednesday morning, several hundred people were still inside the Garden, which remained open continuously throughout the race. The band had packed up its instruments and the vendors had gone home. The bar was closed. Occasionally the arena would fall so silent that the spectators could hear the clomp-clomp-clomp of the pedestrians' footsteps as they plodded around the sawdust oval. For long stretches when all the pedestrians were in their tents sleeping, there was nothing to watch at all, and only the hiss of the arena's gaslights was audible.

Some of the night owls in the Garden were fat cats looking for a little late-night entertainment. Others were factory workers coming off the second shift. And a few were squatters, living at the Garden for the week. They had been there since the race began on Sunday night and would remain until it ended on Saturday night, making beds of their seats each night. "I had but a dollar," one of the weeklong denizens explained to a reporter, "and I paid half of it to get into this place. Here I can stay until next Saturday night. The seats are comfortable and I can get a good night's rest. I can go downstairs and for ten cents I can get a sandwich; which is a better dinner than I can count on many days of the year. In the meantime I can have as good entertainment as the people who have thousands in their pockets to bet on Rowell."

By the afternoon of Wednesday, March 12, the third day of the race, Dan O'Leary was a spent man. "I don't think I ever felt worse in my life," he later admitted.

"His stomach, head, feet, mouth, tongue, and entire body seemed to have given way," said a doctor who examined O'Leary. The doctor told O'Leary it would be "suicidal" for him to continue. Still, O'Leary refused to surrender. He returned to the track for two more agonizing hours before finally throwing in the towel.

O'Leary was taken to a dingy room in the attic of the arena and laid across a bed. He was said to be "almost unconscious." His body had finally given out, no longer able to withstand the unnatural exertions to which he had subjected it for the past five years. "The trouble with him is that he has done too much walking," said his trainer, Al Smith. "His constitution is gone. He is the greatest pedestrian that the world has ever seen, but now must surrender the championship to younger men."

Rumors began to sweep the city that O'Leary had died. He wasn't dead. He was just dead tired. He would recover his health, but not his position on the pedestal of pedestrianism. Hailed as a hero just a week earlier, Dan O'Leary now experienced the disillusionment that accompanies every champion's fall from grace. The *Spirit of the Times*, the weekly paper that covered sports, compared O'Leary to "a broken down racehorse" that "falls on the track."

"O'Leary has drained his pedestrian cup to the dregs," the paper said. "The clock has run down, and nature, long baffled, finally asserts her rights."

Although the defending champion had withdrawn from the race, the outcome was still very much in doubt. At 6:00 PM on Wednesday, Rowell was just eight miles ahead of Charles Harriman, the lanky twenty-six-year-old from Maine who was taking part in his first six-day race. Harriman was now the crowd favorite and seemingly America's best hope for retaining the Astley Belt.

Once again, the Garden was "filled to the utmost capacity." The balconies that projected over the main floor and offered spectators a view of the entire track "were particularly crowded" on this night. The front of each balcony was divided into boxes. These were the best seats in the house. Each box was furnished with small tables and chairs and was meant to hold perhaps a dozen people, but on this night the boxes were overflowing. "Here a throng of ladies and gentlemen found lodgment," the *Herald* reported, "crowding every available inch of the place, some seated and many perched upon chairs and tables."

At 8:15 that Wednesday night, the three remaining pedestrians were moving around the track as a group. The band was playing. The crowd was cheering and stamping its feet. All seemed normal. "Just as the men were passing the Madison Avenue end," the *World* would report the next day, "and when the cheers and the stamping were loudest, a crackling was heard which sounded as if the roof were falling in." That crackling was actually the sound of a balcony collapsing. Underneath it, scores of people were crushed.

It was the balcony in the southwest corner of the building, the corner nearest Twenty-Sixth and Madison. Martin and Maria Bates were a husband and wife sitting near the front of the balcony when it went down. They both heard a "low rumbling" noise. "We're going," Mr. Bates said to his wife, "the thing is giving way." Martin threw his arms around his wife as the two sank into a terrifying pit of bodies and broken timber.

A *Herald* reporter happened to be in the balcony too.

The first intimation of the danger was the gradual settling of the flooring; then a loud creaking noise, and away went a section of fifteen yards of the gallery, carrying with it over one hundred people. The frail structure broke into small pieces in the descent, and the unfortunate people who were precipitated with it were jammed between the debris, several of them being seriously injured. . . .

A wall of struggling, groaning, maimed and terrified persons of both sexes was piled up in front. They were hurled into all sorts of attitudes. A gashed face here peeped through the broken timbers; an outstretched arm there; feet uppermost in another place; a woman prone face downward, and a man jumping on her back, others struggling forward to a place of security, and in their haste and terror stepping and plunging on and over women and children, and jumping on blanched and bloody faces, presented a scene of indescribable terror and confusion that beggars description. . . . It was not they alone who occupied the gallery who were injured, but a number of people who were beneath the broken section were caught in the ruins and fared badly. . . .

Such a scene of wild and indescribable confusion and alarm as followed the accident had rarely been witnessed inside of a public building.

A cloud of dust rose from the tangle of bodies and debris, a cloud that some mistook for smoke. A voice cried "Fire!" Fearing the wooden building was burning down—or, at the very least, falling down—thousands of terrified and panic-stricken spectators ran screaming for the exits. A few went the other way, climbing to the top of the arena, kicking out windows, and jumping twenty feet to the ground.

The collapse threatened to trigger a deadly stampede. But a quick-thinking Captain Williams immediately dispatched officers throughout the building to urge people to stay put. When a mass of people came surging toward Williams, he put up his hands and pleaded with them to turn around. "Go back, go back!" he shouted. "For God's sake, go back!"

In the chaos, the band had stopped playing, of course. Williams sent one of his men to round up the musicians and order them to resume making music. The hastily reassembled band struck up the traditional Irish jig "St. Patrick's Day in the Morning." The music calmed nerves considerably. "That hundreds of lives were not sacrificed in the rush toward the doors is nothing less than miraculous," said the *Herald*. Captain Williams's quick intervention had averted a catastrophe.

Williams and his men were also credited for "rendering efficient assistance" immediately after the accident. Dozens of people were trapped in the wreckage of the fallen balcony, and police and civilians worked together heroically to rescue them.

The list of the injured reflects the diversity of pedestrianism's appeal. A young girl who had come to the race with her grandmother was pulled free. She was dazed and bruised and her dress was torn, but otherwise she was OK. Others weren't as lucky. A sixteen-year-old boy named Warren Harrigan, who was pinned beneath a large beam, was extracted with great difficulty. He suffered a broken collarbone. A man named H. L. Desoney was pulled unconscious from the wreckage, placed on a stretcher, and rushed to a hospital. A forty-year-old woman named Louisa Ahern

This illustration depicting the balcony collapse at Gilmore's Garden appeared in the *National Police Gazette*, March 22, 1879. The original caption reads, "Terrifying scene at Gilmore's Garden, during the walking match, caused by the crash of an overcrowded gallery, and the precipitation of more than one hundred persons upon the dense mass of spectators, eighteen feet below." AUTHOR'S COLLECTION

suffered a broken wrist. Another woman, Josephine Little, suffered a dislocated arm. At least nine people were seriously injured in all, but, incredibly, nobody was killed.

The scene outside the building was equally chaotic. Hearing the commotion inside and seeing people jumping out windows, the large crowd gathered outside the Garden assumed, like many inside, that the building was on fire. A general panic began to spread, first through the neighborhood and then through the city at large. Firefighters and ambulances were summoned, their arrival signaled by the sounding of gongs on their carriages. People with family and friends inside the Garden flocked to the building, anxious to learn their fate, pressing close against the doors. Once again the police employed the club, this time to clear a path for the injured to be removed. For two or three blocks in every direction the streets teemed with the curious and the concerned.

In the panic the pedestrians sought refuge in their tents. The race was temporarily suspended, and the band continued to play "lively tunes" while the casualties were attended to. The pickpockets, however, carried on. A broker named Lewis Sears would report that, in the excitement immediately following the collapse, two men robbed him of $450 in cash. He said he "felt the hands of the men in his pockets but they disappeared very suddenly, and when he examined his pockets and found his money and papers gone the robbers were gone also."

It would later be learned that Patrick Gilmore had extended the Garden's balconies farther out without adding adequate support beams underneath. At least one civil suit was filed against the venue, but no criminal charges were ever brought in connection with the accident.

The *New York World* noted that it was a good thing the balcony at the other end of the arena hadn't collapsed: that gallery was over the Western Union office, "and a crash there would leave the Garden without means of communication with the impatient outside world."

Thirty minutes after the collapse, the injured had been removed and transported to hospitals on horse-drawn ambulances. All that remained inside the Garden was the pile of debris, "a tangled mass of woodwork." Blood was visible on some of the planks in the tangle. Visible too were broken bottles, champagne corks, scraps of torn lace, a colored petticoat, a crushed hat, and the wiry remains of an umbrella.

Soon, however, this pile of debris was converted into a makeshift concession stand. A young boy selling oranges set up shop amid the wreckage. Following his lead, spectators began climbing on the pile for a better view of the track. "The excitement of the match soon swept away all memory of the accident," one paper reported, "and few of those who were found among the ruins knew an hour later that anything unusual had happened beneath their feet." The race resumed. It was almost as if nothing had happened.

"The hush that fell over the building did not last long," the *Times* reported. "The excitement over the match was too great to be quieted by anything short of some great calamity." About a thousand people had left the Garden after the collapse, but by midnight the building was nearly as full as it had been before the accident—excepting the wrecked bits, of course.

The structural failings of Gilmore's Garden did not negatively impact attendance. In fact, the demand for tickets was still so great that the price of admission was doubled from fifty cents to one dollar beginning at eight o'clock the next morning. While the race continued, repairs were made to the building.

On Friday night, according to the *New York Times*, "The character of the attendance [was] unusually good." Among the

This illustration of the third Astley Belt race appeared in *Harper's Weekly*, March 29, 1879. Rowell is in the lead, with Harriman, O'Leary, and Ennis in the next three places. AUTHOR'S COLLECTION

"gentlemen of distinction" in attendance that night was James G. Blaine, the heavily bearded Republican senator from Maine who was also a presidential hopeful. The 1880 election was only a year off, and Blaine was eager to associate himself with the country's most popular spectator sport. He even brought along a large basket of flowers to present to Charles Harriman, the entrant from Maine who was, after all, one of his constituents. But when Blaine approached Harriman's tent he was disappointed to learn that the pedestrian was resting and did not wish to be disturbed—not even by a distinguished United States senator. Blaine left the flowers on one of the tables that had been set up especially to receive bouquets intended for the competitors.

Blaine, of course, would never become president, but another Republican in attendance that night would—though nobody in the Garden or anywhere else would have guessed it at the time. That's because Chester Arthur was, at that moment, unemployed. Until recently, he'd held one of the most coveted patronage jobs in the federal government: collector of the Port of New York, a position that put him in charge of collecting the import duties on foreign goods that came into the United States through New York and made him one of the most prominent politicians in the city.* But Arthur had ended up on the wrong side of a dispute between rival factions inside the Republican Party. Arthur was allied with the powerful New York senator Roscoe Conkling, who'd run afoul of President Rutherford B. Hayes, and Hayes had fired Arthur.

Over the next two and a half years, however, a series of improbable and tragic events would propel Chester Arthur from the political wilderness to the White House. At the 1880 Republican National Convention at the Expo in Chicago, none of the three

---

* Collector of the Port of New York would remain a plum position until the middle of the twentieth century, when income taxes replaced tariffs as the US government's most important revenue stream. The last collector was appointed in 1966.

leading candidates for the party's nomination for president—Senator Blaine, former president Ulysses Grant, controversially seeking a third term, and John Sherman, a former (and future) senator from Ohio—was able to muster a majority through thirty-five ballots. (None of the three was present in Chicago; at the time it was considered unseemly for a candidate to campaign for the nomination in person.) Weary delegates then turned to a compromise candidate, James Garfield, a rather obscure but well-liked congressman from Ohio, who won the nomination by a landslide on the thirty-sixth ballot. To balance the ticket, the delegates chose a vice presidential nominee from the East: Chet Arthur.

Garfield won the election, but, just four months after taking office, he was shot in the back at a Washington train station by Charles Guiteau, a delusional and almost certainly psychotic drifter who was furious with Garfield for refusing to award him an ambassadorship, despite his obvious lack of qualifications. Garfield died on September 19, 1881, eleven weeks and two days after he was shot. (His death was largely attributable to the abysmal health care he received, but that's another story.)

Garfield's death thrust Arthur into the presidency. Despite his limited experience and a reputation for cronyism, Arthur ended up being a decent president. He reformed the civil service and revitalized the navy. His major failing, according to most biographers—not that he's had that many—was that he didn't do enough to reduce the federal budget surplus, which had ballooned to $145 million by 1882. Arthur, who was suffering from kidney disease, did not run for the presidency in 1884. He would die in 1886.

Instantly recognizable by his fabulous whiskers—a mutton-chops-gone-wild style known as a Franz Josef—Chet Arthur was an avid sports fan; nobody was surprised to see him at the great walking match at the Garden that night.

While the character of the attendance was unusually good, the atmosphere inside Gilmore's Garden was downright foul.

By Friday night, according to the *New York World*, the arena had "turned it into a Black Hole of smoke and stench and general stuffiness which a week's ventilation will not remove." The track itself had deteriorated badly. The pedestrians kicked up fine dust particles with every step. Tobacco-chewing spectators routinely expectorated on the track, causing one pedestrian's trainer to lament, "It has now got to be a regular spittoon."

The putrid conditions were taking their toll on Charles Harriman, the gangly Mainer who'd become the crowd favorite after O'Leary dropped out. "The tobacco smoke and the dust are affecting him very strongly," said a doctor looking after Harriman. "He is not drowsy, but they sicken him and take away the vigor and ability to work." Said one of the scorekeepers bluntly, "Harriman is a dead cock in the pit, and the belt will never stay this side the water by his work."

As it became apparent that Charles Rowell would win the race and take the Astley Belt back to Britain, the Englishman began receiving threats. Early on the morning of Saturday, March 15, the sixth and final day of the race, a "drunken loafer" accosted Rowell on the track. The police subdued the attacker. John Ennis, the Irishman from Chicago, admonished the crowd to leave Rowell alone. "I want you to understand that if this man is injured," Ennis announced, "I will leave the track and not walk another mile." The two pedestrians then joined hands and walked a lap together, amid much cheering.

Extra police were assigned to the Garden for the rest of the race.

At nine o'clock that Saturday night, Rowell completed his 500th mile while the band played "God Save the Queen." He led Ennis by thirty miles and Harriman by fifty. His lead insurmountable, Rowell left the Garden for a luxury suite at the Ashland House. Harriman retired as well. Ennis completed five more miles before surrendering, making the final score Rowell, 500; Ennis, 475; Harriman, 450; O'Leary, 215.

A few days later, the four pedestrians reconvened in an office on Wall Street to divvy up the proceeds. The total receipts exceeded

This Thomas Nast illustration appeared on the cover of *Harper's Weekly* on April 5, 1879. It depicts Rowell as the victorious British lion and O'Leary as the vanquished American eagle. AUTHOR'S COLLECTION

$54,000 (roughly $1.25 million today). For failing to walk the minimum required number of miles (450), O'Leary received nothing. Harriman and his manager split $7,359.32. Ennis took home

$11,938.98. And Rowell received a check for a whopping $18,398.31 (roughly $425,000 today).

When Sir John Astley, who'd sent Rowell across the Atlantic to "bring back the champion belt to England," learned of his minion's victory, he was ecstatic. When he learned of his winnings, he was flabbergasted. It was, Astley said, "a pretty good haul for a man who had seldom had two sovereigns to rub against each other."

O'Leary, meanwhile, announced his retirement from competitive walking. His body simply couldn't take any more. Instead, he was moving into promotion and management. To find new talent, he unveiled plans to stage a competition for the "long-distance pedestrian championship of America." The winner would receive the O'Leary Belt, which, its namesake promised, "shall far exceed in beauty and worth that offered by Sir John Astley." He'd already ordered it from Tiffany. He'd also signed a lease to rent Gilmore's Garden for the first O'Leary Belt race the following October.

On the afternoon of March 17, 1879—two days after the race ended—William Vincent Blake walked into a New York police station and filed a complaint against Captain Alexander Williams for allegedly beating him for no good reason six days earlier during the walking match at Gilmore's Garden. Blake swore an affidavit giving his version of events that night. He also submitted several letters of reference, including one from New Jersey's ambassador to the previous year's Paris Exposition, attesting to Blake's good character. Blake explained that he would have filed the complaint sooner, but "that he did not feel well enough, as he suffered severely from the rough usage he alleges he received at the hands of Capt. Williams."

Many complaints had been filed against Clubber Williams for excessive use of force over the years, but he'd never received a punishment more severe than a reprimand: a slap on the wrist for a club to the skull. But Blake, the immigrant potter from Trenton, was determined to see Williams held accountable this time. His complaint was forwarded to William F. Smith, the president of the board of police commissioners.

Smith was a no-nonsense Civil War veteran who'd risen to the rank of general in the Union army. He'd seen action at the First Battle of Bull Run, Antietam, Fredericksburg, and Gettysburg. General Smith was not intimidated by Captain Williams. The same day Blake filed his complaint, Smith formally charged Williams with conduct unbecoming an officer and forwarded the case to the full commission for a hearing.

> Central Department, March 17, 1879.
> To the Board of Police of the Police Department of the City of New-York:
> I hereby charge Alexander S. Williams, Captain of the Police force of the City of New-York, in command of the Twenty-ninth Precinct, with conduct unbecoming an officer.
>   Specifications—In this, to wit: On the 11th inst., at about 11 o'clock P.M., at Gilmore's Garden, in said City of New-York, the said Alexander S. Williams wrongfully and unlawfully assaulted one W. V. Blake, and beat and kicked him and otherwise maltreated him, and did not arrest him.
> W. F. Smith, Commissioner.

The hearing began on April 3. Blake was the first to testify. He admitted that he was one of several spectators who hissed at Williams after he struck one of the spectators near Rowell's tent. But what happened next, Blake testified, was wholly unjustified. Blake said Williams "singled [him] out . . . clubbed him out of his box, gave him a violent kick, and when he got to the door gave him a violent blow on the shoulder." Blake also testified that Williams used foul language and called him "a —— sneak-thief." After Williams evicted him, Blake said, he went back inside the arena to continue watching the match.

Blake's account was corroborated by six witnesses who testified after him.

Williams was represented at the hearing by George Bliss, one of New York's most prominent defense attorneys. "Our view of this case," Bliss told the commissioners, "is that there prevailed at Gilmore's Garden during the walking match a gathering which required stern and strict treatment." Bliss also questioned why the complaint wasn't filed until six days after the alleged assault occurred, insinuating that Blake had been put up to it, perhaps by a newspaper. Bliss pointed out that Williams had recently had one of the *New York Herald*'s editors locked up for being drunk and disorderly. Bliss then read several affidavits, including one from Charles Rowell, praising Williams "very highly for his executive ability, as shown by his conduct at the Garden." One of Rowell's trainers, John Simpson, said in his affidavit that Williams "had acted rightly, and had not used unnecessary violence toward Blake."

Edward Plummer, one of the judges at the match, then testified that he had called on Williams to evict Blake from the Garden, "because he feared that Blake was trying to create a riot." Several other witnesses testified that they had seen Blake evicted, "and all agreed that there was no clubbing done."

The hearing resumed on April 12. Williams testified in his own defense. Defending himself from charges of using excessive force was not a new experience for Williams, and he looked perfectly at ease as he recounted his version of events at the Garden that night.

> Capt. Williams—I found the crowd on the Twenty-seventh-street side, in the vicinity of Rowell's house, very boisterous; I thought when I first heard it that the hissing was directed toward the walkers; I was walking down the track at the time; one of the judges pointed out Blake as a ringleader in this demonstration; I made my way up through Mr. Gardiner's box and the passageway to the spot where Blake was, and ordered him to vacate and leave the building; Blake refused to go and I took hold of him and urged him down toward the track through the same lane that I had used in coming up; there was a

space between the track and the boxes along which he walked to the Twenty-seventh-street door; I walked on the track, following him along, and wasn't within 75 feet of him when he got out the door; I did not call him a sneak-thief or use foul language.

Col. Bliss—Did you club him?

Capt. Williams—No, Sir, I did not; he was dilatory in his movements, and I touched him with my club to let him know that I was following him to the door; three-quarters of an hour afterward he saw me outside, came up to me and said: "Captain, I am sorry for what I have done. I would like to pay my money and go inside again." I told him if he would behave himself he could go back; he went to the door, bought his ticket, and went into the Garden again.

Col. Bliss—Did you kick him?

Capt. Williams (emphatically)—I did not kick him.

Col. Bliss—Was there any dragging done?

Capt. Williams—I think I took hold of him, but I didn't drag him; he passed down through the boxes ahead of me; there was no necessity for clubbing him anyway.

It was vivid, colorful testimony, and it bore little resemblance to the truth. The part about encountering Blake outside the arena seems to have been completely fabricated. The commissioners called Blake back to testify. He said Williams's testimony "about the interview outside the building" was "incorrect." This, of course, was Blake's polite way of saying that Williams was a liar.

It came down to Williams's word against Blake's, and Williams was counting on the commission to give him the benefit of the doubt, as it always seemed to do.

At the commission's meeting on April 22, Commissioner Joel B. Erhardt introduced a motion to dismiss the complaint against Captain Williams. Erhardt explained his rationale:

> There has been no attempt to impeach the character of any of the witnesses either for the prosecution or the defense, and the weight of evidence being so overwhelmingly in favor of the defense, it is a fair inference that during the excitement attending an international walking match, in which existed national antipathies, personal friendships, and pecuniary wagers, and a turbulent crowd, exaggeration may have colored the honest convictions of witnesses. Prompt action on the part of the commanding officer in this case was required to quell trouble at the outset. While this would not justify unnecessary harshness, it would authorize any commanding officer—and, indeed, it would be his duty—to check instantly any quarrelsome spirit or riotous demonstrations among the spectators. . . . It does not appear that he used unnecessary harshness. It does appear, however, that he was prompt and that a serious disturbance did not take place.

The motion to dismiss the complaint passed by a vote of two to one. William F. Smith cast the dissenting vote. CAPT. WILLIAMS EXONERATED, read a headline in the next day's *New York Times*.

It would be many years before "Clubber" Williams finally met his match. In 1895, after twenty-nine years on the force, Williams was finally forced to retire by a new, ambitious, and reform-minded police commissioner named Theodore Roosevelt. By then, Williams had racked up a staggering 358 complaints, making him, according to *Harper's* magazine, "the most venomously hated" officer in the New York Police Department.

Although involuntary, his retirement would not be uncomfortable. Williams owned a New York townhouse, a sprawling estate in tony Cos Cob, Connecticut, and a steam yacht named the *Eleanor* for commuting between the two. His wealth, he insisted, came not from corruption but from shrewd investments: "I bought real estate in Japan and it has increased in value." When he retired, his annual salary was $3,500. He was allowed to collect his pension of $1,750 a year for life, but only because Roosevelt could find no legal recourse for withholding it.

Williams had become an institution in New York, and even the papers that had editorialized against him and his brutal and corrupt ways over the years sounded sorry to see him go. "In the days of the old walking matches," the *World* recalled wistfully, "when the crowds were packed so dense about the doors that life was endangered, 'Fighting Aleck' and his club could always make a passageway."

9

COMEBACK

or

A GAME OLD PED

Bankrupt and stranded in Britain, Edward Payson Weston spent most of 1878 trying to make money the only way he knew how: by walking. Mostly he performed solo exhibitions, walking against time in music halls all over England. Dressed in his trademark ruffled shirts and wielding his ever-present riding crop, Weston consciously cultivated an image of aristocracy. While most other pedestrians were coarse, hard-drinking products of the working class, Weston came across as the complete opposite. "He was refined, intelligent, and educated," wrote track-and-field historian Ed Dodd. "He gave the upper class a hero with whom they could identify." This was a lucrative niche, and Weston "never failed a draw," as the British sports journal *Turf, Field and Farm* explained in January 1879:

> When he pursued his weary way around the track, the best people thronged the immense buildings and applauded him earnestly. From the dainty hand of fashion he received

many floral tributes, which he gallantly acknowledged, and during the pauses in his walk the profound, the cultivated, and the beautiful gathered around him. Reclining in his chair, he held his court as if he had been a sprig of royalty. He had the shrewdness to see that in order to secure the patronage of the best elements of the social world, he must cultivate the leaders of society and make public exhibitions conform to their tastes. The boisterous classes thoroughly hated him, which hate was returned with interest.

Despite the success of his exhibitions before the profound, the cultivated, and the beautiful, by the beginning of 1879 Weston was still in desperate financial straits. He had racked up several hundred pounds in legal fees just fending off creditors in Britain. So he turned to his old patron Sir John Astley for help. Weston wagered Astley that he could walk two thousand miles over England's country roads in one thousand consecutive hours, excluding Sundays, of course. Along the way, Weston promised to deliver lectures extolling the virtues of walking and temperance in fifty selected towns. Astley accepted the wager, and under very favorable terms for Weston: If Weston succeeded, Astley would pay him £500. If Weston failed, he would owe Sir John only £100.

Accompanied by "competent and trustworthy judges," Weston set off from London on the morning of Saturday, January 18, 1879. His route would take him through nearly two hundred cities and towns in thirty-one counties. It was much like his long overland walks in America, but Britain had never seen anything like it, and, as in America, everywhere he went large crowds turned out to see him. Several times, his attendant, William Begley, was forced to disguise himself as Weston to allow the great pedestrian to escape the throngs.

About halfway through the walk, around midnight on the night of Thursday, February 6, Weston arrived in the city of Preston, in northwestern England—and "a pitiable, rather than an enviable object he looked," according to the *Preston Guardian.* He was three hours behind schedule, and his right arm was in a sling. "He met with an accident" on the way to Preston, the *Guardian* explained, "owing to the very slippery state of the roads." Despite the late hour, the number of people awaiting him was so large that he was escorted into town by "a body of policemen . . . amid the loud cheers of the spectators." At the Corn Palace, Weston delivered a lecture—the twenty-second of the fifty he was required to deliver on the walk. Although he did not begin speaking until 12:15 AM, the venue was still one-third full. By now, Weston had the talk down pat. "With regard to walking," the *Guardian* reported, "he maintained that there was no more healthful, graceful, or dignified exercise, and a love of it could be acquired by practice without any detriment to the constitution."

"It might be thought that he had been under great physical training," the *Guardian* quoted Weston as telling the audience in Preston, "but he could inform them that he had never trained more than five days in his life, and during those five days they would have taken him to be the most wretched candidate for a walker they ever saw." This line never failed to provoke a round of hearty laughter.

Weston was a natural performer, and he excelled at these lectures. "Whether he was speaking to a group of farmers at a local corn exchange or to a group of undergraduates at Oxford or Cambridge," Ed Dodd writes, "the response was always the same— unbridled enthusiasm."

After speaking for twenty minutes at the Corn Palace in Preston, Weston asked the audience to "excuse him at so late an hour for not saying more." Again "escorted by a strong body of police," he retired to the Arms Hotel. At ten o'clock the next morning, he resumed his journey.

But the punishing schedule, inclement weather, and nagging injuries were all too much for Weston to overcome. When the time was up on February 28, he was short of his goal—by less than twenty-three miles. He was also more deeply in debt, as he now owed Astley one hundred pounds.

Weston's gamble had not paid off, but fate threw him a lifeline. His wife, Maria, had come into a small inheritance after her father died, and—somehow—Weston convinced her to give him one hundred pounds so he could challenge Charles Rowell for the Astley Belt. (Astley had raised the entrance fee from ten pounds to one hundred pounds, presumably to discourage "speculators.")

On March 15, 1879, the day the third Astley Belt race ended at Gilmore's Garden with Rowell's victory, Weston sent a telegram to Astley to challenge Rowell for the belt. "I shall be obliged if you would at once inform him of this challenge," Weston wrote, "that he may name the time and place for the contest."

At first Sir John refused to take the challenge seriously. Weston was now forty and an old fashioned "heel and toe" pedestrian. Rowell was twenty-six, a "go as you please" pedestrian who racked up miles by running, an activity that Weston still averred to disdain. "Why not leave well enough alone?" Astley told Weston. "No walker can compete with these runners, and I'm not going to let you throw £100 away in that way." But Weston persuaded his old supporter Sir John to give him a crack at the whippersnapper Rowell.

The announcement that Weston was challenging Rowell for the Astley Belt was greeted with a skepticism that verged on amusement. Weston was written off as washed up, a has-been. He had staged many solo exhibitions, but since losing to Dan O'Leary in their showdown at the Aggie in April 1877, Weston had taken part in just one competitive race, a six-day, "go as you please" affair in which he dropped out on the fifth day with just 365 miles to his credit. It was quite evident that Weston was no longer a world-class pedestrian. It was no wonder that the weekly British sports journal *Bell's Life* condescendingly dismissed Weston as a "game old ped" and a "weary wobbler."

Pedestrianism had become a runner's game. Even Dan O'Leary, once strictly a walker, had felt compelled to run occasionally.

Weston racing Rowell was like Abner Doubleday going to bat against Nolan Ryan. Furthermore, Weston still refused to run. "As Weston is not a runner, his chances of winning the belt are not good," predicted *Turf, Field and Farm.* "Rowell's most dangerous competitors in the forthcoming contest will be English blood. The Astley Belt is likely to remain in England for sometime to come."

But Weston, who had paid close attention to the first three Astley Belt races from afar, was convinced he could keep up with Charles Rowell, who was only too happy to accept his challenge.

The fourth Astley Belt race would take place in June 1879 at the Aggie. Besides Weston and Rowell, the entrants were John Ennis, the Irishman from Chicago; Richard Harding, an English pedestrian; and Henry "Blower" Brown, recent winner of the English championship. Brown, who had finished third in the first Astley Belt race in April 1878, had recently won a six-day race with 542 miles—a new world record.

A few days before the race, Rowell, the reigning Astley Belt champion and overwhelming favorite, was out jogging when he stepped on a sharp stone that pierced the thin sole of his shoe and lodged in his heel. The injury forced him to withdraw from the race.

Around the same time, John Ennis was jogging around a lake just outside London when he heard the cries of two women drowning. Their boat had capsized. Ennis dove into the water and rescued the women, but wrenched his back in the process. Afterward, sopping wet, he walked the five miles back to his hotel and caught a cold.

At 12:55 AM on Monday, June 16, the race began. The bookmakers listed Brown, the English champion, as the favorite at odds of 4 to 6. Ennis was listed at 5 to 1, Harding at 6 to 1.

Weston was the long shot at 10 to 1.

When Weston appeared at the starting line for the beginning of the race, the crowd gasped: Rather than his usual natty attire, Weston was wearing a conventional athletic costume: a tight white shirt and red tights. Not only that, his trademark riding crop was nowhere in sight.

When the race began at Astley's command of "Go!" the crowd was stupefied: Weston, the world-famous walker, was running!

Weston would later explain his transformation from walker to runner in an interview with a *New York Times* reporter. "While I was in this country [the United States] I never believed that running could hold out against walking," he said, "but when I saw the easy pace of some of those runners, I changed my mind. Some of them ran at a ten-mile gait with less apparent exertion than a man makes in walking four miles per hour." One month before the race, Weston had started experimenting with running and, much to his surprise, discovered he enjoyed it. "I fell accidentally into an easy running pace, just as I did in walking."

By the end of the second day of the race, both Ennis, still suffering from a wrenched back and a cold, and Harding, who was hopelessly in the rear, had dropped out due to illness, making it a two-man contest between Weston and Blower Brown. Early on the third day, Brown led by seven miles, 318 to 311. But by the end of that day, Weston, still running occasionally, had overtaken the English champion.

Weston went on to win the fourth Astley Belt race in a rout, 550 miles to 453. His victory was no fluke: Weston had set a new six-day record. As he finished his final mile, Weston was handed British and American flags, which he waved above his head while the crowd cheered and the band played "Yankee Doodle" and "Rule Britannia."

Weston's victory was a shocking upset, truly one of the greatest comebacks in sports history, but his winnings were paltry compared to Charles Rowell's jackpot after the third Astley Belt race in New York three months earlier. Weston's share of the gate amounted to only around $2,000 (roughly $23,000 today). Attendance on the final days of the race was reported to be "meagre in the extreme." In London, at least, it seemed pedestrianism's

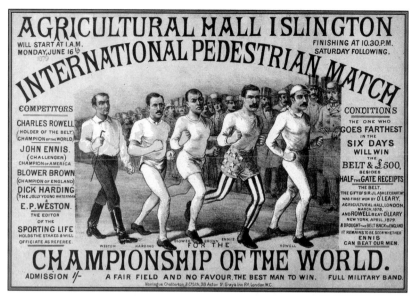

This broadside advertised the fourth Astley Belt race at the Aggie, June 16–21, 1879. Pictured, from left to right, are Weston, Harding, Brown, Ennis, and Rowell. ISLINGTON LOCAL HISTORY CENTRE

popularity was waning. Certainly, the absence of Charles Rowell had a negative impact on the box office. Without Rowell, the *Islington Gazette* wrote, a "great deal of the interest that would have been felt in the affair . . . evaporated."

But larger issues were at work as well. Since the inaugural Astley Belt race at the Aggie a little more than a year earlier, the British Parliament had passed a law giving all factory workers Saturday afternoons off. The Factory Act of 1878 had an unintentional but profound effect on a sport that theretofore had been strictly a gentlemen's game in Britain: association football, now known, in the United States anyway, as soccer.[*]

Spectator sports were banned on Sundays in Victorian Britain, of course, so soccer matches were typically played on Saturday

---

[*] The word "soccer" is widely believed to derive from "assoc.," the common abbreviation for the word "association."

afternoons. The passage of the Factory Act allowed the working class to attend these matches for the first time. "The effect on Saturday soccer was major," wrote Mike Huggins in *The Victorians and Sport*. Between 1876 and 1880, the number of soccer teams in Birmingham alone grew from 20 to 155. Similar increases were reported in other parts of the country.

Almost overnight, soccer became the most popular sport in Britain, both to play and to watch, and that growth would continue well into the twentieth century. "There were less than fifty soccer clubs nationally in the 1860s," Huggins wrote, "but Sheffield alone had 880 soccer clubs in 1899." The Factory Act was an important factor in what Huggins has called "the democratisation of leisure" in Britain. It transformed soccer into a massively popular enterprise that transcended class divisions. Many of the workingmen who'd attended walking matches at the Aggie began turning their attention to what its disciples call the "beautiful game."

Something else had happened since that first Astley Belt race, something that would fundamentally change live entertainment on both sides of the Atlantic. On Saturday, May 25, 1878, inside a rickety theater called the Opera Comique in London, a "comic opera" called *H.M.S. Pinafore* premiered. Written by William Gilbert and Arthur Sullivan, *Pinafore* was positively revolutionary. It was, in a sense, the first modern musical, and it established conventions for musical theater that endure to this day. Before *Pinafore*, musicals were an incoherent mess, with little or no plot. Gilbert and Sullivan wrote lyrics and dialogue that told a story. It was a simple formula, and one that has been copied by everyone from Rodgers and Hammerstein to Andrew Lloyd Webber.

Working with their business partner, Richard D'Oyly Carte, Gilbert and Sullivan exercised what is now known as complete creative control. Instead of working for a theater, they financed their productions independently so they could hire the actors they wanted and design their own costumes and sets. They instructed their actors to act more naturally, instead of in the highly exaggerated style then in vogue. This was extraordinary for the time, and one critic marveled at the "naturalness and ease" with which the duo's actors performed. Gilbert and Sullivan were also meticulous. Before designing the sets for the nautically themed *Pinafore*, they toured a shipyard.

Pinafore was actually Gilbert and Sullivan's fourth collaboration, but it was their first big hit. The plot, as is typical for the duo, is comic and comically simple: Josephine, the daughter of the titular ship's captain, Corcoran, is in love with a lowly sailor named Ralph Rackstraw. But Corcoran wants her to marry Sir Joseph Porter, the head of the British navy. Corcoran, meanwhile, is in love with Little Buttercup, a "plump and pleasing" woman beneath his station. Spoiler alert: Ralph and Corcoran were switched at birth, which means Ralph, being above his supposed station, is free to marry Josephine, and Corcoran, being below his, is free to marry Little Buttercup. Sir Joseph ends up marrying his cousin.

The plot may seem trite, but *Pinafore* was socially relevant, commenting pungently on class and politics in Britain. (The foolish Sir Joseph was based on the real head of the Royal Navy at the time, W. H. Smith, a businessman and politician with neither military nor nautical experience.) Audiences flocked to *Pinafore*, and it ran for an astonishing 571 performances before going dark in February 1880.

The musical was so popular that American theater owners hired stenographers in London to transcribe it so they could produce *Pinafore* stateside. These bootleg productions, the equivalent of today's illegal downloads, were extremely popular in the United States, though neither Gilbert nor Sullivan earned a penny from them. The first pirated version opened in Boston in November 1878, just six months after the original premiered, and soon more than one hundred unauthorized versions were in production across the country. Eight versions of *Pinafore* were in production simultaneously in New York City alone, including one at Gilmore's Garden. In Philadelphia, a young John Philip Sousa conducted the orchestra in a pirated *Pinafore*.

When Gilbert and Sullivan finally premiered the bona fide version in New York on December 1, 1879, the box office receipts were disappointing. By then, everybody had already seen it. So the duo hurriedly completed their next production, *The Pirates of Penzance*, which premiered on December 31 and was another huge critical and financial success.

Which is all a bit of a longwinded way of saying that, by the time the fourth Astley Belt race rolled around in June 1879, there were more interesting things for Londoners to do in their spare time than watch people walk around in circles for days at a time.

But in the United States, pedestrianism remained as popular as ever.

10

BLACK DAN

or

A DARK HORSE

WHEN THE RAILROAD MAGNATE Cornelius Vanderbilt died in 1877, his eldest son, William Henry Vanderbilt, inherited an array of assets totaling $100 million (roughly $2 billion today). Among those assets was a prime piece of real estate in Manhattan: the entire block bounded by Madison and Fourth Avenues and Twenty-Sixth and Twenty-Seventh Streets. This had once been the site of a terminal for the New York and Harlem Railroad, a Vanderbilt rail line. Now, of course, it was the site of Gilmore's Garden.

William H. Vanderbilt, according to one account, "promptly elected to reassert the family's control of its old railroad properties," and when Patrick Gilmore's lease on the Garden expired in the spring of 1879, Vanderbilt assumed control of the venue, declaring his intention to operate it primarily as an "athletic center." The first thing Vanderbilt did was rename the arena after a city square just southwest of the building, a square that itself had been named in honor of America's fourth president. The change was announced in a small item buried on page eight of the *New York Tribune* on Friday, May 23, 1879: "Gilmore's Garden is to be

William Henry Vanderbilt.

known hereafter as the 'Madison Square Garden.'"

Although it had opened just five years earlier, by 1879 the arena was already run-down. Vanderbilt himself was well aware of the building's deficiencies; he'd been in attendance the night the balcony collapsed during the third Astley Belt race. His private box had been damaged, and he'd barely escaped injury.

Vanderbilt ordered major upgrades. "Inside and outside the premises are to be thoroughly renovated," the *Tribune* reported shortly after Vanderbilt took over. A small garden was installed at one end of the building, complete with caged birds, a small waterfall, and a gravel path that wound through "shrubbery, flowers, trees, fountains, statuary, and little bowers." The plaster walls were covered with "handsome wooden wainscoting," a billiard room was installed, the bar was completely refurbished, and the balconies were rebuilt.

But the biggest change was dazzling in every sense of the word: Vanderbilt installed electric lights in Madison Square Garden.

The first electric light had been invented seventy years earlier, in 1809, by a British chemist named Humphry Davy, who, in a moment of inspired curiosity, attached a stick of charcoal to a battery. Then he took a second charcoal stick and touched it to the first one. A spark appeared. But, more remarkably, as he drew the second stick away from the first, the spark grew into a brilliant, buzzing arc of electric light that danced between the two sticks. Davy had accidentally discovered the illuminative power of electrified carbon.

Though spectacular, Davy's discovery was of limited practical use. The light lasted only as long as the charcoal sticks burned or until the battery ran out of power. What was needed, first and foremost, was a reliable and constant source of electricity: in other words, a dynamo. That problem would not be solved until the early 1870s, when the Belgian engineer Zénobe Théophile Gramme invented a machine that used magnets to create a steady electric current. Powered by a small steam engine, the Gramme machine made arc lights practical for the first time, and in 1876, Paul Jablochkoff, a Russian engineer living in Paris, perfected an electric "candle" consisting of a cluster of carbon rods. When one rod burned out, another automatically ignited. Jablochkoff demonstrated his invention for municipal officials in Paris, and soon his candles were brilliantly illuminating the fashionable Avenue de l'Opéra, cementing the city's reputation as the Ville-Lumière, City of Light.

In the United States, meanwhile, an amateur electrician named William Wallace was illuminating his Connecticut brass foundry with eight arc lights powered by a dynamo he had invented with Moses G. Farmer. On Sunday, September 8, 1878, Thomas Alva Edison visited the foundry at the behest of his friend, a University of Pennsylvania physics professor named George F. Barker. Though just thirty-one years old, Edison was already famous for having invented a phonograph just the year before, but he had so far evinced little interest in electricity. That changed with his visit to William Wallace's brightly lit brass foundry.

"Edison was enraptured," wrote a *New York Sun* reporter who accompanied the inventor that day. "He ran from the instruments to the lights, and from the lights back to the instruments. He sprawled over a table with the simplicity of a child, and made all kinds of calculations." As he was leaving, Edison blithely told Wallace, "I believe I can beat you making the electric light. I do not think you are working in the right direction." Wallace, to his credit, "was a good sport" about the challenge.

The right direction, Edison believed, was to make a more practical light. Arc lights were so blinding that they were useless in small, enclosed spaces. As Edison later wrote, "The intense light had not been subdivided so that it could be brought into private houses."

Back at his laboratory in Menlo Park, New Jersey, Edison began pursuing his goal with his usual single-mindedness. Rather than arc lights, however, Edison experimented with strands of fiber inside an airtight glass bulb. When these filaments were heated, they produced "an even, clear light." The trick was finding one that didn't burn out too quickly. Edison and his army of assistants patiently tested hundreds of different fibers, from silk to facial hair, before stumbling upon one made with carbonized bamboo that burned for more than a thousand hours. Unlike the harsh light produced by arc lights, Edison's filament bulb produced a warm, gentle light that glowed "like the mellow sunset on an Italian autumn."

In a staggeringly brief period of time—less than two years—Edison would perfect and receive a patent for his incandescent lightbulb. At the same time, Edison and his assistants also devised an entirely new means of delivering electricity through thin copper wires.

Much like more recent format wars (such as VHS versus Betamax or Blu-ray versus HD DVD), the two competing systems—arc lights and incandescent lights—would fight for supremacy. Incandescence would ultimately win, of course, and remain the world's dominant source of artificial light until the emergence of energy-efficient alternatives such as compact fluorescent lamps and LED lamps in the late twentieth century.*

But in June 1879 the arc light was still king, and the company that William H. Vanderbilt chose to illuminate Madison Square Garden, the Fuller Electric Company of Brooklyn, was on the

---

* Although he won the lightbulb battle, Edison would lose the electric war. He believed direct current (DC) would become the dominant means of transmitting electricity, but ultimately the more efficient system of alternating current (AC) promoted by his bitter rival George Westinghouse prevailed.

cutting edge of that technology. The company's founder, J. Billings Fuller, was a brilliant inventor who had perfected a new kind of arc light as well as a new dynamo. Like other lighting systems at the time, however, the one that Fuller installed in the Garden was rather cumbersome. It was powered by a fifty-horsepower, coal-fired engine that was connected to a dozen electric generators. These generators, which resembled lathes and were "so small that they might be placed in a hat box," produced electricity using magnets, similar to a Gramme machine. All of this machinery was arrayed on a platform in the southeast corner of the arena, near the Fourth Avenue entrance. The generators were connected by wires to eleven massive arc lights arrayed throughout the interior of the building. According to Fuller, each arc light glowed with the intensity of 2,500 candles, and the eleven arc lights together flooded the Garden with the equivalent of 1,840 gas lights. "It is a brilliant opalescent light," one newspaper reporter wrote. "It is so bright that it forces a shadow from a gaslight."

The system required constant monitoring; since the carbon rods burned as they produced light, they had to be replaced regularly. Hedging his bets, Vanderbilt kept the old gas lamps in place for the time being. There would be kinks to be worked out, but eventually the Fuller system would prove reliable enough to permanently replace gas in the Garden, and at a great savings. The Garden's gas bills had averaged between sixty and seventy dollars a night. The electric lights cost just eight dollars a night.

The grand opening of Madison Square Garden was celebrated on Saturday, May 31, 1879, with a "choice program of music by 60 musicians—Harv[e]y B. Dodworth, Director."* Throughout the summer of '79, the Garden hosted concerts conducted by

---

* Harvey Dodworth was the era's preeminent conductor. He had once hoped to rent Madison Square Garden from Vanderbilt and turn it into a "music garden," complete with a 123-piece orchestra under his direction and occasional "battle of the bands" competitions featuring musical groups from other parts of the country. But Vanderbilt had other ideas.

Madison Square Garden in the 1880s. Milstein Division of United States History, Local History & Genealogy, The New York Public Library, Astor, Lenox and Tilden Foundations

Dodworth (admission: twenty-five cents), as well as other events, including a horticultural show, a gymnastics program, and an extended run of yet another pirated version of *H.M.S. Pinafore* (admission: fifty cents). But the first really big event scheduled to take place in the renovated arena was the next Astley Belt race in September. Edward Payson Weston had decided to defend his title in New York. As the *New York Times* put it, the race would be "the first extremely favorable test of electricity for popular uses."

At eight o'clock on the morning of Wednesday, August 27, about twenty invited guests, including former New York mayor William Wickham and several newspaper reporters, gathered on Pier 38 on the North (now Hudson) River to greet Weston upon his return from Britain. Accompanied by his wife, three children—and a valet—Weston was scheduled to arrive on the Guion

Line steamship *Nevada* that morning. It had been nearly four years since Weston had fled the United States for Britain after his ignominious loss to Dan O'Leary at the Expo in Chicago. Now he was returning home a hero, holder of the prestigious Astley Belt, restorer of American supremacy in pedestrianism, and, for the time being anyway, free of debt.

The arrival of the *Nevada*, which had set sail from Liverpool a week earlier, was delayed by headwinds and fog. It wasn't until noon that its single smokestack was spotted, silhouetted against the horizon just off Fire Island. Weston's welcoming party jumped into a tugboat laden with "six kegs of beer, two baskets of wine, and a basket of sandwiches" and chugged out to meet the ship.

Weston was standing on the deck of the *Nevada*, waving his hat at the tug as it pulled up. He was wearing a black suit with red socks and, on a long gold chain, a "handsome, plain gold locket" that had been presented to him by Sir John Astley. (The locket contained a miniature portrait of Astley himself.) "Weston looks younger by some years than when he left this country," one reporter wrote. "His face was shaved smooth, giving him an almost boyish appearance, and the only indications of advancing age were the few gray hairs that showed themselves about his temples."

After the *Nevada* cleared quarantine, the tugboat passengers and their goodies were loaded onto the ship. In the *Nevada's* parlor, Weston proudly showed his guests the Astley Belt, which he kept in a leather case. One of the panels of the belt was engraved:

WON BY EDWARD PAYSON WESTON
OF PROVIDENCE, U.S.A.,
AGRICULTURAL HALL, ISLINGTON, MAY 16–21, 1879.
DISTANCE COVERED, 550 MILES.

Weston should have been in a jovial mood, but instead he was pouty and seemed intent on settling old scores. Like too many of today's pampered athletes, Weston suffered from an acute sense of entitlement and was easily prone to feeling "disrespected." He complained that he'd never received a gold watch he'd been promised after his 500-mile walk in Newark in December 1874. As the *Nevada* made its way to port he told the reporters on board, "If I owned a house in perdition and another in Newark, I'd rent [out] the Newark house." And he still chafed at the criticism he'd received years before in sporting journals like the *New York Sportsman*, which had dismissed him as "a fraud."

"I did not care to bring this belt back to New-York," he said. "In fact, when I went away I had made up my mind not to walk any more in this City. While in many quarters I always received the kindest treatment here, in others I did not."

Weston sounded a little like he wished he'd never returned to the United States at all. "There was a time when I would have considered it the proudest event of my life to bring this belt back to America, but I have got over that," he said. "If I had had my way about it, this next walk would not be in New-York, but in Australia, but my wife and Sir John Astley overcame my wishes." Nonetheless, he said he would "do his best" in the upcoming race, though he insisted he would not walk in Madison Square Garden unless smoking was banned in the building during the race. "It is too hard on the lungs to breathe that foul atmosphere for six days," he said, "and I do not intend to do it."

The *Nevada* docked. Several hundred people were waiting on the pier and several thousand more outside the gates, "all anxious to catch an early glimpse of the walker." Weston and his family climbed into a waiting carriage and were driven to the Rossmore Hotel at Forty-First and Broadway, a cheering crowd following close behind the whole way.

At the hotel, Weston, clearly relishing the attention, couldn't help himself from convening another impromptu press conference. Seated in a rocking chair, he regaled reporters with tales of his unexpected victory in the Astley Belt race, his equally unexpected conversion to running ("I hardly knew that I could run"), and even his financial woes, which he blamed on an unnamed man who "has been persecuting me for years."

"I owed him $350, but he claimed $420. I offered him the $350 half a dozen times, but he would not take it. He said he would have the $420 or ruin me, and his persecutions followed me to England. He has persecuted me for 12 years, and it has cost me over $15,000, but he hasn't got that money yet, and I don't think he will."

On the night of Friday, August 29, Weston was feted at Madison Square Garden. About three thousand people attended the event. A brass band struck up "See the Conquering Hero Comes" as Weston, behind a phalanx of police officers, entered the arena "amid a storm of cheers." As was often the case with Weston, his attire was much commented upon. "He was dressed in a glossy suit of black," the *New York Sun* noted, "with swallow-tail coat, white neck tie, expansive shirt bosom, on which glittered gold studs; a massive watch chain dangled on his vest; over his broadcloth coat he wore a white overcoat of faultless cut; in his hands, which were covered with white kid gloves, he carried a glossy high hat and a natty cane."

Weston climbed the stairs onto a stage that was still festooned with props from the *Pinafore* set. He bowed again and again to the cheering crowd. Then he took a seat while his friend Robert Ogden Dormeus made some introductory remarks. Dormeus, a physician and public health expert, thanked Weston for encouraging New Yorkers to walk, joking that the Vanderbilts "feared that Weston and his competitors will seriously reduce the income of the railroads."

Then Weston stepped forward. The crowd cheered "lustily." When the applause subsided, Weston began, not exactly by apologizing, but by clarifying the remarks he'd made on the *Nevada* two days before, which had run afoul of the patriotism police. He said that "when he went away he was an American, and he came back an American."

He spoke about his Astley Belt victory in London two months earlier, saying he'd "determined to do something worthy of an American, and so made 550 miles, and in doing that did what any young man before him could do who would take as good care of himself as he did."

"I have two faults," Weston added. "One is that of procrastination, the other is in following the advice of that great wit Artemus Ward, 'Always live within your income, [even] if you have to borrow money to do it with.'"*

He ended with another plea for a ban on smoking inside the Garden during the upcoming race. "If you will abstain from smoking in this building during the next match," Weston promised, "you will see one of the greatest pedestrian contests ever attempted in the world."

The race was scheduled to begin on Monday, September 22. Weston, Rowell, and eleven other competitors had each paid the one-hundred-pound entrance fee, and the promoters, two brothers named Joseph and L. F. Kuntz, had signed a lease for the Garden, the going rate being about $10,000 a week.

In late August a contretemps erupted that threatened to scuttle the event. Six months earlier, Dan O'Leary, the recently retired winner of the first two Astley Belt races, had signed a lease to rent the Garden for his first O'Leary Belt race in October—with the understanding, he said, that no other pedestrian matches would be staged in the arena before then. Understandably, O'Leary was not pleased with the prospect of another big six-day race taking

---

* Artemus Ward was a character portrayed by Charles Farrar Browne, a prolific writer and performer who is widely considered America's first stand-up comedian. Browne played Artemus as a simpleton prone to unintentional puns. Browne's performance in Virginia City, Nevada, on December 22, 1863, was attended by a young Sam Clemens, who was inspired to pursue his own career in writing and humor, complete with his own nom de plume, Mark Twain. Browne was also a favorite of Abraham Lincoln, who was known to read his stories aloud to his cabinet.

place in the Garden just a month before his, and he complained
directly to William H. Vanderbilt. The dispute was so serious that it
became front-page news. Vanderbilt threatened to void the Kuntz
brothers' lease if they didn't reach a settlement with O'Leary.

After tense negotiations that included threats of lawsuits and
injunctions, the two brothers and O'Leary finally came to an
agreement early on the morning of Saturday, September 13, just
nine days before the Astley Belt race was to begin. The Kuntzes
agreed to pay O'Leary $10,000 for the bar concession during his
race in October. "As this part of the business has been rated at
about $6,000," the *New York Sun* reported, "the amount properly
credited to the compromise may be fairly stated at $4,000."

So the fifth Astley Belt race began as scheduled at one o'clock
on the morning of Monday, September 22, 1879. In keeping with
the changes made to the Garden, the Kuntz brothers made some
changes of their own. The price of admission was raised from
the usual fifty cents to one dollar—as much as a ticket to see the
comic opera *La jolie parfumeuse* at the Fifth Avenue Theatre. The
increase, the brothers explained, would "keep away an undesir-
able crowd." The tickets themselves were individually numbered
and engraved, and printed by a banknote company to discourage
counterfeiters.

"We don't intend the garden to be a lodging house either,"
the brothers announced. "Every morning at three o'clock it will
be cleared of all loungers and sleepers." A team of "colored" jan-
itors had been hired to thoroughly clean the building each day
at dawn. And, much to Edward Payson Weston's satisfaction and
relief, signs reading NO SMOKING were posted throughout the
building. Although it would not be heeded scrupulously, the ban
was an early and laudable attempt to create a smoke-free environ-
ment in a public building.

The ⅛-mile track was said to be the finest ever constructed
for a pedestrian match: a combination of loam and tanbark covered with sawdust and tightly compressed with heavy iron rollers.

It took nearly a hundred men a full day to build it. The pedestrians' tents were equally fine. Made of blue-and-white canvas and measuring twelve feet by twelve feet, each was surrounded by a stout railing and furnished with a cot, table, two chairs, washstand, gas stove, a piece of carpet, and, presumably, a chamber pot. In an early example of "promotional consideration," the furnishings were provided by an enterprising furniture dealer in exchange for permission to hang one of his placards on each tent. As the race progressed, however, the placards would be obscured by mountains of floral arrangements and other gifts delivered to the pedestrians from well-wishers.

The tents were placed inside the oval. This was convenient for the pedestrians, but less so for the spectators, as the tents obstructed views of the track from every vantage point in the arena. "After the tents were put up the managers were struck by the stupidity of the plan," the *New York Times* reported, "and they sought to change it by placing the contestants in the space under the seats on the Twenty-seventh-street side." The pedestrians, however, would not consent to the change, so the tents stayed put.

A new scoreboard had been erected especially for the race. Written across the top was each pedestrian's name. Underneath each name were two dials; one tallied laps and the other, miles. It was an ingenious device, though it was too small to be read from any appreciable distance.

In anticipation of the great crowds, the Kuntz brothers had added an extra bar to the Garden and hired a small army of vendors to hawk apples, soda water, souvenir photographs of the pedestrians, pickled sheep's tongues, oysters, eggs, clam chowder, and coffee, among other goods. The new electric lights, according to one reporter, made it "as bright as day within the amphitheater." The lights received mixed reviews from the men on the track, however. The *New York Sun* wrote, "Some of the contestants like the electric light and others declare it to be too bright." To soften the light, the Fuller Company covered the arc lights with thick globes of glass.

The start of the fifth Astley Belt race, at the newly christened Madison Square Garden, on Monday, September 22, 1879. COURTESY OF LIBRARY OF CONGRESS

When the race began with the command "Go!" the Garden was packed with more than ten thousand spectators, a complete sell-out. "It has been claimed that the American public has grown very weary of these six days contests," the *Brooklyn Daily Eagle* noted, "but the reverse seems to be the case."

Each of the thirteen pedestrians in the race wore a large red number on a piece of black oilskin pinned to his chest. Among the bookmakers, Charles Rowell was the favorite at odds of 3 to 2. Edward Payson Weston was the second favorite at 5 to 2. As in the previous Astley Belt race in London, Weston was wearing a normal athletic costume ("red trunks and tights, white shirt") instead of his usual black jacket and ruffled shirt. He did, however, carry a cane.

But, from the very start of the race, the pedestrian who captured the imagination of the audience was a Boston grocery store clerk in his early twenties who was competing in his first big walking match. His name was Frank Hart, and what set him apart from the rest of the field was the color of his skin. Frank Hart was black.

African Americans played a pivotal role in nineteenth-century American sports. In 1875, just four years before Frank Hart's appearance in the Astley Belt race, the first Kentucky Derby was run. Fourteen of the fifteen jockeys were black, including Isaac Murphy, who would go on to win three Derbies, including the 1891 race on a horse named Kingman, which was owned and trained by another African American, Dudley Allen. (As of 2013, Kingman was still the only horse owned by an African American to win the Derby.)

And at the very moment Frank Hart was racing around the ⅛-mile track inside Madison Square Garden, twenty-two-year-old Moses Fleetwood Walker was distinguishing himself on the playing fields of Oberlin College. (And in the classroom: Walker excelled at Greek, French, Latin, and math.) Walker was a star catcher on Oberlin's baseball team. In 1881 he would transfer to the University of Michigan, studying law while he played baseball for the Wolverines. On May 27, 1882, Walker hit a game-winning home run against archrival Wisconsin, prompting Michigan's student newspaper, the *Chronicle*, to label him "a wonder."

In 1883, Walker signed with the Toledo Blue Stockings, a minor league team in the Northwestern League, and helped lead them to the league championship. The following year, Toledo joined the American Association, a major league in competition with the National League at the time. Playing mainly as a catcher, Moses Walker hit .264 for the Blue Stockings in 1884, and in the process became the first African American to play in the major leagues, sixty-three years before Jackie Robinson broke in with the Brooklyn Dodgers.

Walker was well received in some quarters. One opposing manager called him "a splendid catcher and batter" and "very much a gentleman." But when the Blue Stockings traveled to Richmond for a game in the middle of the season, Walker received a death threat. A letter sent to the team said there were "75 determined men who have sworn to mob Walker if he comes on the grounds in a [baseball] suit." (Walker, who was injured at the time, did not play.) A few opposing players objected to Walker's presence as well. Cap Anson, an outstanding first baseman for the Chicago White Stockings, refused to take the field against Toledo when Walker was in the lineup.*

A handful of black ballplayers would follow Moses Walker into the major leagues, including his brother Weldy. After the 1887 season, however, the major leagues, under pressure from Cap Anson and other white players, systematically banned African Americans. By then, Moses Walker had returned to the minor leagues. He retired from baseball in 1889 and returned to his hometown of Steubenville, Ohio, where he owned a hotel and, later, a movie theater.

In 1896, in the infamous case of *Plessy v. Ferguson*, the United States Supreme Court upheld the constitutionality of segregation. Jim Crow was legitimized, and black athletes were marginalized, effectively barred, often by law, from participating in athletic events with whites.† It can be argued that African American athletes enjoyed more opportunities in the second half of the nineteenth century than in the first half of the twentieth. By the time sports finally reintegrated in the middle of the twentieth century, the great black athletes of the Gilded Age were long forgotten.

Athletes like Frank Hart.

Like many famous pedestrians, Hart rose from impoverished obscurity, and details about his early life are sketchy. He was born

---

* Anson, a notorious and unapologetic racist, is in the baseball hall of fame. At least he was never accused of using steroids.

† After *Plessy*, events in which black and white athletes competed together (most notably boxing matches) were staged surreptitiously or in remote jurisdictions where law enforcement officials were either sympathetic or pliable.

Fred Hichborn (or Hitchborn or Hickborn) around 1857, probably in Haiti. In his late teens he moved to America, and by 1877 he was in Boston, where he worked in a grocery store.

The first race Hart entered was a thirty-hour "go as you please" at the Boston Music Hall in April 1879. During the race, a spectator tried to throw pepper in Hart's face, though for reasons unclear. The attack may have been racially motivated, though it may have just as well been motivated by gambling. In any event, Hart, who hadn't even trained for the race, won with 119 miles and collected a hundred-dollar prize. A month later he entered a six-day race in Boston and finished with an impressive 425 miles.

Hart's performances caught the eye of Dan O'Leary, who was eager to find fresh young talent for his first O'Leary Belt race in October. O'Leary took Hart under his wing and began training him. They made an odd couple, the successful Irish immigrant and the poor, black grocery store clerk from Boston. But O'Leary saw something special in Hart. "Hart is a good boy and I am fond of him," O'Leary said. "He will make his fortune at walking."

O'Leary was so convinced of Hart's potential that instead of entering him in the O'Leary Belt race, he decided to enter him in the far more prestigious (and competitive) Astley Belt race in September. It was akin to starting a rookie pitcher in the seventh game of the World Series.

Right from the start of the race, Hart made quite an impression on the denizens of Madison Square Garden. He "dogged" Charles Rowell, employing the same annoying tactic that Rowell himself had used against Hart's mentor O'Leary in the third Astley Belt race back in March. "Rowell does not seem to like it, and runs frequently," one reporter noted, "but Hart also runs, and Rowell cannot shake him off." Hart was giving the Englishman a taste of his own medicine, and the spectators adored him for it. At one point they began chanting his name over and over: "Hart! Hart! Hart!"

"He struck into the upright O'Leary step," one paper noted, "head up, breast out, hands closed as if circling corncobs, eyes

straight ahead, and legs moving like a drum major's." In
fact, Hart's style was so similar
to O'Leary's that the papers
called him "Black Dan."

While Hart and Row-
ell played cat and mouse,
Edward Weston seemed to be
in a world of his own, less concerned with racing than show-
manship. He ran little, but
instead walked imperiously
along the outer edge of the
track, occasionally tossing his
cane into the air and catching
it. At one point he balanced a

In this illustration of the fifth Astley Belt
race, Frank Hart is in fourth place. COUR-
TESY OF LIBRARY OF CONGRESS

cup on the end of the cane, holding it aloft for all to see. His antics
seemed to annoy rather than entertain the great crowd, which
had, after all, come to watch pedestrianism, not a circus act.

Rowell, meanwhile, managed to shrug off Hart's dogging, and
by the end of the first day he led the race with 127 miles. Hart—
"O'Leary's dark horse," as the papers inevitably described him—
was third with 110 miles. Weston was far behind with just 95.

Interest in the race was intense. As usual, thousands lingered
outside the arena at all hours. They looked, according to the
Times, "as if they would pawn the clothes they wore if they could
but pass the vigilant doorkeeper."

Early on the fourth day Hart sprained his ankle badly but raced
on, limping noticeably. His tenacity further endeared him to the
audience. At the end of that day, Rowell was still in the lead with
402 miles—on pace to shatter Weston's six-day record of 550 miles.
The hobbled Hart had dropped to fifth with 339 miles. Weston,
the defending Astley Belt champion, was in sixth place with 322
miles.

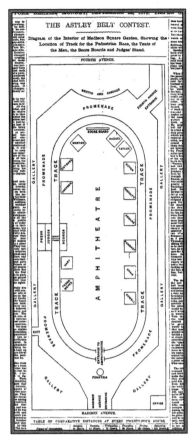

This illustration appeared in the *New York Herald* on September 22, 1879. It shows the configuration of Madison Square Garden for the fifth Astley Belt race. COURTESY OF LIBRARY OF CONGRESS

Weston, now certain that defeat was inevitable, resorted to "queer antics" in a pathetic attempt to amuse the audience, "twisting his body into all sorts of apish forms . . . to the great disgust of the many." Hisses and epithets rained down on him. One reporter speculated that Weston was "insane."

Around 2:30 on the afternoon of Friday, the fifth day of the race, Hart was summoned to his tent by Dan O'Leary, who read Hart a telegram O'Leary had received from the "Young Men's Club (Colored) of Boston."

"At a meeting [of the club] this morning," the telegram read, "it was voted that your interest and gentlemanly politeness and kindness to Mr. Frank Hart, the colored pedestrian, are more the object of our thoughts than you, perhaps, imagine, and that we return our thanks to you, many and sincere. . . ."

The telegram was accompanied by a floral bouquet that Hart carried back to the track, holding it aloft for several laps, amid much cheering. The photograph vendors reported that Hart's photo was the best selling.

Still, all was not brotherly love. An undercurrent of prejudice was persistently palpable. When Hart began racing another pedestrian, the band struck up "Pop Goes the Weasel," which includes the line "The monkey chased the weasel." Hart would later say that racial epithets were often hurled at him by spectators when he competed, and some of his fellow pedestrians would refuse to shake his hand at the start of races. John Hughes, a rival pedestrian who spoke with an Irish brogue, referred to Hart contemptuously as "the nagur."

Near the end of the sixth day, Weston completed his 450th mile. When the crowd responded to the milestone with only tepid applause, Weston was distraught. He broke down in tears and retreated to his tent, where he was said to be "quite hysterical," sobbing so hard that his attendants feared he was suffering convulsions.

The match ended at eleven o'clock Saturday night. Rowell was the winner with 530 miles. Hart finished fourth with 482 miles. Weston was a distant sixth with 455.

Although Rowell was the new champion, the post-race talk was all about Hart. On Sunday, the *Brooklyn Daily Eagle* published an editorial entitled "The Pedestrianism of Our Friend Mr. Hart." His performance proved, the paper said, "that there is nothing in a black skin or wooly hair that is incompatible with fortitude."

The total gate receipts for the six days were $73,932—roughly $1.7 million today. Rowell's cut was $19,500. Coupled with his winnings from the Astley Belt race in the Garden six months earlier, Rowell's cumulative earnings for the year were nearly $38,000—about $880,000 today. It was an astonishing figure.

On Tuesday, September 30, Rowell was feted before three thousand fans at the Garden, where he was to be formally presented with the Astley Belt. But there was a problem: the belt, which Weston had been holding, had been "attached" by creditors and could not be surrendered to Rowell. Weston's money problems had returned. Six days later a court ruled that since Weston never actually "owned" the belt, it could not be attached, and it was finally handed over to Rowell.

The fifth Astley Belt race was another spectacular financial success, but it was subsequently mired in controversy. After the race it was discovered that the track was more than seven feet short of

⅛ mile, meaning the pedestrians' final tallies had to be revised downward. Rowell's total, for instance, was reduced from 530 miles to 524.

But the controversy hardly seemed to dampen the public's enthusiasm for pedestrianism. On October 2, several prominent pedestrians took part in a kind of celebrity cruise. For fifty cents, fans could mingle with the athletes and enjoy the music of a military band on a steamer that sailed from Manhattan to Bridgeport, Connecticut, and back.

And just four days after that, on Monday, October 6, 1879, the first O'Leary Belt match began at the Garden. The belt itself was described as "far superior in artistic execution and elegance of design" to the Astley Belt. Thirty-five pedestrians entered the race. Although it followed the conclusion of the Astley Belt race by just nine days, the attendance was nearly as great, in no small part because O'Leary returned the price of admission to fifty cents.

The winner of the first O'Leary Belt race was Nicholas Murphy, an eighteen-year-old novice from Haverstraw, New York, who completed a very respectable 505 miles. Murphy was awarded $5,000 for his efforts. (O'Leary, apparently, kept most of the gate for himself.)

Later that month, the *Brooklyn Daily Eagle*, indulging in the then-popular pastime of predicting the future, speculated on what a "walking match of a hundred years from now" might look like. According to a faux letter to the editor dated October 27, 1979, "The 146th international contest for the pedestrian championship terminated at 3 o'clock today, and Shang Smith retains the belt and earns $98,762.52 as his share of the gate money." The letter noted that the winner completed 1,095 miles, and that the aggregate attendance for the six-day race was two million.

In 1879, it seemed the future of pedestrianism was limitless.

11

ANTI-PEDESTRIANISM

or

BODILY EXERCISE PROFITETH LITTLE

ON SUNDAY, MARCH 16, 1879, the Reverend Dr. John Philip Newman mounted the pulpit inside the rambling, gothic Central
Methodist Episcopal Church on Seventh Avenue in Lower Manhattan to deliver his weekly sermon. Broad-shouldered and barrel-
chested, Newman cast an imposing figure, though he was said
to be "one of the kindliest of men." Once described as among
"the greatest orators of the American pulpit," Newman delivered
booming sermons that, according to one biographer, "were ring-
ing and spirited, resembling in many of their forceful character-
istics the speeches of Calhoun, Webster, and other orators of the
older type." Throughout his ecclesiastical career, Newman had
never shied away from addressing controversial and important
social issues in his sermons: slavery (he was against it), temperance
(for it), and polygamy (against it). But on this Sunday he would
address what he believed to be a new menace: pedestrianism.

Born in 1826, J. P. Newman had been called to God by a "mysterious occurrence" when he was sixteen. According to one account,

"On the streets of New York one day he was suddenly accosted by a stranger of impressive mien, who, without a single word of salutation, simply said, 'God wants your heart,' and then vanished as abruptly as he had appeared." On a Sunday two weeks later, the stranger reappeared on the street and, again without preamble or introduction, handed the young man a slip of paper on which was written, "God wants your heart."

"His message was obeyed," Newman recalled many years later, "and within a month thereafter I was received into the Methodist Episcopal Church." (The M. E. Church was a predecessor of today's United Methodist Church.) At twenty-two, Newman was ordained a minister. In 1864, with the Confederacy in its death throes, he was assigned to organize the M. E. Church in Louisiana, Mississippi, and Texas. Over the next five years he founded an orphanage and a seminary, and built nine churches for freedmen.

Newman's work in the South brought him into contact with Republican politicians overseeing Reconstruction, and those contacts would prove useful in his next assignment: in 1869 he was appointed the first pastor of a new M. E. Church in Washington. The church soon became the spiritual home of many leading Republicans in the capital, including numerous members of Congress, Chief Justice Salmon P. Chase, and, most prominently, President Ulysses S. Grant. (Newman and Grant became close friends, and Newman would be at Grant's bedside when he died in 1885.) Newman's popularity among high-ranking Republican officials earned him the nickname the Court Chaplain, and in 1869 he was appointed chaplain of the United States Senate, a position he held for four years.

In April 1878, Newman was appointed pastor of Central Methodist Episcopal Church in New York, perhaps the most important pastorate in the M. E. Church at the time. He was now one of the most influential Protestant ministers in the country. His sermons were published in the New York papers, and Ulysses Grant, now retired in New York, regularly attended his services. Newman's

The Reverend Dr. John Philip Newman, photographed in the 1860s.

words carried weight, and when he began speaking on that Sunday in March 1879, his congregants listened intently.

The third Astley Belt race, won by Charles Rowell and marred by rioting and the balcony collapse, had concluded at Gilmore's Garden just the night before. Newman could not have avoided hearing about the race. It was, as the reverend himself noted, "the engrossing topic of conversation on our thoroughfares, in the cars, at business places, in our public schools, at home and even at church."

"The press," he said, "published the results of each day's contest as if a nation's life were at stake on the field of battle."

In his sermon, entitled "The Brutal Contest," Newman said New York—a "great Christian metropolis"—had been "shamefully disgraced" by the race. "Law has been held in contempt, decency at a discount and human life as a thing not worth a thought. Disorder has been rampant, the midnight air has resounded with the yells and execrations of a maddened crowd and the holy Sabbath trampled in the dust."

"What was at stake?" he asked.

Four men were testing their capacity of physical endurance—that is all. Pride, ambition, and love of gain gave inspiration to the strife. By force of national pride the brutal contest was clothed with international dignity. England and America, the two great Christian nations of the globe, were pitted on a sawdust track and represented by animals in human form. The interest in the result felt and manifested on both sides of the Atlantic is the shameful count in the indictment against our Christian civilization. Public opinion should have been so strong in advance as to render the race impossible, and public indignation should have flamed forth at the mere proposal of such a contest in our city.

Pedestrianism, the reverend thundered, was sinful—sinful because it was wasteful, and God abhors waste. Citing Matthew 26:8 ("To what purpose is this waste?"), Newman said walking matches were a waste of physical force, a waste of happiness, and a waste of money. They were also magnets for "a whole brood of vices," such as gambling, intemperance, and profanity. "But there is one great lesson taught by this contest," he said in conclusion, "namely, if men can train themselves to endure so much in a bad cause they can do the same in a good cause, and God and society hold them responsible."

J. P. Newman was not the only minister to preach against pedestrianism that Sunday. At the Methodist Society's Third Street Chapel in Brooklyn, the Reverend W. C. Steele delivered a sermon entitled "The Evils of Pedestrianism." Steele said the sport was "born of and productive of evil," and it was "the duty of the censors of public morals appointed by the Almighty to point out the danger arising from it."

"We remember when the ladies of the Temperance Union protested against the open violation of the Sunday law by that coarse rough woman Mme. Anderson at Mozart Garden; how they were treated and the sophisms with which she replied to them. Since that time she has had hundreds of imitators, and every village of any size has had a touch of the walking mania, which has culminated in the international match, with all its evils, the first of which is physical abuse." Here the reverend cited 1 Timothy 4:8: "Bodily exercise profiteth little."

"Open air exercise is good," he said, "when not excessive."

"Another evil is its injury to the morals by promoting Sabbath breaking, filling, as it did on Sabbath evening last, Madison Avenue with a drunken ribald mob, that made the night hideous with their noise and obscenity."

And at the Second Baptist Church in Newport, Rhode Island, that Sunday, the Reverend N. B. Thompson told his parishioners that pedestrians had "broken the laws of health and nature."

"[The] walking fever was spreading like an epidemic," Thompson warned, "and . . . no good would come of it."

Moral crusaders like the Reverends Newman, Steele, and Thompson found much to dislike about pedestrianism: its profligacy, its close association with vice, its "scandalously indecent walking costumes," its supposedly corrupting influence on the children who idolized its stars. But an even greater concern was the sport's perceived cruelty. It was, they believed, a sport unbecoming of a

Christian nation, certainly no better than cockfighting, dogfighting, or prizefighting. Rev. Newman likened pedestrianism to "a revival of the brutal sports of pagan Rome, when the gladiatorial combats were at their height," and Rev. Steele said it was "barbarous and never ought to have a place among civilized amusements."

It was no secret that many fans of six-day races reveled in the spectacle of sleep-deprived and bedraggled pedestrians pushing themselves to the very limits of human endurance. To these spectators, the staggering pedestrians were a source of great amusement, and a six-day race was not an athletic event but a freak show.

"The poor wretches struggled around, every step a torture, their haggard faces covered with cold perspiration and their glazed eyes looking appealingly at the mob of spectators who alternately cheered and jeered them," one attendee recalled of a six-day race. "One of the walkers whom I met a few days after the last match told me that he knew nothing of what was going on in the last days of the race, except that he was walking, and that he would give all the world to be allowed to lie down on the ground and go to sleep."

"I went to the walking match at the Madison Square Garden the other day while it was in full heat," an Ohio newspaper reporter recalled of a six-day race. "The first thought that a man has when he looks down on the weary wights pegging away for dear life is that of pity. Then he laughs. Why? Because it's funny."

What some found amusing, however, others found dangerous and possibly even deadly. The physical toll the six-day races took on the competitors was, of course, extreme. Sleep-deprived, malnourished, dehydrated, and out of their minds, many pedestrians pushed themselves to the very edge of physical and mental endurance. One British newspaper wrote of the effects on a hypothetical pedestrian:

It is about the fifth day that the sleeplessness and fatigue tell on him, and the sport begins. He limps along, suffering torments from a festering heel. His brain is bemused with exceeding toil; and, as he staggers mechanically round, it is said that curious visions beguile him. He does not see the crowd, which stares, smokes, and drinks. He does not hear the music, which mixes in a dream of his past life. He thinks that he is working in some country place that he knew long ago before he was a long-distance walker, and a mirage floats before him, like that which cheats wanderers in the desert. When his hour is up, he staggers into his bedroom, and there, let us hope, has the good fortune to become quite senseless and indifferent. As the last day of the competition approaches the softer-hearted lookers-on wish to have some of the walkers removed; but their backers will not permit this. Men are compelled to subject themselves to this voluntary torture, which equals those to which Red Indian braves expose themselves.

Sometimes it seemed like the spectators were circling the track like vultures anticipating carrion. A well-known pedestrian named Patrick Fitzgerald reported being shadowed during a race by a mysterious man in a cream-colored slouch hat. "He is clad in a respectable suit of black, and often carries a long cape over his shoulders," the *Boston Globe* reported.

He is about 65 years of age. His hair is long and gray, and he has intelligent features, lighted by restless and piercing black eyes. He had never been known to speak to any person during a race, but always keeps his eyes on the weakest-looking man. When Fitzgerald appeared particularly weak and tottering, the mysterious man crossed the main floor quickly and noiselessly, intercepting him in his laps. It is said that the mysterious man is a wealthy and eccentric citizen, residing in Harlem, who has laid a wager of $10,000 that he will yet see a pedestrian die on the sawdust.

Pedestrians' trainers often came in for special scorn. The trainers of lesser pedestrians were often nothing better than henchmen hired by gamblers to keep their charges on the track by whatever means necessary. One eyewitness described a pedestrian, in a state of delirium for want of rest, being refused entry to his tent by "the fierce oaths of his trainers and the men who had risked their money on his success."

In the winter of 1878–79, a pedestrian named Peter Van Ness attempted to walk two thousand half miles in two thousand consecutive half hours (more than forty-one days). On the thirty-sixth day, Van Ness cracked. He was said to be "suffering terribly" and "out of his mind." But his trainer refused to let him quit. "Harsh treatment had to be used to compel him to walk," one eyewitness recalled. After completing his 1,718th half mile, Van Ness, "behaving like a madman," grabbed a revolver he kept in his tent and shot his trainer, taking a chunk out of his arm.

This, many long-distance pedestrians could empathize with. But then Van Ness, utterly raving, started shooting wildly into the audience until he ran out of bullets and collapsed to the floor, apparently comatose. The trainer was not seriously wounded, and, remarkably, no spectators were injured. Even before his arm was tended to, the trainer ordered "morphine and hot drops" to be administered to Van Ness. This revived the pedestrian well enough to send him on his not-so-merry way. He completed his 1,719th half mile without missing a beat. Police were summoned to the venue, but Van Ness, who probably would have preferred to be arrested, was allowed to continue his tramp.

Influential newspapers editorialized against pedestrianism. In January 1879, the *Saturday Review*, a highbrow British weekly, published a lengthy editorial entitled "A Stupid Sport."

"We do not see the fun of 'long-distance walking,'" the paper said, calling it "stupid, dangerous, and brutal," "monstrous and degrading," and "a despicable exhibition of silliness and ruffianism," before laying the blame squarely on the New World:

Long-distance walking was imported from the United States of America, where it seems to have come into existence about the time when negro slavery was abolished. Perhaps in viewing the agonies of a half-dead man staggering along a track to the music of a band, and much to the anxiety of a doctor, the public found some compensation for the loss of the privilege of thrashing its own nigger.

Long walking . . . is scarcely more diverting than the slower tortures of the Inquisition, which only began to afford the spectator entertainment after the victim had suffered for some considerable time.

The similarity to medieval forms of torture was also noted in an editorial that appeared in the *New York Times* later that year.

As for the performance, if the rack is torture and is demoralizing, what is walking? The thing is a provoking of nature to interpose—a deliberate attempt to see how much abuse the human frame will endure. The interest lies in watching that attempt, for while the alertness of the stride and the physical beauty of the work are at their best the interest is least. People go to see the thing after it becomes torture, as they do to see the acrobat walk on a high wire and the trainer put his head in the lion's mouth—in the half-hope of seeing the one fall and the other lose his head. . . . But saw-dust rings, foul air, weary assistants and spectators, and worn-out trampers, abusing their bodies because a depraved appetite enjoys it, form a scene in which all elements of athletic interest and manhood are wanting.

These rebukes were indicative of an emerging backlash against pedestrianism. Most pedestrians, however, failed to appreciate the threat this posed to their sport and, indeed, their livelihoods. When he returned to the United States in August 1879, Edward Payson Weston was asked what he thought of J. P. Newman's sermon. "I have walked 53,000 miles in the last 14 years, and I don't look much like a used-up man, do I?" he answered dismissively.

"If the ministers would pay more attention to theology, and less to walking matches, there would be fewer ministerial scandals."

Like today's professional athletes, pedestrians occasionally got caught up in scandals that damaged their sport's reputation. In 1880, a pedestrian named William H. Davis was sentenced to eighteen months in prison after pleading guilty to theft. The *New York Times* described his fall from grace:

> He was formerly a respectable man, and did a good business as [a] truckman, having in his employment at one time a dozen teamsters. In an evil hour he became affected with the pedestrian craze, and allowed his business to go to ruin. He was one of the contestants for the Rose belt, in Gilmore's Garden, but after two days' tramp, withdrew from the track. He has since lived an idle, dissolute life, apart from his wife, who earned an honest living as a tailoress. On May 18 Davis went to the clothing manufactory at No. 541 West Twenty-third street, from which his wife was in the habit of obtaining garments to finish, and informed the superintendent, Charles M. Dewey, that his wife had sent him for some work. Mr. Dewey, believing his statement, gave him 12 pairs of cassimere pantaloons. It was subsequently discovered that Davis had not been sent for work by his wife, and that he had pawned the garments which he had fraudulently obtained.

A much more notorious scandal involved a well-known pedestrian named George Cameron, who raced under the name "Noremac" ("Cameron" spelled backward). Born in Edinburgh in 1854, Cameron was a lithographer by trade who began competing in pedestrian events in his midtwenties.

In the first half of 1880, Cameron won three consecutive seventy-two-hour races in Scotland. He caught the attention of George Beattie, a fellow native of Edinburgh and recently retired British

Army sergeant who was eager to capitalize on the pedestrianism craze. Beattie was forty-four, a decorated veteran of Britain's war in Afghanistan, and "a fine specimen of physical manhood." He was also an alcoholic. Beattie offered his services to Cameron as a trainer, and Cameron accepted. It was likely Beattie who convinced Cameron to adopt his cacophonous nom de plume.

In late 1880, Cameron and Beattie sailed for New York. Though he never won a major race in the United States, Cameron managed to earn enough prize money to buy a saloon he named the Walker's Rest on the corner of Prince and Mulberry Streets in Lower Manhattan. He hired Beattie as a bartender, which, in hindsight, was probably a mistake. "For a year Beattie kept sober and attended strictly to business," it was later reported, but then he became "excessively intemperate in his habits."

Beattie shared an apartment with Cameron, his wife, and their two small children, and, as his drinking worsened, Beattie became "a nuisance, and . . . greatly annoyed the Camerons by his conduct." While under the influence, Beattie was said to have a "very ugly disposition," and he "made mischief between Cameron and his wife by telling the former that she was in the habit of going out at unseemly hours and remaining out late, and although Cameron was convinced that his wife was an honest, faithful woman, yet the insinuations of Beattie had the effect of making husband and wife unhappy." Unsurprisingly, Beattie's rumor-mongering infuriated Elizabeth Cameron, and she came to despise him.

In August 1883, Cameron sold the Walker's Rest and opened a new bar he called the Midlothian Arms at 466 Eighth Avenue. Pointedly, he did not ask Beattie to tend bar at the new establishment, instead only offering him "charge of the pool-room." This infuriated Beattie, who "wanted to be head bar-keeper or nothing."

Around nine o'clock on the morning of Wednesday, August 22, 1883, Elizabeth Cameron got into an argument with her husband about "some domestic matter" while she was preparing breakfast for him and Beattie. Cameron stormed out of the apartment as Elizabeth shouted after him, "I know what's the matter, George; this man [Beattie] has been talking about me again."

Precisely what transpired between Elizabeth and Beattie after Cameron left will never be known, but about five minutes later neighbors heard two gunshots in quick succession. Elizabeth, "a buxom Scotch woman of twenty-eight years," was found dead on the floor in a corner of the kitchen, her two children crying over the corpse. A single bullet had entered her mouth, breaking her two front teeth, then exited the back of her skull. In another corner lay the body of George Beattie, also dead of a bullet through the brain, an entrance wound above the left temple, an exit wound above the right. On the floor next to his left hand was the pearl-handled .38-caliber revolver that he always carried.

"The crime is regarded as a bit of drunken rascality on the part of Beattie," the *New York Herald* reported the next day, "who allowed his bad temper and vindictiveness to make him a murderer, and then his cowardice and fear of the consequences of his act made him a suicide."

Although much sympathy was extended to the bereaved husband, "who was a well behaved man in every way," the shocking incident—involving a nefarious trainer, gross intemperance, murder, and suicide—did nothing to improve pedestrianism's standing among its growing number of critics.

12

THE NATIONAL PASTIME

or

KING OF HARTS

AROUND ELEVEN O'CLOCK ON THE MORNING of Saturday, March 15, 1879, three newsboys named James—Fitzgerald, Murphy, and Thompson—snuck into a coal yard at Cherry and Rutgers Streets on the Lower East Side of Manhattan. The lads had been at Gilmore's Garden for the Astley Belt race earlier that week, and they were determined to emulate their heroes. They would be Rowell, Ennis, and Harriman. A track was marked off in the black dust: eighty-four laps to the mile, according to their calculations.

Friends from the neighborhood tagged along to lend support. Mike O'Connor, "a little cool headed lad," would keep score with "a dirty piece of paper and a stump of a pencil." Three other boys formed an impromptu band with a mouth organ, a beat-up accordion, and the bones. More than a dozen other children took seats on the edge of coal bins to watch the great walking match. Behind a tattered piece of carpet hung in one corner of the yard, the three budding pedestrians dressed for the race. The band struck up a tune as the pedestrians emerged from their makeshift dressing room. A *New York Herald* reporter who happened upon the scene recorded it for posterity:

> "Rowell" was barefoot, the only article of clothing upon him being a pair of light linen pantaloons, which had long since seen their best days. His hair was frowzy and his eyes crossed. "Ennis" was an interesting object to look upon. He wore a pair of shoes several sizes too large, and a shabby shirt and pair of trousers. His step was that of a fighting cock; and, as he walked, he puffed away at the stump of a choice "Havana," enveloping himself in smoke. Harriman's face sadly needed washing. His "walking suit" was not very striking, and on his feet he wore a pair of rubbers.
>
> Everything being ready, the band led off with a selection from *Pinafore*, to the delight of pedestrian and betting men. The music attracted the attention of the proprietor of the coal yard, who, as luck would have it, was prejudiced against walking contests, especially on his own premises.

The proprietor summoned a police officer, who apprehended "Rowell," "Ennis," and "Harriman" before any of them had even completed a mile. The three boys, still in their walking costumes, were taken to the Essex Market Police Court, where they appeared before a magistrate who told them, "If you boys promise me to go right home, go to school, and never again attempt to become pedestrians, I will let you go."

The boys unanimously accepted the magistrate's proposal.

Though they usually didn't end up in court for it, boys and girls in every corner of the country pretended to be champion pedestrians in the late 1870s and early 1880s, walking on improvised tracks and even imitating the gaits of their heroes: Weston's distinctive wobble, O'Leary's piston-like perfection. Children went to bed dreaming of becoming stars of the tanbark. That's how popular pedestrianism was at the time.

———•·•·•———

The National League of Professional Base Ball Clubs had been founded in 1876 with teams in eight cities—Boston, Chicago, Cincinnati, Hartford, Louisville, New York, Philadelphia, and Saint Louis. But it was a ragtag outfit. The ballparks were little more than wooden grandstands and weedy fields. After the first season, New York and Philadelphia were expelled from the league for refusing to complete road trips at the end of the season.

"There were fifteen different clubs in the first four years of the new league," wrote historian Steven A. Riess, "and by 1881 Boston and Chicago were the only surviving original franchises." (Those two franchises are now the Atlanta Braves and the Chicago Cubs, respectively.) Besides, professional baseball players were regarded as uncouth, tobacco-chewing, low-class ruffians. Pedestrians, on the other hand, were considered the embodiment of American masculinity—healthy and virile.

Baseball was not the national pastime in the late 1870s and early 1880s. Pedestrianism was. It was the most popular spectator sport in the United States. Its athletes were the highest paid, its contests the best attended and most profitable. When the Thomas H. Hall tobacco company began inserting trading cards into its cigarette packs in 1880, the athletes portrayed on the cards were pedestrians, including Edward Payson Weston, Dan O'Leary, Charles Rowell, and Frank Hart.* These were some of the very first sports trading cards ever produced, and Hart was almost certainly the first black athlete portrayed on a trading card. (These cards are now worth roughly one hundred dollars apiece.) Prominent pedestrians were handsomely paid for endorsements, often in the form of testimonials published in newspapers:

———

* Their images were used without their permission. Weston detested smoking and certainly would have objected to his likeness being used to promote the habit.

MR. A. J. DITTMAN,

Dear Sir—I feel that it is but justice to you as the proprietor of a valuable article to state that I have found your SEA SALT an indispensable article in our pedestrian outfit, and I would not think of entering a match or moving without it. Yours, very sincerely,

DANIEL O'LEARY.

Newspapers were filled with reports of walking contests in Baltimore, Boston, Chicago, Newport, Philadelphia, Poughkeepsie, Providence, Syracuse, and Washington. The papers were also filled with letters from readers arguing the merits of various pedestrians and commenting on all aspects of the sport, a precursor to sports radio, though in more restrained and elegant tones:

New York, March 13, 1879.

To the Editor of the Herald:—

"Fair play is a jewel," and I hope it will be shown by all Americans to the plucky little Englishman [Charles Rowell] who is contesting at Gilmore's Garden. I observed him closely yesterday for a long while, and could only notice that he did his work steadily and fairly and apparently indifferent to the proceedings of others . . .

(signed) Looker-on.

The second O'Leary Belt race began just after midnight on Monday, April 5, 1880. It was the fourth six-day race held at Madison Square Garden in just eight months, following the Astley Belt race won by Charles Rowell the previous September, the first O'Leary Belt race the following month, and another "championship walk" in December. Yet hundreds of people were already waiting outside when the Garden doors opened at eight o'clock on Sunday night, and, according to the *New York Times*, by 11:45 "there were more persons in the Garden than ever before at the start of any walking match." Clearly, the public's appetite for these events had not been satiated.

Eighteen pedestrians had entered the contest, each paying an entrance fee of $500. Dan O'Leary was more generous with the revenue this time: Half the gate receipts would be divided among the pedestrians who completed at least 450 miles, with the winner of the race receiving the largest share. The winner would also receive the $9,000 in entrance fees, as well as a $1,000 bonus if he beat the six-day record of 553 miles set by the Englishman Blower Brown just two months earlier in London.

The incumbent holder of the O'Leary Belt, Nicholas Murphy, was there, but he was in poor shape. "I was at a fire up in Haverstraw," he explained to reporters just before the race began, "and the boys turned the hose on me." As a result, Murphy said, he'd caught a bad cold, had been unable to train, and didn't expect to last more than "a day or two."

The most mysterious entrant was a man who appeared to be in his fifties and was identified only by his initials, J.B. The man, whom the papers dubbed "Jaybee," was said to belong to a "prominent Knickerbocker family" and feared he would be disowned if it came to be known that he was engaging in such a plebeian enterprise.

But the pedestrian attracting the most attention going into the race was Dan O'Leary's African American protégé, Frank Hart, who'd won the six-day race held at the Garden the previous

DANIEL OLEARY
Champion Heel and Toe Pedestrian.

This trading card depicting "Champion Heel and Toe Pedestrian" Dan O'Leary was issued by W. S. Kimball, a tobacco company, in 1887. Pedestrians were among the first athletes to be portrayed on trading cards. AUTHOR'S COLLECTION

December with 540 miles, setting an American record. "Black Dan" was the bookies' favorite at odds of 3 to 1, and he was determined to win the race promoted by his mentor O'Leary. "I'll break those white fellows' hearts," he promised beforehand, "I will—you hear me!"

Hart was actually one of three African Americans in the race. The others were William Pegram, who, like Hart, hailed from Boston, and Edward Williams, a New Yorker one paper described as being "as black as a length of stovepipe." (Williams was also perspicacious. "When there was a discussion about setting men to watch the managers in the interests of the pedestrians," the *New York Sun* reported, "Williams said he wanted to know who would watch the watchmen.")

"The building never looked so attractive," the *Times* said of the Garden that Sunday night. The new electric lights were working perfectly, and the arena was "ornamented with the usual number of advertising signs and glass cases containing samples of all sorts of wares." The pedestrians' comfortably furnished tents were arranged in four neat rows at one end of the arena, leaving the area within the track unobstructed and giving spectators an unimpeded view of the entire track. O'Leary had introduced a tiered pricing system for tickets to the race. A general admission ticket to the lower level of the arena was fifty cents, while a reserved seat in the balconies was a dollar extra.

Around five minutes before midnight, the pedestrians emerged from their tents dressed in the "gayest of colors."

"If Grant and Blaine and the rest of our future Presidents* had been preparing for a race for the White House," said the *Times*, "there could hardly have been more excitement. Everybody was wild. The mere sight of the men set the people crazy."

---

* In 1880, a presidential election year, Grant and Blaine were considered early favorites for the Republican nomination. Of course, at the party's convention (at the Interstate Exposition Building in Chicago) the nomination ended up going to a dark horse, James A. Garfield, who went on to win the election, get assassinated, and be succeeded by noted pedestrianism devotee Chester A. Arthur.

When the eighteen competitors were sent on their way, one eyewitness wrote, "The Garden was turned into a lunatic asylum." Much of the crowd's attention was directed at the mysterious Jaybee, who wore a fancy white vest emblazoned with a blue dart on the front and a blue horseshoe on the back. The dart, he said, represented speed. "The horseshoe," he explained, "is a token of my wishes for good luck to those behind me." Jaybee walked "like the pretty man at a picnic" and "furnished the amusement that every walking-match crowd has to have." It was rumored that he had hired an electrician to administer electric shocks to him during the race, believing they would increase his endurance.

"He was greeted everywhere with invitations to 'brace up,' 'strike out bold,' and 'pull down his vest,'" the reporter for the *Times* wrote, "but he took the jibing good-naturedly, and kept on at his work."

By two o'clock in the morning, Frank Hart was in the lead, and at least a thousand spectators were still inside the Garden, many of them stretched out on the floor or on benches. Unlike during some previous six-day races, the Garden would not be cleared of "loungers and sleepers" each night. Once again, for just fifty cents, one paper noted, these "patient lodgers" could "sleep under cover for a whole week—an unusual circumstance with them."

By Tuesday evening, six of the eighteen starters had already dropped out of the race, including the ailing belt-holder Nicholas Murphy. The supposedly aristocratic Jaybee, however, soldiered on, much to the delight of the crowd. "His score crept up very slowly," one reporter noted, "and he has a fine chance, if he does not give out, of winning the last place." Jaybee would dodder on until Thursday, when a carriage pulled up to the rear entrance of the Garden and swept him away.

The *New York Sun* would later reveal that Jaybee's real name was John Brinkerhoff, and he was no aristocrat. He was a fifty-six-year-old Columbia grad who'd gone to San Francisco, made a fortune, and then lost everything in one of the city's periodic fires. Returning to New York, he started a venture publishing advertising circulars. "In the course of his business he walked a great deal without fatigue," the *Sun* reported. "Becoming reduced in circumstances, his friends thought that, even at his time of life, he stood a good chance of winning first prize in a big walking match." His friends were wrong. When he left the race, Jaybee had completed just 140 miles and was in last place among the remaining competitors.

Madison Square Garden in the midst of a big-time walking match was still a place to see and be seen, and on Tuesday night two of the biggest celebrities in the country were spotted at the Garden. They were also two of the smallest: General Tom Thumb and Commodore Nutt. The two little people, forty and forty-three inches tall, respectively, came to fame with P. T. Barnum, who exploited their diminutive stature for colossal profit. Tom Thumb, born Charles Sherwood Stratton in Connecticut in 1838, was just five years old when Barnum, a distant relative, taught him a routine that included singing, dancing, and impersonations and took him on a tour of America. Stratton became a staple of Barnum's circus as well as his freak show in New York. George Washington Morrison Nutt, born in New Hampshire in 1844, was seventeen when Barnum hired him to join the freak show. Stratton and Nutt became close friends and often performed together. (Nutt was Stratton's best man when he married Lavinia Warren, another little person, in 1863. Nutt's wife, Lilian Elston, was an average-sized woman and a devoted wife.)

By the time they stopped by the great walking match at Madison Square Garden on that cold Tuesday night in April of 1880, Tom Thumb and Commodore Nutt were in the waning stages of their careers. Barnum's freak show had closed years before. Tom Thumb and his wife now traveled the country "placing themselves on exhibition." Commodore Nutt was planning to open a saloon on Sixth Avenue.* But their celebrity was still firmly intact, and when they were spotted at the Garden, according to one account,

---

* Sadly, in a little more than three years, both men would be dead. Commodore Nutt died of kidney failure on May 25, 1881. He was thirty-seven. Tom Thumb died of a stroke on July 15, 1883. He was forty-five.

"a rush was immediately made for them, everybody being anxious to see them."

At midnight on Tuesday night, after two days of racing, Frank Hart was still in the lead with 225 miles, though he was only a single mile ahead of his nearest rival. By midnight Thursday night, Hart had racked up 405 miles and stretched his lead to ten miles. Hart was averaging more than a hundred miles a day, a pace that would shatter Blower Brown's world record. "To all appearances the darkey was as fresh and walked with as much ease as when he started the first night," the *New York Tribune* reported. But Hart was not as fresh as he appeared. In his tent at one point he fell asleep so deeply that his trainer, Jack Smith, was unable to awaken him. Alarmed, the trainer "went to work in earnest" on Hart, who finally staggered to his feet.

"Where am I?" Hart asked.

"You are in the walk for the O'Leary belt," Smith answered.

"How far am I behind?" asked Hart, who was, in fact, leading the race at the time.

"Ten miles," said Smith, not hesitating for an instant to seize the opportunity to motivate his charge.

William Pegram, one of the two other African Americans in the race, was in second place, and the headline in the next day's *Tribune* read, THE NEGROES LEAD THE WALK. Several times during the race, Hart and Pegram, along with the third black pedestrian, Edward Williams, circled the track together in a show of solidarity, demonstrating, as one paper put it, "their constitutional right to walk in public, without regard to any previous condition whatever." (The Thirteenth Amendment had been adopted only fifteen years earlier, so all three men had been born when slavery was still legal in the United States.) "Pegram and Williams frequently kept by Hart's side as he ran," the *Times* noted, "and gave him such encouragement as they could, evidently wanting to see a man of their own color carry off the honors."

It was turning out to be another profitable week at the Garden. The concessions were booming. The bar was the "busiest part of the whole place." A lunch counter reported brisk sales as well, though some customers complained about the "extravagant prices." At the tobacco stand, it was said that a good five-cent cigar could be had—for fifteen cents. Only the sales of reserved seats were disappointing. It would be too much to say the arrangement was rejected as undemocratic, but, as one reporter wrote of the more expensive seats, "Not more than a dozen of the chairs have been occupied at any one time, for the view from there is no better than from many parts of the floor, and there is no chance to walk about and see the sights." In New York, at least, the wealthier spectators seemed to prefer to be on the floor, closer to the action, rubbing elbows with the hoi polloi.

At ten o'clock on Friday night, Hart was at 488 miles, twenty-nine more than his nearest competitor. His victory was no longer in doubt. It only remained to be seen whether he would break Blower Brown's world record. To do so, he only needed to complete 66 miles over the next 26 hours. His prospects seemed good. "His trainers said that he never was in better condition," the *Times* reported, "and his face and general appearance indicated that this was true." At 4:22 on Saturday morning Hart completed his 500th mile, putting him nearly two hours ahead of Brown's record pace. But he seemed to be running out of gas. Around noon, he staggered back to his tent, where his trainer, Jack Smith, was waiting for him.

"Jack, I'm terrible sick," Hart said.

"What's the matter with you?"

"I'm awful dizzy."

"I'll fix you," said Smith, who drenched Hart's head and neck with water, then made him lie down with a wet towel wrapped around his head. After about twenty minutes, Smith sent Hart back out. Apparently he was rejuvenated, for it was said that he was soon sailing around the track "with the gallant strut of a gamecock." During the last hours of the race, Hart would also be "stimulated with champagne."

Later that afternoon, Hart received a telegram from a friend who owned a restaurant in Boston, who told the pedestrian how his performance was being received in his hometown:

> The West End is all excitement over your wonderful achievement. Wipe out the English record, and give Boston the greatest pedestrian of the world. It looks like a holiday on Cambridge street.
> Henry P. Kelly.

By now Hart had been presented with so many bouquets that one onlooker said his tent "looked like a florist's shop." Dan O'Leary, the Irishman from Chicago who had mentored Hart, was bursting with pride at his performance. "Hart is a wonderful walker," O'Leary told a reporter. "He has the strength and vim to do anything, and I am sure that he has not yet put his best foot forward."

By 5:00 PM on Saturday the Garden was already filled with spectators, nearly all of whom intended to remain in the building until the race ended late that night. "There were many ladies in the pack," the *Sun* reported. "The first question asked by women who visit the walk for the first time is: 'Which is Hart?' When pointed out to them their eyes follow him around the sawdust for hours." At 5:50 PM Hart completed his 550th mile, a neat coincidence that was much remarked upon by those in attendance. Hart was now dressed in his finest walking costume: a blue-and-white striped satin shirt, with black velvet trunks over white tights. On his head he wore a black-and-red cap.

At 6:33 PM on that Saturday, April 10, 1880, Frank Hart surpassed 553 miles, eclipsing Blower Brown's six-day record. The crowd cheered ecstatically. Even the other pedestrians stopped racing to acknowledge the achievement. His trainer, Jack Smith, handed him a broomstick to which the Stars and Stripes had been attached. Hart ran around the track with it. "From this time on," the *Sun* reported, "there was not an instant of time in which a roar was not echoing through the Garden."

After his 563rd mile, Hart tied the flag around his waist and completed two more miles while the band played "Yankee Doodle." At nine o'clock he made his final lap, wearing around his waist the O'Leary Belt that was now his. The *New York Sun* described the scene:

> While he made that final tour of the track the noise of the vast throng of spectators was almost deafening. Men cheered, shouted, clapped their hands and pounded the floor with their canes; ladies stood up in the boxes waving their handkerchiefs and hurrahing; even the officials connected with the match, the reporters and the policemen caught the inflection, and vied with each other in adding to the uproar. That wound up the great walk, and then, while the band played "Home, sweet, home," the spectators slowly departed.

Hart finished the race with 565 miles, besting the world record by an astonishing twelve miles. William Pegram, one of the two other African Americans in the race, finished second with 543 miles. Edward Williams, the third black entrant, finished in seventh place with a commendable 509 miles—enough to take home a share of the prize money.

The secret to Hart's success in the race was simple: he almost never rested. During the week he was absent from the track for a total of just 23 hours and 23 minutes. That meant, on average, he was locomoting more than twenty hours a day for six straight days. It was a punishing pace, and it was the third time he'd done it in less than eight months. It seemed unsustainable.

For his efforts, Hart would collect $7,967.86 in gate money, the $9,000 in entrance fees, and the $1,000 bonus for breaking the six-day record. It was also reported that Hart had bet $3,600 on himself, bringing his total earnings for the week to $21,567.86 (roughly $480,000 today).

Frank Hart was the first African American to win such a prestigious championship in American sports. He was now not just the most celebrated black athlete in the country—he was the most celebrated athlete of any color. The stunning news of his record-breaking victory in the second O'Leary Belt race was headlined in papers from coast to coast the next day: HART LEADS THE WORLD (*Lancaster [Pennsylvania] Daily Intelligencer*). THE COLORED BOY GETS AWAY WITH THE BELT (*Salt Lake Daily Herald*). THE TWO NEGROES THE BEST TWO MEN (*New York Tribune*). THE KING OF HARTS (*Kennebec [Maine] Journal*). The *New York Sun* published on its front page a full-length illustration of Hart wearing the O'Leary Belt, standing with his arms folded across his chest. Hart's achievement was widely hailed, though a few papers refused to recognize the superiority of this black athlete. One New York paper attributed Hart's victory to "a strong admixture of French blood in his veins." Even if true, this failed to explain why Pegram, an African American with no such "admixture," finished second. Hart's success also nettled some of his fellow African Americans. "In speaking of himself and achievements he invectively denounces the colored people of the North," an African American newspaper called the *New York Freeman* later reported, "declaring that they are prejudiced to him and have at no time treated him with the courtesy which he has received from his

FRANK H. HART, of Boston.

This image of Frank Hart appeared on the front page of the *New York Sun* on Sunday, April 11, 1880, the day after he won the second O'Leary Belt race at Madison Square Garden. COURTESY OF LIBRARY OF CONGRESS

people in the South. He remarks that white men made him what he is and as long as he can get support from that source he will be found among them."

On the afternoon of Thursday, April 15, Frank Hart was honored as "champion pedestrian of the world" in a ceremony at the Fifth Avenue Theatre in New York. (Charles Rowell, the holder of the Astley Belt, undoubtedly would have taken exception to the title, which was rather nebulous, to be sure.) "Frank looked as bright and spry as a West Point cadet on evening dress parade," a *Boston Globe* reporter who was in attendance wrote. "The audience greeted him with a storm of applause." Unfortunately, Hart had caught a cold and was unable to address the audience. Instead, the theater manager made a few complimentary remarks, after which Hart "gracefully bowed his acknowledgement" and was sent off with a rousing rendition of "Yankee Doodle" by the orchestra.

Back home in Boston, Frank Hart received a hero's welcome, complete with a public reception fit for "such an athlete as the champion pedestrian of the world, who was honest under every temptation and is a living example of what temperate habits and uprightness of character will do for a man in his walk of life" (no pun intended, presumably). The O'Leary Belt was put on display at the restaurant owned by his friend Henry Kelly on the corner of Cambridge and Temple Streets.

Hart did not long revel in the adulation, however, for in July, just three months after his record-shattering performance at the Garden, he was reported to be "dangerously ill." At one point he was said to be "out of his head." The diagnosis was "congestion of the brain," a common medical term at the time that described a variety of ailments, including cerebral hemorrhage, hydrocephalus, meningitis, and stroke. (The cause of Edgar Allan Poe's death in 1849 was determined to be "congestion of the brain.") A *Boston Globe* reporter who called on Hart at his home on North Anderson Street on July 25 found him to be suffering from a fever.

"I feel much better today," Hart told the reporter, "but my physician says I must keep quiet. Ice seems to be the only comfort that I have. My head worries me considerably, but I am satisfied that I will come out all right."

Not surprisingly, Hart's physician attributed the malady to the patient's occupation. "Dr. Stackpole ascribes Hart's present trouble to overexertion," the *Boston Herald* reported, "as well as to a continual strain on his physical powers before properly recuperating after each of the severe trials he has subjected himself to during the past year. Added to this, the great strain that he has endured by loss of sleep in his tasks has been sufficient to affect his nervous system."

For weeks the Boston papers carried regular updates on Hart's health. On July 27 his condition was reported to be "if anything, worse," with symptoms resembling typhoid fever. On August 4 he was said to be "rapidly improving." On August 6 he told a reporter, "I'm all right now, but I've had a siege of it." His trainer, Jack Smith, who was nursing him, said, "The crisis is past . . . and you can bet your bottom dollar that he will win another race."

On August 21 a *Globe* reporter who went to Hart's home found him sitting in a chair chatting quietly with some friends. "I am getting along nicely and improving daily," Hart said. "Every day this week I have gone out for an hour or two's ride in a carriage. In fact I am a hundred percent better than I was a week ago." But the illness had clearly taken a toll on Hart. He had lost about twenty pounds and was apparently suffering from vertigo, as he reported some difficulty getting around the house. He said he would not resume training until late fall at the earliest. That meant he would not be able to take part in the next Astley Belt race, scheduled for November in London, but he said he still expected to win "a few more trophies" after he was fully recovered.

On September 26 the *Globe* reported that Hart had "thoroughly recovered from his late serious illness, but will require some time yet ere he can undertake another six days 'go-as-you-please.'" The precise nature of Hart's illness can never be known, but doctors who have recently studied his case believe he may have suffered from viral encephalitis. Hart had hoped to go to London to watch the sixth Astley Belt race in November, but he was still not well enough to travel. It's probably just as well, for Charles Rowell won the race with 566 miles, breaking Hart's own six-day record by a single mile. The victory was Rowell's second consecutive in an Astley Belt race, and if he won the next one, the belt would be his to keep forever.

Frank Hart would eventually return to the tanbark, but he was never the same pedestrian he had been before the illness, and he never won another major long-distance race.

13

HIPPODROMING

or

THE SUSPICION WAS VERY GENERAL

By EARLY 1881, WITH THE SPORT at the height of its popularity, a specter loomed over pedestrianism that threatened to destroy it: rumors were rife that races were being fixed.

At the time, gambling existed in a gray area. In New York, as in most other states, there were laws banning lotteries, but none that specifically prohibited other forms of gambling. In New York City, bookmakers, usually in cahoots with corrupt police officials, operated with impunity. At Madison Square Garden, the bookies were under the aegis of the notorious Captain Alexander "Clubber" Williams, who probably received a kickback on every bet placed. There was even a section of the arena specifically reserved for bookmakers. Working with their sleeves rolled up, they scrawled their odds on blackboards and traded betting slips as nimbly as a cardsharp dealing a hand of poker.

In fact, bookmakers made up a powerful and influential lobby in New York. When the city attempted to explicitly ban gambling inside the Garden, a group of bookies went to court seeking an injunction, which was granted. "What wonder that there is so little respect for the law in New York," the *Brooklyn Daily Eagle* lamented, "when even the courts exercise their powers in behalf of those who are seeking to evade it."

As pedestrianism grew more popular with the public, it naturally grew more popular with gamblers. Inevitably, there were reports that unscrupulous pedestrians were colluding with bookmakers to "hippodrome" races. At the time, the common term for an athletic venue, "hippodrome," was synonymous with fixing matches—a measure of how prevalent the practice was. The bookies took wagers not only on winners and losers but on everything from the number of laps a particular pedestrian might complete in a given amount of time to which pedestrian would be the first (and second, and third) to drop out of a race. And as many ways as there were to wager, there were opportunities for hippodroming.

After the fifth Astley Belt race in September 1879, a rumor circulated to the effect that the winner, Charles Rowell, had collaborated with gamblers. After the fourth day of that race, Rowell had been on pace to complete 600 miles. Yet he finished with just 530 (or 524, as it turned out, owing to the short track). It emerged that bookmakers had taken many bets that Rowell would complete more than 530 miles. The suspicion was that Rowell colluded with the bookies for a share of the wagers by intentionally completing no more than 530 miles. A similar suspicion arose after Frank Hart's victory in the second O'Leary Belt race in April 1880. At 7:30 on the final night of the race, the *Brooklyn Daily Eagle* reported,

> The bookmakers threw out as a bait to the uninitiated bets of 3 to 1 that Hart would beat 565 miles, 3 to 2 that he would beat 567 miles, and 6 to 1 that he would not beat 570 miles. It was whispered that the champion would stop at 565 miles, thus giving the bookmakers an opportunity to win on the second and third bets. This suspicion was justified by the result.

It must be emphasized that neither Charles Rowell nor Frank Hart was ever proven to have colluded with bookmakers, and Hart, for his part, always insisted he competed scrupulously. "I must go straight and win," he once said, "or I'll go back to groceries."

But there were numerous reports that lesser races were definitely fixed. In July 1880, a referee overseeing a match in San Francisco resigned in disgust after denouncing the affair as a hippodrome.

In an effort to reassure the public before the third O'Leary Belt race, scheduled to begin on February 28, 1881, at Madison Square Garden, the match referee, William B. Curtis, bluntly promised reporters, "There will be no hippodroming in the O'Leary Belt contest." The promise proved to ring hollow.

It should have been an auspicious week. The presidency transferred from Rutherford B. Hayes to James A. Garfield. It was the twentieth anniversary of Edward Payson Weston's famous walk from Boston to Washington for Lincoln's inauguration, the walk that had launched pedestrianism in America. But what happened in Madison Square Garden that week was not auspicious for pedestrianism.

In the first two days of the race, twelve of the nineteen starters dropped out, some under suspicious circumstances. Frank Hart, competing in his first six-day race since winning the last O'Leary Belt contest eleven months earlier, dropped out before noon on the first day after completing just 63 miles. Even considering his recent health problems, this raised eyebrows. Hart was one of the favorites going into the race. He blamed his withdrawal on "neuralgia" (nerve pain) and even produced a note from his doctor, Alexander B. Mott:

> This is to certify that I have examined Hart and find that he is suffering from intercostal neuralgia caused by taking cold during the walk from wearing too light clothing, and that the trouble would be increased by his continuing to walk in the match; but he will be relieved by rest and treatment in a few days.

Nonetheless, "the suspicion was very general that he had been bought off." It was said that Hart had "never looked better" when he started the race and "showed no signs of suffering while on the track."

"Skeptical persons believe that there is a little secret history behind Hart's action," the *New York Sun* reported. "The bookmakers as usual reaped the benefit of the surprise."

The skepticism only intensified later that first day when John Hughes, another favorite in the race, "began to show signs of intense suffering." Around ten o'clock that night he began to stagger and "fell to the ground in a swoon." A doctor pronounced that Hughes was suffering from "'acute stomachic rheumatism,' resulting from over-exertion." Hughes abandoned the race after completing just 115 miles. After his withdrawal he was said to be "the very picture of a man in perfect health."

"At the time of Hughes's mishap the betting was greatly in his favor," the *Sun* drily noted, "and his retirement will cause much money to change hands abruptly."

With two of the sport's biggest names out of the race and charges of hippodroming abounding, attendance plummeted. The total number of tickets sold for the six days was 21,101, with about a quarter of those sold before Hart and Hughes withdrew. After expenses, the race netted a profit of just $650. As his share of the receipts, the winner, a Minnesotan named Peter Panchot, received $300, as well as the $1,800 in entrance fees paid by the other runners, for a total of $2,100 (roughly $47,000 today). Not too shabby for 1881, but a far cry from the heady paydays of Charles Rowell just two years before.

Three months later another six-day race sponsored by Dan O'Leary was held at the Garden. Early on the morning of the final day of the race, the *Boston Globe* reported, "an utterly unexpected and exciting incident occurred":

Ephraim Clow of Boston, who had been backed heavily to secure second place, and who stood third on the score-sheet, with every prospect in his favor, as he was undoubtedly the freshest man on the track, suddenly left the track and went to his room. Inquiries were at once made as to the reason for his action. He gave various excuses, all of a flimsy character, and finally bluntly said that he would not stay in the race unless $500 was placed in his hand. He was told that O'Leary would give him a check for $500 if he would stay on. Clow curtly answered that checks were no good, and, donning his every-day clothes, left the garden. The impression prevails that Clow has been captured by the bookmakers. Certainly his conduct afforded good grounds for such a suspicion.

Of this particular race the *Spirit of the Times* said, "This affair was, in its inception, management, and results, a striking specimen of the degradation into which six-day pedestrianism is speedily sinking."

These hippodroming scandals gave the moral crusaders seeking to ban long-distance races even more ammunition. The scandals also highlighted a weakness of pedestrianism that would eventually contribute to its downfall: it had no central governing authority. Unlike baseball's National League, which was overseen by a powerful governing body, pedestrianism was leaderless. On the contrary, dozens of promoters and managers competed with each other for a piece of the action. Without the equivalent of a modern-day commissioner or ruling body, there was no single entity charged with rooting out hippodroming and punishing violators, or banning unscrupulous promoters, managers, and trainers. In short, there was no one to ensure the legitimacy of the sport and foster public confidence in it. The absence of a central governing authority would be felt most acutely in the ensuing years, as pedestrianism faced increasing competition and economic uncertainty.

In June 1881, Charles Rowell won the Astley Belt race for the third consecutive time, giving him permanent possession of the celebrated belt and putting an end to the greatest series of races in the history of pedestrianism.

The end of the Astley Belt races marked the end of pedestrianism's golden age. All sorts of new belts were contrived to replace it—the Ennis Belt, the Fox Diamond Belt, the Rose Belt, etc.—but none could match the Astley's popularity and prestige. In fact, the myriad six-day races concocted to replace the Astley only oversaturated the market, fatiguing aficionados.

There would be no more O'Leary Belt races either, for Dan O'Leary, the Irishman from Chicago, had decided to get out of promotion. He was coming out of retirement to return to the tanbark.

14

BICYCLES AND BASEBALL

or

TOO FREE USE OF STIMULANTS

IN NOVEMBER 1885, EXACTLY TEN YEARS after their first epic encounter at the Interstate Exposition Building in Chicago, Edward Payson Weston and Dan O'Leary, those two great old rivals on the tanbark, surprised the sports world by announcing a rematch of sorts. They would walk twelve hours a day, "fair heel and toe," until one of them reached 2,500 miles. The match would unfold in two- to six-day increments from December 1885 to February 1886 in nine cities throughout the Northeast and Midwest.

The event was sponsored by New York temperance advocates who offered a $3,000 purse on the condition that Weston and O'Leary walk only in venues where alcohol was not sold. The winner would receive two-thirds of both the purse and the gate. It was a peculiar arrangement, for, while Weston was a well-known teetotaler, O'Leary's fondness for "stimulants" was legendary. Maybe old Dan just needed the money.

The traveling match commenced on the morning of Monday, December 7, at the Metropolitan Rink in Newark. Weston wore a blue cloak over a ruffled shirt and slapped his riding crop against his leather leggings as he walked. He was his usual showboating self, chatting with spectators and occasionally playing the cornet. O'Leary, who wore a flannel shirt and black trunks over white tights, seemed like the O'Leary of old, looking straight ahead and walking "like a piece of machinery."

The match was akin to an old-timers' game. By now Weston was forty-six and O'Leary thirty-nine. The two pedestrians were long past their prime, although one thing hadn't changed: their mutual antipathy. In fact, if anything, it seemed that Weston was getting on O'Leary's nerves even more than usual. At the Cosmopolitan Rink in New York in late December, the *New York Times* reported, "Weston sang snatches of songs in a cracked and uncertain tone of voice."

"Shut up, you jumping-jack!" shouted O'Leary across the rink in the evening, when Weston was at his musical exercise.

"I'll take my oath," retorted Weston, "that that man has no ear for Eye-talian opera!"

A decade earlier, thousands of people had packed the largest venues on both sides of the Atlantic to watch these two men walk in circles, but now there was little nostalgia for them. Attendance was meager. On their last day in New York, fewer than one hundred people paid to see them. "I have seen more money in a single night than we've taken in here all the week," O'Leary grumbled as he left the rink.

By early January, when the match reached Rochester, New York, O'Leary had opened up a sizable lead, 1,292 miles to 1,260. But by the middle of that month, O'Leary's lead was dwindling and he had started acting erratically. There were whispers that he was drinking heavily. In Erie, Pennsylvania, O'Leary was "terribly abusive" toward Weston. "O'Leary became troublesome and pushed Weston off the track twice," one paper reported. The spectators hissed O'Leary, but Weston exhorted them to excuse his opponent "on account of his condition."

By the time the tour reached its final stop in Chicago on January 30, O'Leary's lead had shrunk to just nine miles (2,067 to 2,058). On February 2, O'Leary collapsed on the track, due to, according to one account, the "too free use of stimulants." In other words, he was drunk as a skunk.

O'Leary never returned to the race. It was an inglorious end for one of the giants of pedestrianism. Weston kept walking, alone on the track, until, on February 6, he completed his 2,500th mile to collect his two-thirds of both the purse and the gate.

After the match, Weston announced his retirement from pedestrianism. "It became such a business for gamblers and other disreputable people that I am glad to be out of it," he said.

A little less than three years later, in the autumn of 1888, in a "go as you please" race at Madison Square Garden, an Englishman named George Littlewood set a new six-day record with a whopping 623 miles. It would stand as the last great record in the history of pedestrianism.[*]

The following July, Madison Square Garden (formerly Barnum's Grand Roman Hippodrome and Gilmore's Garden), the scene of so many historic pedestrian matches, was demolished. By then, according to *Harper's Weekly*, it had become a "patched-up, grimy, drafty, combustible, old shell."

The dilapidated rattrap was replaced by a magnificent new arena on the same site. Designed by the renowned architect Stanford White,[†] the new arena, also called Madison Square Garden (and known to historians as Madison Square Garden II), opened

---

[*] Littlewood's record would stand for nearly a century, until 1984, when a twenty-eight-year-old Greek marathoner named Yiannis Kouros, who'd doubted such a record was even possible, covered 635 miles in six days.

[†] White, a notorious philanderer with a humongous mustache, would later be murdered in the building's rooftop restaurant. He was shot by the jealous husband of a woman with whom White had had an inappropriate relationship when she was sixteen.

on June 16, 1890.* It was a Beaux Arts masterpiece, topped with a thirty-two-story tower on which was perched an eighteen-foot bronze Augustus Saint-Gaudens statue of a nude Diana, goddess of the hunt, who acted as a weather vane, her bare breasts pointing whichever way the wind was blowing.†

But, by the time the new Madison Square Garden opened, pedestrianism had been eclipsed by a new sport: bicycle racing. The first major bicycle race in the new Garden began shortly after midnight on Monday, October 19, 1891. Adopting the pedestrians' six-day format, fourteen riders on "penny-farthing" bicycles—the kind with the absurdly oversized front wheel, so named for the British penny and farthing coins, the former being much larger than the latter—raced around a wooden oval with banked turns, racking up as many miles as their bodies would allow, until just before midnight the following Saturday.

"The six-day bicycle race is an interesting novelty to New Yorkers, and there is much about the tournament to recommend it," a *New York Sun* reporter wrote halfway through the race. "It is a clean sport, and the natty, tireless wheelmen, with their unceasing spurts, coupled with a fascinating fear of an accident whenever the riders dash around the steep inclined corners at full speed, are a vast improvement over the six-day pedestrians, who were wont at this stage to become dirty, haggard, footsore, and weary, inspiring nothing but sympathy as they hobbled around the track in agony."

---

* In 1925, Madison Square Garden II would be replaced by Madison Square Garden III, which was situated farther uptown, on Eighth Avenue between Forty-Ninth and Fiftieth Streets. In 1968, Madison Square Garden III would be replaced by the current Madison Square Garden (IV) between Seventh and Eighth Avenues and Thirty-First and Thirty-Third Streets.

† In 1892, Saint-Gaudens, who felt the statue was too big for the tower, replaced it with a smaller copper version. The original Diana has been lost, but the second Diana now resides comfortably inside the Philadelphia Museum of Art.

The second Madison Square Garden, which was built on the site of the first, opened in 1890. It was known for its distinctive tower, on top of which was perched a statue of the goddess Diana. Here the building is pictured around 1905. COURTESY OF LIBRARY OF CONGRESS

An Irish immigrant named William Martin won the race with a world record 1,466 miles. "At the finish," the *New York Times* reported, "the building was crowded and hundreds were clamoring for admission."

By the end of 1891, pedestrianism was a fad whose time had passed. Even boxing, once considered nothing better than a brutal blood sport, had eclipsed it.

In the late 1880s, prizefighters in the United States began adopting the Marquess of Queensberry rules, which had first been published in Britain in 1867. The rules, named for the Scottish nobleman who promulgated them, revolutionized boxing. They established three-minute rounds with one-minute intervals, and a ten-second count for boxers who were knocked down. Most significantly, the Queensberry rules required fighters to wear "fair-sized boxing gloves of the best quality." These padded gloves were intended to make the sport less brutal, though, as the historian Elliot Gorn wrote, "Gloves protected fighters' hands more than their heads, added weight to each punch, and allowed men to throw innumerable blows to such hard-but-vulnerable spots as the temples and jaw." In Gorn's estimation, the gloves actually made boxing more dangerous; the Queensberry rules "merely pasted a thin veneer of respectability over the brutality."

Nonetheless, the Queensberry rules improved boxing's image and prompted many jurisdictions to relax their laws against the sport. Prizefighting began to move from the back rooms of saloons to the center of giant arenas like Madison Square Garden, from the margins of society to the middle. In 1890 the New Orleans City Council authorized "glove fights," and, on September 7, 1892, the city hosted the first legal heavyweight championship fight in the United States: "Gentleman" Jim Corbett knocked out John L. Sullivan in the twenty-first round before ten thousand frenzied spectators at the Olympic Club. The legalization of boxing transformed the sport. "Boxing was becoming commercial entertainment," Elliot Gorn wrote, "more accessible than ever before to all classes."

Bicycle racing's popularity, meanwhile, continued to skyrocket, largely due to the introduction of the "safety bicycle," the kind with two same-sized wheels and a chain drivetrain, which we still ride today. An Englishman named John Kemp Starley is widely credited with inventing the first practical safety bicycle, which he dubbed the Rover, in 1885.* By the end of 1893, bicycle racers had adopted the much faster and more nimble safety bicycle, and watching the "safeties" race was even more thrilling than watching the old penny-farthings.

As pedestrianism's popularity declined, a few prominent pedestrians abandoned their sport's sinking ship and jumped on the bike-racing bandwagon, most notably Astley Belt champion Charles Rowell, but none enjoyed appreciable success. Frank Hart, Dan O'Leary's African American protégé, even tried his hand at six-day roller-skating races, which were briefly in vogue. (Hart also played shortstop for an all-black baseball team called the St. Louis Black Stockings.)

In the early 1890s, pedestrianism also faced increasing competition from team sports, especially baseball. In 1879, the National League introduced the notorious "reserve clause," which bound a player to his team in perpetuity, unless he was traded or released.† The owners said this prevented the richest teams from signing all the best players. But it also kept salaries low by eliminating free agency. The owners also imposed a $2,500 salary cap.

These measures were unpopular with the players, naturally, but they were good for the league's bottom line. According to historian Steven A. Riess, "Overall, the National League made seven hundred and fifty thousand dollars in the period between 1885 and 1889, a 300 percent increase over the early 1880s. By contrast, players' salaries rose by just 30 percent." By 1890, the National League had become a stable, profitable enterprise. Of the eight

---

* In the early twentieth century, Starley's company would begin manufacturing automobiles under the Rover name, and automobiles would continue to be manufactured under that name in Britain until 2005.

† The reserve clause would survive nearly a century, until 1975, when it was finally struck down by a federal mediator.

clubs in the league that season, only one, the Cleveland Spiders, is not extant today.*

But, ultimately, what killed pedestrianism was legislation—ironically, legislation that was designed to restrict bicycle racing. As bicycle racing grew in popularity throughout the 1890s, the sport faced the same backlash that pedestrianism had faced a decade earlier. Moral crusaders decried bicycle racing as inhumane, even worse than pedestrianism. Indeed, bicycle racers faced greater dangers than the pedestrians in six-day races, with "spills" not uncommon, especially in the latter stages of a race, when the riders were delirious with exhaustion. Numerous bicycle racers were injured in accidents. There were also rumors that some riders were using strychnine to stay awake and on the track.

As the decade progressed, the calls for the abolition of the sport intensified, with many influential newspapers joining the chorus. "An athletic contest in which participants 'go queer' in their heads, and strain their powers until their faces become hideous with the tortures that rack them, is not sport," wrote the *New York Times* in 1897. "It is brutality."

A December 1898 six-day bicycle race at Madison Square Garden was especially brutal. Several riders were injured in accidents, and several others "went to pieces."

"Few more hideous and revolting struggles have been seen in this city than the exhibition of torture which was going on last week," the *New York Tribune* wrote after the race in an editorial headlined SIX DAYS OF TORMENT. "Under the laws of this State it is a crime to attempt suicide," the paper noted. "Ought it not to be a crime under our laws to promote a six-day cycle race or to take part in it?"

A New York state assemblyman named Cornelius Collins believed it ought to be, and in early 1899 he introduced a bill to

---

* The other seven clubs were (and still are) the Braves, Cubs, Dodgers, Giants, Phillies, Pirates, and Reds.

ban six-day racing in the state. Although it specifically targeted bicycle racing, the bill aimed to ban "any contest of skill, speed, or endurance, which shall continue for more than forty-eight hours." After forty-eight hours, the bill continued, "it shall be unlawful for any contestant . . . to continue in such a race or contest for a longer time than twelve hours during any twenty-four hours."

Surprisingly, one of the bill's staunchest supporters was the League of American Wheelmen (now known as the League of American Bicyclists), the leading national organization for cyclists. The LAW believed six-day races were giving bicycling a bad name. It's also possible that baseball's National League, now facing competition from the Western League (soon to be renamed the American League), might have lobbied for the bill as a way to kill off another rival for the attention—and dollars—of sports fans.

In any event, the Collins bill passed the New York legislature and was sent to the governor, a hearty man who never shied away from feats of physical endurance. In fact, he liked sports very much. "There is a certain tendency . . . to underestimate or overlook the need of the virile, masterful qualities of the heart and mind," this governor had once written. "There is no better way of counteracting this tendency than by encouraging bodily exercise and especially the sports which develop such qualities as courage, resolution and endurance."

Yet he signed the Collins bill anyway.

And so, American pedestrianism, which began with Abraham Lincoln, ended with Teddy Roosevelt.

EPILOGUE

THE LAST PEDESTRIANS

or

NOW ABOUT EVERYBODY RIDES

IN 1880 PEDESTRIANISM was the most popular spectator sport in the United States, indeed in all the English-speaking world; its fans were so passionate that they were not averse to rioting.

Twenty years later, it was dead.

The Collins law effectively killed pedestrianism. With six-day races, the most popular iteration of the sport, banned in New York City, the country's largest and most lucrative market, the sport didn't stand a chance.* While six-days continued to be staged from time to time in smaller cities such as Philadelphia and Saint Louis, the purses were too small to justify the pedestrians' efforts. A few six-day "relays" were staged at Madison Square Garden, with teams of two pedestrians each competing for no more than the legally permitted twelve hours a day, but the races failed to generate the excitement, or the gate receipts, of the old-fashioned

---

* The Collins law is still on the books in New York (under "Offensive Exhibition" in the penal code), so six-day races are still illegal in the state. Violators can be sentenced to a maximum of fifteen days in jail.

six-days. (The bicycle racers, however, fared much better; their six-day relays turned out to be quite popular, and remained so until the onset of the Great Depression. In fact, six-day bicycle races are still popular in Europe, though the racers usually compete only from 6:00 PM to 2:00 AM each day.)

On April 1, 1906, the *Salt Lake Herald* published a small article headlined SIX-DAY WALKERS OF OLD. "Six-day pedestrians," the piece began, "popular in the days of old, are now forgotten." The article went on to update readers on the whereabouts of some of the old pedestrians. Daniel O'Leary, the Irish immigrant from Chicago who'd won two Astley Belt races, was back in the bookselling business, working in the South for a large publishing house. "He is past 60 years of age," the paper reported, "and although he made at least $60,000 in matches he has none of his fortune left."

"Frank Hart, the negro wonder, is dying with consumption in Colorado." Hart would linger for two more years before succumbing to tuberculosis in 1908 at the age of fifty or so. Although he was once the most famous black athlete in the country, his passing elicited little notice. Only a handful of African American papers acknowledged his death. The *Cleveland Gazette* estimated that Hart earned more than $100,000 in six-day races. "Like many other sporting men," the paper noted, "he was a high liver and good spender." For the last twenty years of his life, the paper said, Hart "lived off the charity of his friends."

Charles Rowell, the Cambridge rower who'd won three consecutive Astley Belt races to take permanent possession of the belt, would die a year after Hart at the age of fifty-three. Although his career winnings easily amounted to more than $1 million in today's money, Rowell had a gambling problem, and according to one newspaper report, he was "face to face with poverty at the time of his death." He'd even been forced to pawn off the Astley Belt at one point. (It was later claimed out of hock and is now on display at the Cambridge & County Folk Museum in Rowell's hometown. The fate of the O'Leary Belt, however, is a mystery.)

In 1906, only Edward Payson Weston, ever the restless tramp, was still walking. Although retired from competitive pedestrianism, Weston had returned to his roots, undertaking long overland walks. In May 1906, at age sixty-seven, he walked more than ninety miles from Philadelphia to New York in less than twenty-four hours, stopping to rest just once, for thirty minutes in New Brunswick, New Jersey. On this walk, however, Weston was forced to contend with something new on the roads: automobiles, an innovation he detested because they caused people to walk less.

A large crowd greeted him when he arrived in New York, but by now Weston was regarded as something of a relic, like the last living veteran of a long-forgotten war. As he climbed the steps of City Hall, a voice cried out, "Good work, old man!"

Commenting on the walk, the *New York Mail* praised Weston for having aged more gracefully than most other professional athletes. "Mr. Weston is neither a saloonkeeper nor a sot," the paper said. "He did not burst upon the world for a year or so, 'go the pace' while the pride of youth was upon him, and, like some scores of prizefighters, become a 'good old has-been' at thirty-five. . . . For his demonstration that unusual physical gifts are not of the moment and need not be squandered, but may be husbanded to make old age admirable and delightful, Mr. Weston has laid all men in his debt."

The walk rekindled nostalgia for the bygone era of professional pedestrianism and for the days when America was still a walking nation.

"Remember Edward Payson Weston?" began an editorial in the *Des Moines News*.

The older ones do.

It was back in 1867 that Weston walked from Portland, Maine, 1,237 miles to Chicago, in twenty-six days. And what a stir he made at the county fairs where he gave exhibitions of his walking in the early years following his great feat!

If you were a boy at the time you remember how you ran around on the inside of the racing ring and how you were obliged to run a pretty good lick to keep up with the long-striding pedestrian. How carefully you measured the stride, numbering the inches from heel to toe of the footprints that were left in the soft earth. The measurements were data that furnished topics of dispute with the other boys for many a day.

Well, Edward Payson Weston is close to his seventieth year and still a champion pedestrian.

The other day he completed a walk of nearly one hundred miles, coming into New York from Philadelphia in twenty-three hours and seventeen minutes. . . .

And it would be a good thing if old man Weston's latest stunt would give an impetus to the walking industry in this country as his feats did forty years ago.

Many persons have almost forgotten how to walk. In the cities the street cars have sapped the vitality of a generation because of their ever present invitation to ride. Formerly everybody walked. Now about everybody rides.

After all is said about exercise the old-fashioned habit of long walking on one's legs is about the best sort known to men.

The following year, Weston repeated his famous Portland-to-Chicago walk of 1867, completing the trip in less than twenty-five days (not counting Sundays, of course), more than twenty-four hours faster than his previous time. "From the time that Edward Payson Weston began his 1,230-mile tramp from Portland, Me.," a newspaper in Weston's hometown of Providence reported, "the septuagenarian [sic] pedestrian was greeted everywhere by the townspeople of the hundreds of towns, many of whom had seen him pass through their villages on his similar journey four decades ago."

"What were stray hamlets then are sizable towns now," the paper continued, "and the changes wrought by the nearly half century of time have been of constant interest to the hardy old veteran of the road as he has responded quaintly to the hearty greetings and cheering." In the forty years between the two walks, the nation's population had doubled from thirty-eight million to seventy-six million. Chicago's population had grown fivefold, from 300,000 to 1.7 million. Indeed, the city that Weston entered on November 27, 1907, bore practically no resemblance to the Chicago of 1867. Completely reborn after the Great Fire, the city was now the second largest in the country; its skyline was jagged with skyscrapers, its stockyards were the largest in the world, and a network of elevated rail lines covered it like a spiderweb.

Weston in 1909.
COURTESY OF LIBRARY OF CONGRESS

Although his reception in Chicago was less raucous than it had been in 1867, an "immense throng" still awaited Weston's arrival at the city's new Federal Building on the corner of Jackson and Dearborn. A delegation led by Mayor Fred Busse waited inside the imposing granite structure to greet the famous pedestrian. But when Weston attempted to enter through the employees' entrance, a security guard blocked his way and directed him to the public entrance, piquing the notoriously prickly pedestrian. "Weston apparently misunderstood the situation, and his pride was touched," according to one account. "He cancelled on the spot the arrangements for the reception by the officials."

Once in Chicago, Weston found himself in financial trouble yet again. Like many modern professional athletes, he blamed his agent, a man named Dana Albee Patten. "That fellow has not been a bit of good to me," Weston complained to a reporter. "He has been a detriment. I discharged him at Buffalo after a public reception he arranged there proved a failure. Instead of charging an admission fee, he took up a collection and my share was practically nothing." Patten, for his part, claimed it was Weston who had acted unprofessionally, and he sued the pedestrian for $500.

In Chicago, Weston had planned to earn money by making public appearances, just as he'd done at the old opera house back in '67. But he overestimated the city's appetite for long lectures about the virtues of walking, which had waned considerably in the intervening forty years. For a time, Weston was stranded in Chicago, and the *New York Times* reported that "the indications were that Weston would go out of the city the same way he came in—on foot, and broke." A benefit was eventually organized to raise funds for his return trip home to New York.

—•••—

Perhaps inspired by Weston, perhaps eager to erase the memory of his ignominious performance in his 2,500-mile race with Weston twenty years before—or, perhaps, just to make a little money— Dan O'Leary emerged from retirement in 1907.

That September, O'Leary embarked on an attempt to duplicate Captain Barclay's historic feat of walking one thousand miles in one thousand consecutive hours. At sixty-one, O'Leary was more than twice the age Barclay was when he accomplished the feat in 1809.

"I am an Irishman, you know, and like all true sons of the ould sod, I have my own ideas about doing things," O'Leary explained. "When it was suggested that it would be next to impossible for any man to walk 1,000 miles in 1,000 consecutive hours I made up my mind that I would do the trick."

The event took place at a ballpark in Norwood, Ohio, an enclave of Cincinnati. An organization raising awareness of tuberculosis promised to pay O'Leary $5,000 if he was successful.

Before he embarked, O'Leary was asked, "What would you suggest to the weakly men and women who need exercise?"

"Walk: that is what they need," Dan answered. "Get out and walk. Do not take strolls. Vigorous breathing is what builds up a healthy life. The physical need for air is the best tonic that will help produce a graceful development of the body. . . . If walking exercises were taken oftener by men, women, and children life could be prolonged and the body preserved by certain attention. Ease and grace would come to the person, and instead of seeing so many wrecked and bent forms, there would be healthier people. I have found walking to be the staff of life."

He began the walk at 4:00 PM on Sunday, September 8, 1907, completing his first mile in ten minutes. Rather than employing Captain Barclay's strategy of walking consecutive miles before and after the top of every other hour, O'Leary chose the more taxing method of walking a single mile just after the start of every hour.

"Small of stature and rather slender," a *Cincinnati Enquirer* reporter observed, "the famous old long-distance champion is still as supple and as graceful as in former years, and walked the distance with a swinging, strength-conserving step which gave

Dan O'Leary in 1908. CHICAGO HISTORY MUSEUM, *CHICAGO DAILY NEWS* NEGATIVES COLLECTION, SDN-006847

many spectators full confidence in his ability to accomplish the gigantic task he has picked out for himself."

Between miles, O'Leary rested or regaled visitors with "reminiscences of the golden age of pedestrianism as far back as the old days in Chicago, when, as he expresses it, he 'got bees in his bonnet' and came to the conclusion that walking was more lucrative than selling Bibles to the household trade."

Bald and bespectacled with a bushy white mustache, O'Leary still walked like a piece of machinery, arms pumping like pistons, eyes fixed straight ahead. He walked on a ⅛-mile cinder track laid over the baseball diamond. A gong sounded at the top of every hour to signal the start of his next mile. Occasionally he allowed members of the audience to join him on the track, but only on one condition: "Dan insists that all who accompany him on his tiresome journey must conform strictly to the rules of the heel and toe step," the *Enquirer* reported. "As this is a great novelty to many who do not understand how to walk correctly, they soon find themselves falling back into their old habit and so become disqualified."

O'Leary's attempt was successful: He completed his thousandth mile at 7:12 AM on Sunday, October 20. The *Enquirer* called it "the crowning effort of his long career—a feat demanding for its accomplishment the plodding patience of the ox, the gameness of a fighting cock, the tenacity of the bulldog and the aggressive courage of the gladiator."

But it didn't come easy.

"O'Leary's willpower throughout the last, awful hours of the feat was wonderful," one reporter wrote. "His flesh had wasted away, his eyes were far back in his head and he could not see to read even coarse print."

"I have never in my life seen the man who withstood anything like the physical strain undergone by this man here," said G. W. Hale, one of O'Leary's doctors. "But he couldn't have stood it much longer. Something would give way if he continued the strain many more hours."

After he recuperated, O'Leary challenged his old nemesis Edward Payson Weston to a six-day "walking contest." Weston, however, flatly rejected the offer, noting that O'Leary was seven years younger and, besides, "not in his class."

"He talks about walking 1,000 miles in 1,000 hours," Weston told a reporter, "why, the only trick in doing that is to keep awake. A woman could do it."

Although Weston and O'Leary would never again meet in direct competition, for the next fifteen years the two old pedestrians would attempt to outdo each other with remarkable feats of walking.

In 1909, the centennial of Captain Barclay's thousand-mile walk, Weston walked some four thousand miles from New York to San Francisco in 105 days (excluding Sundays, as usual)—five days longer than his goal, but, at age seventy, an outstanding accomplishment nonetheless. San Francisco, still rebuilding after the 1906 earthquake, gave Weston a rapturous welcome.

"He is probably the greatest athlete of the age, everything considered," declared the syndicated newspaper columnist Willard W. Garrison. The *New York Medical Journal* opined that Weston's achievement repudiated the theory "that a man's best work has been accomplished when he reaches the age of fifty." For good measure, four years later, in 1913, Weston walked the 1,546 miles from New York to Minneapolis. Ironically, one of his main sponsors on that walk was the Hudson Motor Car Company, whose advertisement in the ten-cent souvenir program that Weston sold along the way promised THREE HUNDRED MILES A DAY AND NO FATIGUE.

Four years later, in 1917, Dan O'Leary returned to his hometown of Chicago, where he arranged what one paper called "freak affairs," such as challenging roller skaters and bicyclists to races with O'Leary walking one mile while the others traversed two-and-a-half. He lost more often than not, but the matches rekindled

Edward Payson Weston sets off from the plaza in front of the College of the City of New York at noon on June 2, 1913, on his walk to Minneapolis. COURTESY OF LIBRARY OF CONGRESS

nostalgic feelings for the glory days of pedestrianism in Chicago four decades previous. O'Leary also organized walking clubs throughout the city, a sweet but ultimately futile attempt to rejuvenate the sport. When he sponsored a three-mile race in Forest Park, he stipulated that all entrants must "use the heel-and-toe method."

In the autumn of 1922, meanwhile, Edward Payson Weston embarked on what he advertised as his "Final Example" and promised would be his "last hike," a 495-mile walk from Buffalo to New York City. He completed the trip in twenty-nine "walking days" (again no Sabbaths), averaging more than seventeen miles a day. Not bad for an eighty-three-year-old. Along the way, Weston was much amused by the number of gray-haired men who told him they remembered seeing him pass through their towns on one of his famous walks when they were children.

On the morning of Tuesday, October 7, 1922, Weston began the final leg of the hike, walking down Broadway from 125th

Street. At Seventy-Second Street he was met by a military fife and drum corps, which led the old Union messenger the rest of the way down Broadway to City Hall. Soon a large crowd was following Weston, hooting and hollering for this pied piper of pedestrianism, now taking the final steps of a career spent on his feet. Office workers leaned out the windows of buildings on both sides of Broadway, craning their necks for a glimpse of the "Grand Old Man of Walking," as one paper described him.

It had been sixty-two years since Weston's fateful wager with his friend George Eddy over the outcome of the 1860 presidential election. Now Lincoln's visage was on the penny and the five-dollar bill. Warren Harding was in the White House, and women could vote.

Around 1:00 PM, Weston and his ragtag entourage arrived at City Hall Park, where a large crowd had gathered, not to greet the hoary pedestrian but to follow the third game of the World Series between the Giants and the Yankees, which was being played uptown at the Polo Grounds. The *New York Evening World* had erected a giant mechanical scoreboard in the park on which were posted pitch-by-pitch updates. (The Giants would go on to win the series, denying Babe Ruth and the Yankees their first world championship.) The baseball fans in the park that early autumn afternoon must have been bemused by the shambling old man with the wobbly gait, unaware that he had once been one of the most famous athletes in the country.

When Weston announced that this would be his final walk, the news was met with incredulity. To generations of Americans, a world without Weston the Walker seemed unimaginable. "To-day most people consider it an imposition if they have to walk a few hundred yards to get to a station or a trolley line," the *New York Tribune* editorialized. "Even in the country the flivver has made walking a chore. The country needs Weston's inspiration. Without him there is a serious danger that walking will become a lost art. Isn't he still too active to quit?"

Less than five years later, in early March 1927, Weston, now nearly eighty-eight, was found wandering the streets of Greenwich Village, dazed and destitute. By then he had long been estranged from his wife and children and was living with a woman named Annie O'Hagan, whom he alternately introduced as his niece, his secretary, his adopted daughter, and his housekeeper. An old fan named Anne Nichols heard of Weston's plight and came to his rescue. Nichols was a Broadway producer and playwright, famous for the enormously successful play *Abie's Irish Rose*. She raised $30,000 to establish a trust fund for the aged pedestrian.

Later that month, Weston was hit by a car. He was crossing a street on his way to church in Manhattan when a taxicab plowed into him. Felled by one of the machines he so despised, Weston was left crippled and would never walk again. Two years later, on March 15, 1929, Weston turned ninety. Confined to a wheelchair, he declared it "the bitterest day of my life." Two months later he died.

Daniel O'Leary's reaction to his longtime rival's death is unrecorded, but, at eighty-three in 1929, the old Irishman from Chicago was still going strong. To support himself, O'Leary had become a "baseball pedestrian." He staged exhibitions of pedestrianism before major and minor league games in ballparks all across the country. Sometimes he challenged one of the ballplayers to run around the bases twice while O'Leary walked around them once. Other times, he walked against time, attempting to circle the bases, fair heel and toe, four times in less than three minutes. More often than anyone expected, O'Leary was victorious.

After each performance, O'Leary stood at home plate, smoothed his bushy white mustache, and bowed grandly to the crowd. Then he would walk through the stands, hat literally in hand, collecting nickels and dimes. "Give if you want to," he would say, and, even in hard times, the fans were generous. Sometimes he collected a hundred dollars or more in spare change. "That keeps me in pin money," he told a reporter. It also subsidized his winters spent in Southern California.

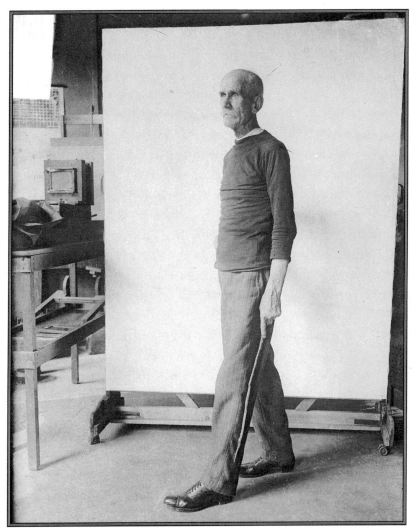

Dan O'Leary in 1917. Chicago History Museum, *Chicago Daily News* negatives collection, SDN-061225

On September 21, 1927, O'Leary walked the bases against time before a game between the Chicago White Sox and the Philadelphia A's at Chicago's Comiskey Park, one of baseball's gleaming new steel and concrete ballparks. By now, of course, baseball was firmly entrenched as America's national pastime, and pedestrianism was but a distant memory.

But the crowd cheered warmly for the superannuated pedestrian as he circled the bases and beat the clock. One imagines the ballplayers lounging in their dugouts, languid in the summer heat, amused by the spectacle of this old man, arms pumping like pistons, rounding third and heading for home. They would have been forgiven for not knowing who he was; after all, they'd all been born well after pedestrianism's heyday. But the ballplayers would have been dumbfounded to learn that way back in 1877, half a century before, that old man earned more in six days than most of them would earn for the entire 1927 season.

O'Leary predicted he would live "six score years," and his doctors weren't inclined to doubt him. But on May 30, 1933, at the hotel where he lived in Los Angeles, O'Leary's seemingly indestructible body finally succumbed to the unstoppable forces of nature. The official cause of death was hardening of the arteries. He was eighty-seven. It was estimated that he had walked more than three hundred thousand miles over the course of his lifetime.

He didn't make it to 120, but Dan O'Leary had long surpassed his biblical allotment of three score and ten years.

Which is rather amazing since, as one obituarist bluntly put it, "He liked the grog."

ACKNOWLEDGMENTS

IN PREPARING TO WRITE THIS BOOK, the most important resource was *King of the Peds* by Paul Marshall. Paul's book is a veritable encyclopedia of nineteenth-century pedestrianism, and an outstanding resource for anyone interested in learning more about the sport. I met Paul while researching this book; he was kind and encouraging, and I am grateful for his support.

Also generous with his time and expertise was Peter Radford, the Captain Barclay biographer who won four track medals for the United Kingdom at the 1960 Olympics. Peter is a world-class athlete, scholar, and gentleman. He and his wife Margaret opened their home to me and my wife Allyson, welcoming us strangers as if we were old friends. Peter was also kind enough to allow me to use images from his vast collection of pedestrianism memorabilia in the book. Thank you, Peter.

Mark Aston, local history manager at the Islington Local History Centre in London, was likewise indispensable. He helped me research the history of the Royal Agricultural Hall and dug up some wonderful images for the book.

Dr. John S. J. Brooks, head of pathology at Pennsylvania Hospital in Philadelphia, kindly reviewed Frank Hart's medical records for me.

Frances K. Browne, an excellent attorney and an old family friend, helped me research the Collins law banning six-day races in New York State.

Rory Coleman, who has completed more than two hundred ultramarathons, graciously answered my many questions about endurance athletes and competitions.

Special thanks to Josh Podwoski for research assistance and to Henry Potts for contributing the photograph of the interior of the Royal Agricultural Hall as it appears today.

As they have for my previous books, my brother Jim (Dr. James H. Algeo Jr.) and my college buddy Gregor (Dr. Gregory N. Prah) patiently answered all questions pertaining to medical matters.

My sister Ann Algeo read an early version of the manuscript and offered valuable advice. For example, she radically reduced my use of parentheses. (Thank you, Ann.)

The following institutions provided substantial support: British Library Newspaper Reading Room; Chicago History Museum; Library of Congress Main Reading Room and Newspaper and Current Periodical Reading Room; New-York Historical Society; and New York Public Library.

I am, as always, deeply indebted to my agent, Jane Dystel of Dystel & Goderich Literary Management, who has worked tirelessly on my behalf for nearly a decade. I couldn't have done it without you, Jane.

Same goes for Jerry Pohlen, my editor at Chicago Review Press. Working with Jerry is simply a pleasure. I am also indebted to his colleagues at CRP, especially Mary Kravenas and Kathryn Tumen.

Finally, while I was producing this book, lovely Allyson was producing our firstborn, a beautiful baby girl named Zaya Theresa. It suffices to say that my production pales in comparison to hers. Thank you, Allyson. And welcome to the world, Zaya. It's a good place.

CHRONOLOGY

1861

FEBRUARY 22–MARCH 4
Edward Payson Weston walks from Boston to Washington, DC, approximately 478 miles, in 10 days, 4 hours, and 12 minutes.

1867

OCTOBER 29–NOVEMBER 28
Weston walks the approximately 1,200 miles from Portland, Maine, to Chicago in less than thirty days (excluding Sundays) to win a $10,000 wager.

1874

JULY 14–15, CHICAGO, WEST SIDE RINK
Daniel O'Leary walks 100 miles in 23 hours and 17 minutes.

DECEMBER 14–19, NEWARK, NEW JERSEY, INDUSTRIAL EXPOSITION BUILDING
Weston walks 500 miles in 5 days, 23 hours, 34 minutes, and 15 seconds (25 minutes and 45 seconds less than six days).

1875

APRIL 24, PHILADELPHIA, CHESTNUT STREET RINK
O'Leary walks 116 miles in 23 hours, 12 minutes, and 53 seconds.

MAY 17–23, CHICAGO, WEST SIDE RINK
O'Leary walks 500 miles in 5 days, 21 hours, 31 minutes, and 50 seconds (2 hours, 28 minutes, and 10 seconds less than six days), more than two hours faster than Weston had walked that distance in December 1874.

NOVEMBER 15–20, CHICAGO, INTERSTATE EXPOSITION BUILDING
O'Leary defeats Weston in a 500-mile race billed as "The Great Walking Match for the Championship of the World."

1876

FEBRUARY 8–9, LONDON, ROYAL AGRICULTURAL HALL
Weston defeats William Perkins in a 24-hour race.

FEBRUARY 15–17, LONDON, ROYAL AGRICULTURAL HALL
Weston walks 180 miles in 47 hours and 40 minutes (20 minutes less than 48 hours).

FEBRUARY 22–25, LONDON, ROYAL AGRICULTURAL HALL
Weston defeats Charles Rowell in a 75-hour race.

APRIL 4–9, SAN FRANCISCO, HORTICULTURAL HALL
O'Leary walks 500 miles in 5 days, 19 hours, and 8 minutes (4 hours and 52 minutes less than six days), breaking his own 500-mile record.

1877

APRIL 2–7, LONDON, ROYAL AGRICULTURAL HALL
O'Leary defeats Weston in a six-day race, 519 miles to 510.

1878

MARCH 18–23, LONDON, ROYAL AGRICULTURAL HALL
O'Leary wins the first six-day Astley Belt race with 520 miles, setting a new six-day record.

SEPTEMBER 30–OCTOBER 5, NEW YORK, GILMORE'S GARDEN
O'Leary wins the second Astley Belt race with 403 miles.

DECEMBER 17–JANUARY 12, 1879, BROOKLYN, NEW YORK, MOZART GARDEN
"Madame" Ada Anderson walks a quarter mile every fifteen minutes for one thousand consecutive quarter hours.

1879

MARCH 10–15, NEW YORK, GILMORE'S GARDEN
Charles Rowell wins the third Astley Belt race with 500 miles. His winnings total $18,398.31 (roughly $425,000 today).

JUNE 16–21, LONDON, ROYAL AGRICULTURAL HALL
In a stunning comeback, Weston wins the fourth Astley Belt race with 550 miles, setting a new six-day record.

SEPTEMBER 22–27, NEW YORK, MADISON SQUARE GARDEN
Rowell wins the fifth Astley Belt race with 530 miles (later reduced to 524 miles after the track was found to be short).

OCTOBER 6–11, NEW YORK, MADISON SQUARE GARDEN
Nicholas Murphy wins the first O'Leary Belt race with 505 miles.

1880

APRIL 5–10, NEW YORK, MADISON SQUARE GARDEN
Frank Hart wins the second O'Leary Belt race with 565 miles, a new six-day record.

NOVEMBER 1–6, LONDON, ROYAL AGRICULTURAL HALL
Rowell wins the sixth Astley Belt race with 566 miles, a new six-day record.

1881

FEBRUARY 28–MARCH 5, NEW YORK, MADISON SQUARE GARDEN
The third O'Leary Belt race is mired in charges of "hippodroming," with twelve of the nineteen starters dropping out in the first two days, some under suspicious circumstances.

JUNE 20–25, LONDON, MARBLE RINK
Charles Rowell wins the Astley Belt race for the third consecutive time, giving him permanent possession of the celebrated belt and putting an end to the greatest series of races in the history of pedestrianism. The end of the Astley Belt races marks the end of pedestrianism's golden age.

SOURCES

THIS BOOK IS BASED PRIMARILY on contemporaneous newspaper reports. I searched hundreds of papers online, mainly through free websites such as the Library of Congress's Chronicling America, the Brooklyn Public Library's Brooklyn Daily Eagle Online, the National Library of Australia's Trove, and the Google News Archive. These are priceless resources. The paid website newspaperarchive.com was also helpful. In addition, I searched dozens of newspapers and periodicals in bound volumes and on microfilm at the British Library, the Islington Local History Centre, and the Library of Congress. Most of the papers quoted in the text are named in the text. The following titles proved especially useful:

Anglo-American Times (London)
Atlanta Constitution
Australian Journal (Melbourne)
Bell's Life in London and Sporting Chronicle
Boston Globe
British Medical Journal (London)
Brooklyn Daily Eagle
Cedar Falls (Iowa) Gazette
Charleston (South Carolina) Daily News
Chicago Daily News

Chicago Evening Journal
Chicago Tribune
Cincinnati Enquirer
Daily News (London)
Davenport (Iowa) Daily Gazette
Des Moines (Iowa) News
Dubuque (Iowa) Herald
Eau Claire (Wisconsin) Free Press
Erie (Pennsylvania) Dispatch
Hagerstown (Maryland) Mail
Harper's Weekly (A Journal of Civilization) (New York)
Holloway Press (London)
Illustrated London News
Illustrated Police News (London)
Irish Times (Dublin)
Islington Gazette (London)
Janesville (Wisconsin) Gazette
Lancet (London)
Los Angeles Times
Milwaukee News
National Police Gazette (New York)
New York Evening World
New York Freeman
New York Herald
New York Mail
New York Sportsman
New York Sun
New York Times
New York World
Observer (London)
Ohio Democrat (New Philadelphia, Ohio)
Penny Illustrated Paper and Illustrated Times (London)
Philadelphia Times
Preston (England) Guardian

Reynold's Newspaper (London)
Rochester (New York) Journal
St. Louis Post-Dispatch
Salt Lake Herald
San Francisco Chronicle
Saturday Review (London)
Semi-Weekly Wisconsin (Milwaukee)
Spirit of the Times (New York)
Sporting Gazette and Agricultural Journal (London)
Sporting Times (London)
Times (London)
Titusville (Pennsylvania) Morning Herald
Turf, Field and Farm (London)
Washington Post
Weekly Irish Times (Dublin)
Worcester (Massachusetts) Evening Gazette

BIBLIOGRAPHY

Adelman, Melvin L. *A Sporting Time: New York City and the Rise of Modern Athletics, 1820–1870.* Urbana, IL: University of Illinois Press, 1986.

Amato, Joseph. *On Foot: A History of Walking.* New York: New York University Press, 2004.

Astley, Sir John Dugdale. *Fifty Years of My Life in the World of Sport at Home and Abroad.* London: Hurst and Blackett, 1894.

Bernstein, Walter. "A Walking Fever Has Set In." *Virginia Quarterly Review*, Autumn 1980.

Bond, Gregory. *Jim Crow at Play: Race, Manliness, and the Color Line in American Sports, 1876–1916.* Unpublished dissertation, University of Wisconsin, 2008.

Cashman, Sean Dennis. *America in the Gilded Age: From the Death of Lincoln to the Rise of Theodore Roosevelt.* New York: New York University Press, 1984.

Collins, Kelly. "Old Time Walk and Run." Remarks delivered at Bethlehem Six-Day Extravaganza, Bethlehem, PA, December 11, 1996.

Cumming, John. *Runners and Walkers: A Nineteenth-Century Sports Chronicle.* Chicago: Regnery Gateway, 1981.

Davies, Richard O. *Sports in American Life: A History.* Malden, MA: Blackwell, 2007.

Dowdeswell, G. F. "The Coca Leaf: Observations on the Properties and Action of the Leaf of the Coca Plant (*Erythloxylon Coca*), Made in the Physiological Laboratory of University College." *Lancet,* April 29 and May 6, 1876.

Durso, Joseph. *Madison Square Garden: 100 Years of History.* New York: Simon & Schuster, 1979.

Forshaw, Alec. *The Building That Lived Twice: The Story of the Royal Agricultural Hall and Its Rebirth as the Business Design Centre.* London: Business Design Centre, 2011.

Gac, Scott. *Singing for Freedom: The Hutchinson Family Singers and the Nineteenth-Century Culture of Reform.* New Haven, CT: Yale University Press, 2007.

Gems, Gerald R., Linda J. Borish, and Gertrud Pfister. *Sports in American History: From Colonization to Globalization.* Champaign, IL: Human Kinetics, 2008.

Gordon, John Steele. *A Thread Across the Ocean: The Heroic Story of the Transatlantic Cable.* New York: Walker Publishing, 2002.

Gorn, Elliott J. *The Manly Art: Bare-Knuckle Prize Fighting in America.* Ithaca, NY: Cornell University Press, 1986.

Harris, Nick, Helen Harris, and Paul Marshall. *A Man in a Hurry: The Extraordinary Life & Times of Edward Payson Weston, the World's Greatest Walker.* London: De Coubertin Books, 2012.

Huggins, Mike. *The Victorians and Sport.* New York: Palgrave Macmillan, 2004.

Jonnes, Jill. *Empires of Light: Edison, Tesla, Westinghouse, and the Race to Electrify the World.* New York: Random House, 2004.

Kellogg, John Harvey. *Plain Facts for Old and Young: Embracing the Natural History and Hygiene of Organic Life.* Burlington, IA: I. F. Segner and Company, 1892.

Lamb, Edward. "'Weston the Walker' Made Pedestrianism a Way of Life." *Smithsonian,* July 1979.

Lewis, Guy M. "The Ladies Walked and Walked." *Sports Illustrated,* December 18, 1967.

Lucas, John Apostal. "Pedestrianism and the Struggle for the Sir John Astley Belt, 1878–1879." *Research Quarterly*, October 1968.

Marshall, Paul S. *King of the Peds*. Bloomington, IN: Author-House, 2008.

Milroy, Andy. "Pedestrianism in America." Ultra Legends, November 22, 2008. www.ultralegends.com /pedestrianism-in-america/.

Nicholson, Geoff. *The Lost Art of Walking: The History, Science, Philosophy, and Literature of Pedestrianism.* New York: Riverhead Books, 2008.

Noakes, Tim. *Lore of Running*. Champaign, IL: Leisure Press, 1991.

Norridge, Julian. *Can We Have Our Balls Back, Please? How the British Invented Sport.* London: Penguin, 2009.

Osler, Tom, and Ed Dodd. *Ultramarathoning: The Next Challenge.* Mountain View, CA: World Publications, 1979.

Pavy, Frederick W. "The Effect of Prolonged Muscular Exercise on the System." *Lancet*, February 26, March 4, March 11, March 18, and March 25, 1876.

Radford, Peter F. *The Celebrated Captain Barclay: Sport, Money and Fame in Regency Britain.* London: Headline, 2001.

Reel, Guy. *The* National Police Gazette *and the Making of the Modern American Man, 1879–1906.* New York: Palgrave Macmillan, 2006.

Riess, Steven A. *Sport in Industrial America: 1850–1920.* Wheeling, IL: Harlan Davidson, 1995.

Schwartz, David G. *Roll the Bones: The History of Gambling.* New York: Gotham Books, 2006.

Segrave, Kerry. *America on Foot: Walking and Pedestrianism in the 20th Century.* Jefferson, NC: McFarland & Company, 2006.

Shaulis, Dahn. "Pedestriennes: Newsworthy but Controversial Women in Sporting Entertainment." *Journal of Sport History*, Spring 1999.

Smith, Gene, and Jayne Barry Smith, eds. *The Police Gazette*. New York: Simon & Schuster, 1972.

Tansey, John E. *Biographical Sketch of Daniel O'Leary, Champion Pedestrian of the World*. Chicago: publisher unknown, 1878.

Thom, Walter. *Pedestrianism; Or, an Account of the Performances of Celebrated Pedestrians During the Last and Present Century*. Aberdeen: D. Chalmers and Company, 1813.

Thompson, J. Ashburton. "Weston's Fourth Walk." *British Medical Journal*, March 11, 1876.

Thoreau, Henry David. *The Maine Woods*. New York: AMS Press, 1982.

Trent, George D., ed. *The Gentle Art of Walking: A Compilation from the* New York Times. New York: Arno Press/Random House, 1971.

Wallace, William Gordon. *Race Walking in America: Past and Present*. Unpublished dissertation, University of Texas, 1989.

Weston, Edward Payson. *The Pedestrian; Being a Correct Journal of "Incidents" on a Walk from the State House, Boston, Mass., to the U.S. Capitol at Washington, D.C., Performed in "Ten Consecutive Days" Between February 22d and March 4th, 1861*. New York: printed for Edward Payson Weston, 1862.

Wiggins, David K., ed. *Sport in America: From Colonial Leisure to Celebrity Figures and Globalization*. Champaign, IL: Human Kinetics, 2009.

Zacks, Richard. *Island of Vice: Theodore Roosevelt's Doomed Quest to Clean Up Sin-Loving New York*. New York: Doubleday, 2012.

INDEX